BLASPHEMY

A VERY CLEVER SEMIOTIC TRICK

MARTIN CROGHAN

SIGN POST INK

PREFACE

BLASPHEMY IS ONE OF THOSE PECULIAR WAYS OF THINKING found in the beginnings of recorded history. It has consistently killed more people and blighted more lives than anything else in the history of the various known worlds. Cities, towns, villages and houses have been reduced to rubble, and arable land has been rendered infertile.

It is structured in the form of a circle with various segments. In the centre stands belief, sometimes religious, sometimes secular, and sometimes a peculiar blend of the two which may alternate in terms of dominance.

The case studies are from my own religion and from Communism. The book started out life as class notes in Dublin City University in the 1980s, but the content has been revisited and revised, and now also serves as an overview of how Catholicism and Communism have changed radically in the last thirty years.

BLASPHEMY, A VERY CLEVER SEMIOTIC TRICK

A religion assigns meaning to a vast host of different phenomena... It may also routinely attach additional markers such as inspired and absolute to these meanings... (and) also tag meanings given by others... individuals or groups, secular or religious, as false. These semantic riders appended to the base meaning by religious authorities can function like flash warnings... if you comment on, question, criticise, a particular meaning... some absolutes of the secular variety may also often assume the same level of supreme status as some religions or denominations of religion...

A RELIGION ASSIGNS MEANING IN MANY DIFFERENT WAYS to a vast range of different things, including those that would be regarded in other traditions as having nothing to do with religion. In addition, it may attach markers such as inspired and absolute to these beliefs which can result in ever more complex, layered sets of related messages. In addition, other religions and secular beliefs and ideologies, may be tagged as false which can add all kinds of dangerous complications. These semantic riders appended to the base meaning by religious authorities can function like flash warnings, to be very careful of the consequences, if you comment on, question or criticise, a particular meaning associated with a religion or specific denomination, or the value and authenticity of any particular meaning, or of the totality of meanings which is that religion or denomination. Questioning the authority of the officials of the religion who decree that something is blasphemous is also regarded as blasphemy, and not only when they regard themselves as intermediaries between the divine and the secular sphere or when they present themselves as representatives of the divine. The Christian section of the *Good Book* has its own expression for such authority. *Μὴ γένοιτο, It is not to be, it will not be,* is a very curt, absolute warning, that there is (to be) no dialogue, no analysis, unless I - an individual or group, which also usually has an individual as primary - say there can be, and that any dialogue, commentary or analysis will follow his rules. The religious bureaucracy of sanction in the context of orthodoxy and blasphemy, has a long history, Catholicism's sometime triple system of approval for publication, for example, might be regarded as the historical heir of rabbinic sanction.

The religion says what the meaning is and that is the end of the discussion, as one of the less impolite of the many such informal clichés in English says, and if you are new to this world, you should know that religions which do not do this are never very long for this world. End in the phrase end of discussion in contexts such as this, can also mean before any analysis of meaning or any review of possible meanings can begin. One of the implications of any proposition such as *Religion says what meaning is,* gives us the stark chain, you should know this, you should have known this, you should know that a failure to know this has consequences which can range from exclusion of some kind to very painful mortal retribution. This is as true now as it was in the past, but, for obvious reasons, not really anymore in places where the intensity of religious belief and adherence has declined radically. The exclusion can also have a very wide range, and not just the ceremony of excommunication which had its own dramatic ritual in Catholicism.

(Note: Since this was written quite some time ago, the world of Islam has given the world a wide range of dramatic lessons on what can happen within a religion and not just between religions when orthodoxy becomes a major issue. This is also the first period in history when the foreign, heretical kuffar from very different political and religious Christian cultures, is taking opposing sides within warring Islamic groups, which evokes ominous feelings among those of us brought up in various Christian traditions in the first fifty, sixty years in different parts of twentieth century Europe).

WHAT I AM WRITING NOW about blasphemy would not be welcome in a very large number of societies, it could not be published in very many societies, and in some of the latter, I would be severely sanctioned, including the ultimate penalty, for daring to think such thoughts. Or because such thoughts are imputed to me and not only for writing explicitly about them in a public or private context. If religion is a gold-mine for semiotics, blasphemy is a *Garden of Eden* for learning about semiotic games in a host of areas. Some of you may have a certain attitude towards religion and may agree with some of what I say - some is an important codicil - and how I say it, but the bad news for most people who regard themselves as liberals, the strategies and tactics used in blasphemy are ones we all use in many different areas of our lives, so the usual rule applies. Semiotics sits poorly with all of us, some of the time, and with some of us all of the time, unless it is what we say, and exactly what we say. I am using this case study from religion because religion is usually more explicit and open than many other worlds of meaning, which may carry high emotional value, and that is the only reason. Some religions, especially the monotheistic religions, generally work with an assumption about the absolute true foundation of their own religion which means they are also very explicit about the rules of the game (game can have very important and sometimes, ultimate consequences in these worlds). Which may also mean they may never feel the necessity to be coy or timid about applying the accusation of blasphemy here, there and everywhere, including about what might seem trivial to those outside a particular religion or religious denomination (using this last term to refer to a peculiar group, can also be regarded as a very hostile act). Some may also engage in discussion, to show how reasonable they are or in the hope of winning someone over to their side, but there is no intention of engaging in an open discussion with no pre-assumptions or conditions which might result in a *volte face* change of mind. The term *game* is being used just above in its usual sense and not in any vague transferred way, and I should have used italics to mark it. If you have played sports or chess or scrabble etc., you will know that playing a game can be a very serious pursuit - including down to the level of small villages and even townlands in Ireland, for example, where particular games become an integral part of historical memory, including quite recent memory - and breaking rules or cheating can be very injurious to your health in all kinds of ways. Game theory assumed a very traditional Catholic role in my life a long time ago, and it now keeps me humble and very conscious of how *not very clever* I can be in exploring meaning, but then, whenever I want, I also have the luxury of reminding myself that I am often in good company, among the dead and the living.

What I am saying here now about religion applies to the Catholic religion of my youth in Ireland but would not necessarily apply in the same way to religions or religious denominations which are often popularly called a broad church, a phrase in the English manner, which is often used to describe certain Christian denominations in particular. These may allow for a certain variation in terms of doctrine and do not always insist on applying in any explicit and consistent way, an absolute truth hallmark or tag, even to what might have been considered primary doctrines in the past, including the very near past. Nor do they necessarily apply any sanctions to those who question these fundamental truths, as they would have been imperiously called in a very explicit and public fashion in the Catholicism of my upbringing; we would have been told, for example, in a blessed metaphor from the Bible, that these are the foundations of the building itself, which guarantee the stability of the whole structure. But, if you are an outsider, do not be too carried away with seeming liberal attitudes to doctrine in English Anglicanism, for instance, to give just one example at random. It has had, for instance, *a human being* as Head of what is its Established Church for centuries. It also features a host of legal details that may often exploit the benefits of being concealed in an implicit cloud of complexity and historical provenance which would now be regarded in many other such contexts in English culture itself, as bordering on sorcery and black magic. England in its purely constitutional capacity as a sovereign state has guarded what is, *de facto* and sometimes *de iure*, a structural amalgam of the religious, the ecclesiastical, the political, and the secular very zealously. It stages grandiose theatre productions with real life characters playing the principal roles in grandiose cathedrals serving as a gigantic stage which were themselves often misappropriated from another, much older Christian faith hundreds and hundreds of years ago, and which predates the English one by much more than a millennium. The great and the good are also often chosen as extras in these extravagant productions which make the modern day staging of opera in the ruins at Luxor or in *Oper Gratz* look like a preview in a crumbling provincial theatre in Argentina.

Seeming openness and liberalism in closed contexts, secular or religious, are of particular interest to semiotics when they serve as a hide for snakes in the grass whose bite is toxic but no longer fatal, especially in those peculiar Western cultures which consider themselves above such chicanery. You will know, however, that such metaphorical snake bites can still be fatal in many places in the world. As the sometime archetypal *bad boy* of intellectual disciplines, semiotics often plays a very mean game, and it has always loved stalking meaning underneath the façade, every façade, including those of religion, in its man made manifestations. England, for example, functions as a theocracy in small - and does this particularly well when there is a female monarch, but maybe this is because historically, males on thrones everywhere have a sometime reputation for behaving like asses or crude tyrants or sexual hyenas - and also prides itself, with its very matriarchal *Mother of Parliaments* as the stellar exemplar of democracy. It may also be often touted as a prime example of a post-religious society, which, taken all together, makes for an interesting mix for semiotics, which as English likes to say when it wants to show its popular credentials, *you couldn't make it up.* And to add to all this, it also explicitly discriminates against those of a particular religion in a manner which might serve as a banal example in the world of blasphemy, but one which is of particular importance because it is not regarded and treated as blasphemy - I have not heard it called blasphemy or racism, or any such negative term, for instance - and because it serves as an early warning of the crucial role the distinction between explicit and implicit often plays, and not just in this very particular complex world of religion.

In teaching semiotics, my only mantra is to be aware of the explicit and implicit, if we are to understand how meaning manifests itself in all the multiple worlds which make up our lives; and that when one of these worlds assumes that it is the most important or even the only important one - which we all do in some form, even in a periodic way - that the purpose of attaching this additional semiotic tag is to announce I am the important one.

FREQUENTLY, we do not understand the most simple, basic things about violence and not just because it may hide in the implicit, because we play tricks on ourselves to make sure we do not understand. In so many different areas of our lives, we do not understand because we do not necessarily want to understand, and, sometimes, we go to very elaborate lengths to hide from reality. Certain religions and certain denominations of religion, on the other hand, can be open, honest and very explicit, which is why I am giving this example of blasphemy from religion as a case study in semiotics in general, and the semiotics of violence in particular. Some people will dismiss what I am saying as a diatribe against religion, which is a common tactic with a long, tried and tested history in many religions for not having to consider what is being said. Others, who regard religion as beneath consideration, even contempt, intellectually, may even read on in the hope of finding support for their views and may find it when it is not there. Which means I may find myself being clamped in a very narrow space between the classic *rock and a hard place* with no room to manoeuvre, which, you will know is not a good place to be if you have done even any modest rock climbing as I have often done badly; neither can *there must be something in what you say if both sides are against you* be considered much of an endorsement either, in this precarious and potentially very dangerous context.* Semiotics is fanatically democratic, however, and will not be hesitant about looking at manifestations of secular type blasphemy either, and not only of the so-called *right* variety which are usually nothing if not loquaciously explicit. The varieties on the right are sometimes so absolute about being right, they regard it as a given, and often see no need to defend their *rightism*; the real fascist varieties in power, both on the left and right, however, do not always bother with anything that would be regarded as justification, which is very telling in any analysis of blasphemy, and not just in the context of the semiotics and politics of freedom.

*(Note: I take my lead from 1920s and early '30 Italy and use fascism and fascist freely in these essays, I am not using it as a type of curse word, as it sometimes is now. It is to be noted as well that this essay was written long before the implosion among Muslims in various places in the second half of the second decade of the first century of the third millennium, which itself has echoes of a sentence which talks in an extravagant manner about time in the early books of the Bible. Which might also be a good place to say that the way we talk about time now, is no different from how time has always been configured).

But, as you might expect, semiotics too can be very devious, and is not some innocent wandering around in a big bad world. It never stays, for example, on what is usually regarded as the main road too long, it twists and turns, and the most brilliant semioticians of all, the great writers and artists, often take inordinate pleasure in taking us down roads which are not on any of the usual maps and which go around in ever shrinking circles or which just end in a *cul de sac*; they are the ones who lay bare like no one else, the illusions and deceptions we all use all of the time, to protect what is of significant value to us. Semiotics is the surgeon of the disciplines outside the natural sciences, and sometimes it uses very sharp instruments which can draw a lot of blood very quickly. It can also be arrogant beyond belief, like the surgeons who used to wield absolute authority with the scalpel (this was when they tired of being classed as common or garden butchers and began what was a very successful campaign to present themselves as a most special elite deserving of absolute obeisance in the old manner of the aristocracy and even royalty). Comics and children are also experts of note; they break the rules about what meanings can be exposed and get a laugh; both, however, can sometimes be severely reprimanded and punished for their trouble. Taking the rules of meaning for a walk in the fresh air can be funny and cruel, but if the religion has a certain standing in a society, getting it wrong about religion *is not allowed to be funny* - and itself a strange expression which *kind of* came through my fingers all by itself - especially in a national context. It is blasphemy, the sin of sins, as Latin with its ridiculously long vowels says in the majestic *peccatum omnium peccatorum*. The Bible might say greed and desire are the root of all evil, but in the real religious world, blasphemy stands alone as the sin of sins; theology might say otherwise, but in that world too, semiotics rules, absolutely, which itself, will not be very popular in certain societies, but how could it not, if we, common or garden human beings, are the ones who create theology and decide how religion is to be practiced. Blasphemy might be ranked as an archetypal case-study to expose how meaning is assigned and manipulated, if only because the elite and the humble both play this very serious game (but not equally, of course). It may also be the only game played by both these constituencies.

———

WHEN YOU PEEL AWAY the covers, the accusation of blasphemy can sometimes be the most revolting form of censorship, and not only when it is an expression of anti-thought. Accusing someone of blasphemy can be an unforgivable act which cries out to God for justice and retribution, to use a form of language from my own happy childhood; it can also be a form of symbolic aggression of paralyzing complexity which often threatens to spill over into any number of very different forms of violence. Dismissal from employment, eviction from house and home, imprisonment, exile, murder, war of all kinds, including civil war, when, for instance, one denomination of a particular religion accuses another of blasphemy and *Holy War* ensues; death or worse may also come into play even against those who would be foolish or brave enough to call this ominous phrase itself, a blasphemy. I might primly call it an example of a classic oxymoron in a lecture, but it is one which has wreaked absolute destruction throughout history, in repetitive, endless cycles of the massacre of the innocents everywhere, and not only those poor children who featured again and again every year in that awful story of my otherwise happy childhood Christmas.

The semiotics of violence featured very strongly and cleverly at Mass in our very first religious lessons in story form outside the home in Ireland, when we listened to readings from the *Good Book* before we ever went to school at the age of three or four. One time when I was talking about the Irish love for the story, I mentioned we could hardly be other than story people, seeing that we were schooled from infancy every Sunday in a crowded *one book* book-club attended by everyone in the community; and this was not just another book suitable for small children, this was story time for everyone in the town together. The story of *the* innocents was classic *cinéma vérité* long before the cinema was invented. It was the true story of a real pogrom - but not the first by any means - visited on all Jews under two years of age, but it was our story because the purpose of the savage hunt was to kill Jesus Christ while He was still a baby and stop Him saving us by becoming our Saviour and Redeemer. But this was not the only story involving children. In the Sunday matinee before the main film, we would also sometimes see the haunting images of Jewish boys our age being dumped out of trains and marched in a kind of frenzy to the camps with their mothers gripping their hands tightly. We were hardly yet teenagers and mothers dragging boys our age along by the hand like this, were also a part of my religion. In the first story they wanted to kill the baby Jesus because he was a Jew, in the second story they wanted to kill all Jews. I could not ever have been called a sensitive little boy but I found the words *all children under two years of age* awful every time I heard the story, and only God knows how many times I heard it. The story also very cleverly told us about the semiotics of time, that time is not always measured by a clock or a calendar, when meaning is all that matters. Millennia and endless miles might separate us from the children in both stories, but that did not matter, they were part of us, in the deepest sense. And we knew this before we could tell the time, not to mention what a month was, and before we could count the syllables in millennium, if we knew what a syllable was.

We also knew very early on that there are two kinds of stories, one was real - the story we heard in the Church was real, as everything else in our Catholic religion was, and we heard it again and again, which is the way children like to hear stories, when they are of particular import - the other was what we called *pretend* stories, that we made up, and we also used a special category transfer from Irish, *mar dheadh*, to say this in our English. Children are very clever, they know from when they are quite young what categories might be of interest to them; they also begin to ask more and more explicitly, in their own particular ways, if what seems to be is all there is, or if there is more than this in our worlds of meaning, which is also a discussion which often leaves me feeling very dim when I am trying to teach semiotics. I am also now asking you not to reject immediately what I have just said because of the language used in this last sentence - *if what seems to be is all there is* - but what children do mentally is sometimes too complex for language. That language can never capture human reality needs to be featured prominently in upper case everywhere. We all know this in various ways, but it should be made explicit more often as well, if only to make us more conscious of *the good times*.

BLASPHEMY IS A VERY complex chapter in the semiotics handbook, and each page is marked for danger with a skull and crossbones. That someone, for example, including a nobody like me says anything about religion may be regarded as blasphemous unless it tracks what is said officially, which means by those who regard themselves as officials and the elite, and it you want to disentangle these last six words, get up very early in the morning and have no other pressing commitments for the rest of the day. Ironically, it was in the story of the Innocents - itself a most beautiful word in English - I first learned that the very person of Jesus was a blasphemy to Herod, and that this was why He was to be massacred. The story would move very slowly over the years and then also become horribly explicit in my young teenage years, in the story of my own people and in the story of the Holocaust which was already in its awful rage when I was just two years of age. This last part always somehow added to the unspeakable sorrow of the story because it raged during the time of my very early innocent life. When I was a little boy, I regarded those who Herod wanted to kill as my family and when I found out that there also had been a way of thinking when I was a child which said all Jews were to be killed I had nowhere to go with the story. I have no idea how to say what I want to say. It is not that I now have some- where to go, there is nowhere to go, as sometimes happens in violence, and especially when blasphemy has a major role in the story. To be a Jew became a blasphemy for Herod because of the story that the Messiah had been born. *Story* is usually the driving force of blasphemy and many other kinds of violence as well.

This then became the ultimate absurdity as often happens in the world of blasphemy; in case there might be something in the story, it had to be killed in the bud, literally, by killing the Messiah, in case he, whoever he might be, happened to exist. The Nazis, however, believed in nothing that might be regarded as religious, and certainly not anything which might remotely be thought of as Christian, especially by Hitler himself, who wanted to kill all Jews because they were Jews, and the primary obstacle to how the world should be, which ultimately meant a world where there could only be Nazis. I said one time that anyone that thought there could be only one story about human beings were also telling us at the same time that they were not just not very clever, but that they were also the worst story tellers ever in the history of the world. I did not say it again because some - and may God forgive them their sin even before they commit it - might think I was trivialising the Holocaust by calling it a story. I always knew from very young that story was part of our life and not just a pleasant way to pass the time. Again, this was because I absolutely loved stories and not because I was or, God forgive me my sins, because I thought I was an intellectual.

***

BLASPHEMY CAN ULTIMATELY TELL ME, I do not have the right to talk, to think, to speak or to write, and it will use every emotional card from the ancient index of intolerance when it says, *See how you are insulting my god, look at the suffering you are causing* us, associating themselves with the divine, in the very same sentence, which is as good an example of blasphemy as any. In Ireland, we *wrote the book* on blasphemy, in every sense. We wrote books which indulged in strident blasphemy and we created a culture after independence in 1922 which cried out blasphemer, and every variation of the term, at everyone who dreamed of asking a question not already in the relatively new official catechism of the Catholic Church; but also, to complete the circle, at anyone who had the audacity to suggest an answer not in the catechism, whatever the question. This could apply as well in many aspects of the social arena as well as in matters of religion, as the Catholic Church in Ireland sought to spread its influence and power to more and more areas of life in the pursuit of establishmentarianism in its absolute form, as it ironically set out, in practice, to ape and surpass the political and constitutional position of the Church of England in the immediate years after Ireland gained its independence. Which was rather a bizarre thing to do, given the history of the two islands, one small, the other bigger, but, in the scale of things universal, not actually that large either. Because England conquered the world in a way nobody ever did before and will never do again - and anyone that tries will witness the end of the world as we know it - it is easy to assume that because England was *so great and so mighty*, that it was also colossal, in some way or other.

———————

Swift in his utterly blasphemous and pornographic Tale of a Tub, used language most foul in his blasphemy against both the Catholic Mass and sacrament of Holy Communion, but also against some of the teachings of the protesting (Protestant) Dissenters who were outside the pale of the (Protestant) Established Church whose titular Head was the reigning British Monarch. In the very important transit years of twelve and thirteen when my friends and I thought we were quite funny - this, of course, is modesty speaking, we knew with absolute surety that we were very funny - I remember asking the others who were with me one day, if Henry the Eight, who everyone knew was in Hell, was still the Head of the Church of England and if that was not embarrassing to English people. Swift, of course, also wrote the book of books on secular blasphemy. In the ordinary day to day lives of many in some countries today in Europe, secular blasphemy in the context of certain types of beliefs is now much more relevant than religious blasphemy, although our recent and predictable preoccupation with blasphemy in the context of Islam, sometimes makes me wonder whether some people in what is commonly called post-religious Western cultures, are implicitly using this now as a distraction from having to look at how we ourselves use the same type of stratagem in areas outside religion; not to mention not having to look at aspects of religious blasphemy which are still very much a live semiotic issue in certain so-called Western cultures such as America. In Gulliver's Travels, which is the major work against intellectual correctness in modern times and maybe every time, Swift became the creator of modern satire, when he invented the obscene and dangerous trick of doing what he wanted to satirize. Doing what you want to ridicule and blaspheme makes great satire, if you are a brilliant intellectual with teeming torrents of talent in a wide variety of literary genres. It can also be highly dangerous, and sometimes mortally, depending on the particular culture in a particular time frame, including now again in various countries in the so-called West, when individuals or small groups may engage in random acts of violence on a small or large scale, in the name of their religion, and where those to be killed are deemed to be the enemy simply because they are in a particular country where the immigrant perpetrators also live.

Other Irish writers would later follow Swift in this unholy tradition. Oscar Wilde would use the talents of a formidable fencing master to prick the habits of the bourgeoisie with a finely honed épée, but James Joyce, the Jesuit boy, was much more ambitious, and had much higher targets. He would also use any and every weapon available, heavy and light; being consistently more vicious than any of his contemporaries also became his trademark. Sometimes when I read snatches of Ulysses at random in a pretend game of lucky dip - it is not the only book where I do this, I do it with some poets as well, but that does not count - I am still sometimes shocked as we come into a new millennium at how revolutionary he can be, even if I have come upon a section I already know rather well. He also had and probably more than most of his peers writing in French or German at the time, a far superior knowledge and more sophisticated and extensive understanding of, religious culture, including the minutiae of practice, which especially delighted his undercover admirers and added to the annoyance of the Church at the same time, and sometimes the political authorities as well. His hapless religious mentors in the Jesuit schools he attended in Dublin must have been attacked by the long dark nights of the soul and the pitch black days as well, when they wondered how they could have produced such a monster. And why they had ever allowed him to transfer from a very ordinary Catholic boys' school where any *notions* that he might have would have been well beaten out of him by the time he came into second year. Joyce, and this is just one example, would take the sacred teaching of the Catholic Church that we are made in the image of God, and in page after page of Ulysses, tell us in graphic detail - matching and sometimes surpassing Swift, the theologian, in obscenity, pornography, and blasphemy - how this image of God manifests itself in the daily lives of the men and women in the *dear old dirty* Dublin of maudlin ballads. Like a morganatic blend of an old style Scottish Puritan and a Franciscan preacher in sandals who could do fire and brimstone on cue any time of day or night, Joyce never misses an opportunity to fire wave after wave of arrows dipped in noxious satire, at the very secular, sacred myths of love and romance between the sexes; sometimes, and very savagely, all sexual relations are dismissed in the manner of the old nasty, brutish and short expression, despite his own *happy days* on the side of Howth Hill which I can see in all its Spring glory a short distance up the road from where I am writing.

P.S. We love the word *field* in Ireland, maybe because for a long long time and well into my adulthood, having a field of any kind saved you from having to *take the boat* and go into the unknown with your family in a foreign country, near or far. A play called *The Field* appeared in 1965 and went straight into the canon of Irish writing. The writer would later enter the exaltation of Irish writers.

In contrast, it may seem in bad taste to say that in *the blas-*

phemy business, the author of the <u>Satanic Verses</u> at the end of the 1980s was an innocent amateur, but there is not much point in worrying about good taste or indeed bad taste either, if you want to talk about the semiotics of blasphemy [1]. If the usual rules of accepted good manners have to be abandoned completely in the discussion of some aspect of the world of meaning, it can sometimes be a clear signal that this may be something of special importance - semiotics is no exception - which may also be very threatening to some people. Most of those in Europe and America who rushed to defend the writer seemed to ignore this, but also, more importantly, not to understand what blasphemy is and what blasphemy does; nor, even worse, did their arrogant ignorance allow them to understand that, in some contexts, there is no defense against blasphemy, in any normal, expected sense of the term.* Swift, the ordained clergyman and Protestant divine, and Joyce, his very Catholic, Jesuit successor, knew what blasphemy was, and both of these indefatigable thinkers used their expertise to create the most extreme, violent, and sometimes even quite exotic blasphemy. Whatever the two Dubliners were, they could never be accused of innocence or naïvety.

*(Note: This was written some twenty five years ago and everything has completely changed - was Yeats a genius or just lucky to have coined the phrase all changed - since then because of the violence perpetrated in the name of Islam in North America and Europe by various groups and also lone individuals who want to leave some mark to compensate for their hapless lives as someone called them. There is no discussion about lines in a book or any other kind of blasphemy, the violence is carried out in principle against people but also physical places deemed not us, which is one of most abrasive and comprehensive couple of words in the semiotics of violence. These last sixteen words will not win me any prizes in any deep

and insightful category, but I do not seem to be able to find any better ones, again. I often think I am in a fight to the death contest with violence because I always fail to capture it in words, as if I need any more reminders about how different verbal and non-verbal can be).

Their theses on blasphemy which were hundreds of years apart, were an exercise in extreme blasphemy and are also regarded as among the great works of world literature which is itself beyond strange. The irreverent duo would freely indulge in gross exaggeration, firing wave after wave of ordnance at their enemies, to make sure their readers and their immediate foes, would have no problem understanding what they were doing. Swift was at war with a known and sometimes named foe, Joyce was doing battle against history and whatever culture which happened to come into sight as a target; this would include religious cultures, and not only those which want to include everything secular as well, under their jurisdiction. In the twinned, sometime scurrilous London and Dublin traditions of the early eighteenth and early twentieth centuries, respectively, neither of the two ever overestimated the intellectual capacity of their opponents. The hyperbole had multiple purposes, but one constant objective was to signal that they would not pay their target the respect of quoting their beliefs accurately, because if something is nonsense to begin with, it would be *below their dignity*, to pay it any respect, of any kind: *infra dig* was even a popular pretentious abbreviation for the more august *infra dignitatem* when I was a student *up from the country* (as was said then in Dublin and not always meant as a compliment). This contrasts absolutely with how blasphemy is now talked about by particular groups of Muslims who shout blasphemer as if the whole world itself was their pulpit. There is, however, no *as if* in their language, their world is the whole world. The whole world, whatever and whoever it is, is their world, and their communication comes primarily in the form of what you are not to do or say, which may include *you are to say nothing,* and also in the form of the most terrible, cruel violence which is its own very frightening, dramatic communication, including by individuals of any age, at any time, anywhere.* I should have made it much more explicit earlier that behaviour can also be included in the censorious circle which is blasphemy, including violence of any and every kind.

*(Note: This was written a long time ago, relatively, but what you are not to do or say has always been the case, it is just that we are now all more aware of it unless you live in a retreat from all media in a deep bunker in the bowels of Inis Tuaisceart off the Southern Coast of Kerry. What is now happening in the lands of Syria, for example, is a wholesale massacre of Muslims by Muslims which is aided and abetted by outside forces which are using the various conflicts in the Middle East as proxy for their own internecine political and economic conflicts. I risk being accused of being an unreformed '60s something or other, which I still am in many ways, and sometimes in a much more pronounced way, but outside forces interfering in the affairs of another country still has peculiar resonance for those of a certain age in Ireland. Meddling with force was many bad and sad centuries ago in what I sometimes lovingly call my place).

The writer of the Satanic Verses, in contrast, tried to assuage his accusers and kept pleading his innocence, not seeming to understand anything about blasphemy and, worse, not seeming to know that it is not in his power to make such a plea of innocence; and never is in any context where the accusation of blasphemy is said with serious intent and not only when there is a permanent threat of consequences. The withering Irish expression *He should never have been allowed out* - which says, he is far too naïve to be allowed out on the street alone - for anyone displaying such childish naivety is on the polite extreme of many such expressions in our English. In my young Ireland saying some of what is being said in this essay, even in a deep, hallucinating sleep would count as gross blasphemy, if someone were to hear it, not to mention see it in permanent print.

IN A BRUTAL, colloquial sense, the accusation of blasphemy is *the oldest trick in the book* and all the other less savoury expressions which could match blasphemy in feral violence and viciousness. I declare that what you say is blasphemy and then refuse to discuss it with you. No, worse than that. When there is a serious charge of blasphemy, and many, most people, in many places in Europe now, do not, could not, fully appreciate what this really means or could mean anymore, because it is not part of our *sensus communis*, our common ideational and emotional culture, our communal talk. You are denied the right, *a priori*, to say anything which the guardians of god, some god, any god, of their making, do not want you to say, which itself will not mean much either to those who are part of that peculiar post-religious culture in Europe. And neither are you free to think anything they do not want you to think. *See the pain you are causing*, they will cry, *See the nefarious crime you have committed against our god.* Strange un-English sounding words like nefarious sometimes seem to be especially popular when violence is in play, as if we need to add gravity to what is being said. When they talk about god, they are talking about themselves, which, again, in workaday speak, is somewhat pretentions, at least, but nothing, be it empirical or theoretical, ever causes or needs to cause, a problem for them. That is what must be accepted, if any such charge of blasphemy is to be understood, even minimally. When I use the term accept here, I do not mean you agree. But you have to accept, and in good faith, if that is also not a station too far along the line, that this is how they really think, or else you will not understand, or you will misunderstand; and you are also saying, implicitly, that you do not want to understand, an attitude which seems to be happily abroad in many places as well when blasphemy is addressed. Understanding may not change anything very much, in practice, but, ultimately, there is no point in not understanding. It is also a pity not to understand. Wanting to understand is the glorious miracle we all share, especially when we are young, independently of time and place, but it may be very different, as we all know too well when we are older, and not only when we know what it is not to be said in any circumstance.* Ask those who are shouting blasphemer at you and they will tell you what reality is, what truth is, what being in error means, in no uncertain terms. *No ifs, no buts,* no *on the one hand* or *on the other hand,* or any other tactics you or I might use if we are holding forth in the more polite media or in academia, so as not to (appear to) give offence, or to be politically correct. They may also tell you nothing but you will know, and very clearly, what you are not to say, not to do.

*(Note: Not to be said could take on primary importance in Communist countries such as Romania in Eastern Europe. Sometimes highly educated, clever people in their fifties had no idea what was to be said, which made the situation even worse, because you might put yourself in jeopardy by not being sure what was to be said, or saying the wrong thing, which is itself an awful three word string. They had not been schooled, literally, in the Communist system and did not always know instinctively what was to be said and not to be said. I was much better prepared because Irish Catholicism gave us a very extensive, very detailed, training in what to say and what not to say, even to the self, and sometimes there were the most severe and sometimes absolute, sanctions attached if the rules were broken. The Irish system - and I am talking semiotics here - was ultra-sophis-

ticated, as a system, compared with the boorish, often crass reality of Communist Eastern Europe.

As we come into the third decade of the third millennium, Official Russia is now much more sophisticated in its post-Communist, patriotic, religious garb, but it still says what it likes, but politicians and commentators in the West make a complete neighing ass of themselves and get all hot and bothered and rush to challenge what is said, and then get all tangled up sometimes as well, in semiotic knots. Moscow says what it likes, when it likes, and you saying that what it says is not true has no bearing of anything: we all do this, all countries do this, it is just that Moscow officially plays the game very publicly, explicitly and very blatantly when some international situation or dispute or crisis is in play. This brings us into the semiotic arena where game can also take on very serious meaning, and it is crass intellectual and semiotic immaturity not to understand what game entails and what it can sometimes mean when lives and people's welfare are at stake. It is a very old, Catholic theological principle and by now a well-honed Communist one as well - they have been doing it for a hundred years now - that a lie is only a lie when the listener is entitled to the truth. No person, no group, no country, is entitled to the truth or anything else, when Moscow puts on this revered Catholic mantle and decides they have no such rights. I always felt that students often had a problem in really understanding what is said in these last thirteen or so lines, and also its implications, because we all have an implicit belief that something is valid or has some validity of some kind or other, when it is said; life would be impossible in practice, if we had to ask is this true every time someone says or writes something. In the old days, Moscow was always bottom of the class in international communications - and it still has not rid itself completely of the mind-numbing dull, dead and solemn, which was the first rule in Russian electronic communications, and when the weather report was no different from anything else - but now one television spokesman who comments on Russian and foreign affairs for the world's media, also has this quite brilliant and extraordinary gift which seems to be very rare in Russia of also saying without saying it, and also the very Irish and if you believe this you're a bigger idiot than I even thought you were at the same time. The new breed of spolesman is now also, of course, of a certain age which is not the dead liability in Russia and China that it often is in the West, and a consummate actor to boot; his sometime winning smile is rare in international, political communications where dour and wooden is often the universal norm).

You MAY ARGUE, on the basis of human or social decency, that nobody should offend people by talking negatively about their beliefs. Or that nobody should ridicule what people hold sacred, that nobody should ever use scatological language when talking about other people's religion, and that nobody should gratuitously cause such pain and hurt. I agree, wholeheartedly with all four principles. I was brought up in a community where wonderful, good people would be deeply hurt by any such behaviour, people who did not have a shred of hypocrisy or cruelty in their profoundly sincere, religious lives. And I now too have total empathy for such religious believers who are offended by pictorial images - and this is not a ploy to win trust, which, you will learn very quickly, is a waste of time, if you write case studies to explain semiotics, which, sooner or later, will be taken as insulting by everyone in turn, and sometimes everyone seems to take a turn at the same time - and not just those representations which are or which are regarded as, obscene, and which they think debase their founders and sacred figures. These very words, obscene and debase, generate endless and often insuperable semantic and semiotic problems in themselves, and not only in religion, and sometimes they are like unintended explosive devices, which may also sometimes be seriously loaded with intention, of course. But you learn very quickly if you begin to walk the very long, twisting, rough roads which are blasphemy, that the language used, and which may also have to be used in talking about blasphemy, is a specific field like no other, and full of snares hidden in the long grass which skirts the road. But sometimes, the ploys and casuistry used in the accusations of blasphemy are beyond simplistic, which is why informal language may best match the shenanigans I first learned in the *hard talk* of the schoolyard when I was six. Maybe it is the best place still in every society to study such talk.

THE DILEMMA of genuinely not wanting to hurt people, even indirectly or implicitly, lies at the heart of the quandary of blasphemy, and may have no solution. This may, literally, be no solution, not just any easy solution. Certain people who are, deem themselves to be, religious, may accuse you of prejudice and plead injury anyway, not just if you disagree with them, but simply because you are not of their faith, for instance, or, if you are (deemed to be) of their faith and do not fulfill, in their eyes, all of their criteria for being regarded as a proper, true member of the faithful, as this is defined by them. The last part, *as this is defined by them*, is always the operative meta-rule in every semiotic world where blasphemy lives. In turn, they may accuse you of abuse and violence of all kinds, if you dare to contradict, or question, their teaching, including aspects of their teachings which have very practical, everyday expression and interpretations, that may intrude in your life and be contrary to ideas and values important to you, including things which, for you, belong either in your religious or secular world, or both. It is time to plant a red flag here, as something which may be beyond acceptance, beyond understanding. For some, there is no such category as secular and to think this or make such an assertion, may also be regarded as blasphemous, and sometimes very blasphemous. In certain recherché contexts of absolute religiosity which do not cater for any distinction between secular and religious, this is the ultimate blasphemy. Again, another red flag is raised as a warning that the major religions have always had the idea of a unitary world, which includes saying that the world is and always has been, as they say it is. Some within the religions, and especially in Christianity and to a lesser extent within Islam - interestingly, both sometimes also used the most exquisite language - had various mystical ways of thinking which could include saying that God is in all of us, and also, sometimes, that God is in all of nature, which, to add to the never ending circle of complexity, has also sometimes itself been regarded as highly blasphemous by others within their own religion.

Some scholars may rightly tell me that the distinction I make between the secular and the religious is not necessarily always valid historically, and, or, that it is prejudicial to expect all societies to have evolved in the same way; but, as in almost any discussion of blasphemy, there may be dangers hiding in the long grass, and sometimes in the short grass and where there is no grass, and using a term such as evolve, or some close synonym, may also be regarded as a blasphemy. You may now also be accused of saying that they change their beliefs which is also on the extreme end of what anathema could mean. It might be taken that I know this, but it has no relevance here, for the simple reason that this is not a historical or philosophical essay, it is an essay which tries to deal with the very difficult and sometimes impossible problem of how meaning is assigned in the here and now, or with meaning in a particular time frame, and when the sometime strictures about a theoretical logicality have no relevance. We may, for example, believe in a field of related meanings which might be regarded in another context as riddled with gross contradiction, but which, of course, is not regarded as such now; nor is the term evolve used in any way prejudicially here in the sense of necessarily always changing for the better, which also belongs in the realm of history, and one this time with an ethical, eschatological edge. The world of evolution other than in the realm of purely physical change, is a paradise for semiotics because of all the cultural skullduggery often associated with how it plays with meaning, and sometimes very violently.

A certain religion or religious denomination now may resolutely refuse to consider my point of view, and I am marking this again, with another red flag. But it is not simply that talking or writing constitutes blasphemy for them, this also says I have no rights. I am not a person, I am not the type of person - *type* in its original sense of class - who has a right to think, to talk, to write, and ultimately, I am not someone who has the right to exist. This kind of cognitive chain is not as strange as it may seem at first, apart from the last part about the right to exist. But I am afraid you will have to take it on trust - also for the good of your health - if you do not know it already, that if you ever want to explore certain areas of belief in particular areas of our lives, there may also be an absolute *non passaran* rule which mark the lines which cannot be crossed; these are absolutes where an alternative position cannot be considered, even if we are sometimes reluctant to be open and explicit about such demarcation zones. Some of these absolutes may also be very relative, in the sense that they may go in and out of existence and our lives, and, sometimes, very quickly, when it suits us, but this does not take from their absolutist importance at a particular time.

Semiotics is magic because we are magicians. It is the only world where the relative can be absolute, and *vice versa*, and the permanent can be temporary and ephemeral. Those who suffer from a semantic blockage which is sometimes accompanied by an absolute belief in a particular dictionary or dictionaries in general, as the ultimate arbiter of meaning - this can be the cause of very serious problems when various elites, politicians, journalists etc. give dictionaries a kind of sacred status - and who pronounce *ex cathedra*, that the invariable cannot be variable. They are stuck permanently at 6.00 *o'clock* and may suffer severe trauma if they wander by mistake into the sometime mad hatter world of semiotics. Unless, of course, they have a predilection for masochism or if they just enjoy being angry, which is not uncommon when particular meanings are in play; this can often be the kind of anger which also hisses and crackles and rumbles incessantly. In the world of blasphemy, for example, and not just in the one where the *White Queen* reigns, it can be common practice to punish people before they commit a crime rather than after. I do this too in a many areas of my life, and - if you will bear with the insufferable pomposity which must go with the most cursory discussions in introductory semiotics - again, everyone does, which is one of my many not very polite ways of saying, so do you, which students, for some reason, hate. It can be one of the most horrible aspects of growing up for many people to realise at a certain point, that you are the same as everyone else, or that you are ordinary, though some seem to resist it to the happy end, even when they also believe absolutely - and this was the sentence of all sentences in my upbringing, from a very young age, even from before what was regarded officially then in Ireland, as the age of reason - in the idea that we are all created equal by God

Himself. You will have noticed that these paragraphs feature the term absolute rather a lot, in one form or another, but this is not always due to my linguistic ineptitude, it is also because this is the land where absolute rules can rule absolutely sometimes. It can also be very costly not to be aware of this, it is just that one of the first things everyone learns in every society is what not to say.

IT IS USUALLY, but not exclusively, believers in the monotheistic religions, especially the two historically later ones, however, or, rather, certain denominations of them in particular, who have a long tradition of defending themselves against real and notional assault; in addition, impressive sets of defence have always been built up, and usually with a language to match. It is in such contexts that we can see clearly that, in certain contexts, in the field of blasphemy, there is, in principle, no common ground, ever, or, at least, at a particular time and in a particular place, which can, however, also sometimes seem like forever. This is the point of the classic accusation of religious blasphemy. It is, on one level, a defence mechanism, and for the accusers to enter into a dialogue with you - you are the blasphemer, not just someone who blasphemes - would involve them having to acknowledge that their belief is open to discussion, but surely, it is not difficult to appreciate why this in itself poses a threat and a risk which cannot be accommodated. On another level, but at the same time, it is an attack mechanism, and it decrees that you be silent, a term which has always carried a very rich meaning, as witnessed in the first examples of writing in the origins of my particular culture. What I now call *the culture of the two rivers* in the geographical *Middle East*, whose names have always fascinated me since I was a boy looking in my hand me down, dog eared atlas of the world. Little did I know then that this was the culture which had already brought so much magic into my life and which also set out many of the dreaded tropes of violence mapped out in the model of violence presented in the various essays I now write about violence.

Despite the use of such brusque language in the classic charge of blasphemy, this is very sophisticated behaviour. It operates on an evasive, invasive axis, and uses a very clever strategy which has multiple and sometimes variable tactical strands in how it deals with what is regarded as blasphemy. Nor would it be clever to delude yourself and apply fallacious and flattering criteria of cultural and intellectual sophistication and superiority to yourself while you define those who scream blasphemy as primitive, simple souls, or even implicitly, as pre-human, in some vague insulting way. Similarly, if you want to consider blasphemy without prejudice, it is not a bad idea to remember that strands of religions, formal and informal, which are wont to cry blasphemy at every opportunity, may be more honest than certain sections of the secular world which are sometimes prone to indulge in deviant intellectual and moral hypocrisy, and not only to avoid giving offence to others. It is not necessary I hope, to labour the fact that the very loaded meaning of the term hypocrisy, could itself justify an endless semiotic study, for every society, in every era, if only because it is always changing, but also because we are all experts in some form of hypocrisy, and absolutely not only those of us with *book learning*.

THIS LAST SENTENCE opens up a complex series of discussions which is relevant to many of those very ordinary aspects of our lives where we may be reluctant to be explicit about how meaning is assigned. This would include what meaning may be expressed, what meaning may not be expressed, and includes meaning which can be made explicit, in some way, at least, and what part has to remain implicit. Institutional socialisation, for instance, often involves learning, and learning quickly, if you want to survive and progress, about what constitutes secular blasphemy in a particular institution, or sub-group, or group, or nation. And there are no induction courses to guide us; it takes poor innocent children years to learn this, and sometimes at great personal cost and trauma. Groups, including nations, have also suffered terribly as well for being slow learners, when contexts change quickly and radically, as happened in the 1970s in these islands with incessant factional terrorism and also endless *dirty tricks* of every kind by a sovereign government which is also a major power and member of the very small number of major powers which have decided at various times, to call themselves G6, G7, G8 (*the group of* etc.). In easy contrast, however, blasphemy in religion which may sometimes be crude, is often open and explicit, whereas in many different contexts outside religion, in intellectual institutions and the media, to give just two examples, blasphemy is sometimes subtle, implicit, and, of course, ultimately dishonest, and there will not even be a hint that *the truth* will not be told. Frequently we will not ever acknowledge to ourselves, that there is such duplicity, or any such *truth*, but it is precisely because of the fact that something is not said which saves us from having to admit that we are engaged in such self-censorship.

But again, I am not talking up a moral crusade, or condemning pretence, or the strategic use of the apposite tactic of omission. My upbringing and education taught me well about the devilishly difficult to explain concept of the sin of omission. We are, of course, all experts in the practice of omission, and learn the strategy and the tactics that need to go with it, very quickly in childhood - not knowing this in practice, can in certain contexts even be regarded as a mental and, or, emotional problem of some kind - when not learning quickly and making mistakes, can be very expensive. This is behaviour which did not happen, in the usual sense given to the term happen, but, despite it not actually happening in any real time frame, it somehow happens, and you can still be deemed guilty. If there are shades of old, moth-eaten and foolish anti-Catholic prejudices now appearing out of the undergrowth, you might discuss it with someone, not for moral reasons, but because it can block understanding like no other. If you do not analogously understand sins of omission in a secular, everyday context, you are a *walking saint*, as we used to say in Ireland, sometimes sincerely, sometimes *not so much*, as my American cousins might brilliantly say, and have been blessed in your relationships, as we would also have said recently in Ireland. Or you are among those not regarded kindly by Swift in his sometime not so <u>Polite Conversation</u>, *There is none so blind as they that won't see*, who took it rather inelegantly - sometimes, however, his very inelegance also seemed to have had serious intent, as only The Reverend Jonathan would risk doing - from another master semiotician, Jeremiah, in the *Good Book ...foolish people... without understanding; which have eyes, and see not; which have ears and hear not.*

The rules in the world of belief and social communication are often very simple. You have the right to express yourself and others (feel they too) have the right not to have what they hold sacred, mocked and scorned, and most decent people fervently, if implicitly, contribute to a belief in this second part, and not just those who are religious. This is a very common semiotic predicament, and we usually solve the problem by keeping quiet about the beliefs and attitudes of others or certain aspects of them, at least in certain delicate contexts; we do not usually make snide remarks, for instance, about what is important to others, especially those we respect and like, or those who are of benefit to us, unless we are engaged in outright symbolic aggression. The right to express yourself freely is, as Hamlet's old saw rather elegantly said, *a custom more honoured in the breach than the observance.* That is the empirical, semiotic position, this is how we are with our loved ones, our families, our friends, and people at work, and this would need to be considered in any discussion of blasphemy, if we are to be exhaustive and intellectually consistent, and human. Political correctness, however, did not arrive in the world via some American university which is famous in a small corner of its own campus, it is just that it now has a popular name, which makes it somewhat easier to talk about; but it is like poverty, it is always with us, as semiotics will also quickly tell you as well. Socrates who was clever and brilliant and often the friend you might call to explain difficult issues, acknowledged, almost casually, that political and intellectual propriety rule, and should rule, even if it were to cost a person his life. He even thought, again almost nonchalantly, that society could not be, without such a rule. I thought when I first read Plato that Socrates took explicit much too far and that he even sometimes went over to the silly side. I was young then, and thought, as I should, as a young one, but semiotics saved me, somewhat, at least, from the pit of propriety, because it has to regard everyone and everything the same, if it is to do its professed work professionally.

Academics, intellectuals and journalists publish on anything and everything, but I do not know of any study ever, which deals with what you are not allowed to say and with how you are not allowed to say it, in all the very different contexts of the lives of those who inhabit the countries which loudly profess *freedom of expression.* My mentors, who are almost all creative writers of some kind, have harvested these fields, however, for millennia, and, since the advent of the music hall and film as well, contemporary comics, in all their sometime estranged forms, have resurrected the great Greek tradition. What are the countless things you never say, which you are never to say, to your friends, your lover, your mother, your teachers, your father, your wife, your children, your partner, your husband, yourself, or maybe even to Almighty God Himself. Sometimes, I am still shocked by what is not said within universities, the secular institution which has always been rather partial to touting its dedication to the pursuit of truth. I am often equally bewildered by the levels of pretence, which is often the other, often very creative, side of blasphemy, in journalism also.

MOST OF THE discussion in Western cultures about the reactions to blasphemy in certain Islamic countries is often so hypocritical it might rightly be classed as structural racism or some such ugly phrase. But this is not saying that people who shout out in a very loud and threatening voice that you cannot say this, you cannot say that, should be ignored, or not countered in some form, and not only when the voice is backed up by threatening and violent demonstrations, or by extreme forms of physical violence which sometimes has no limits. While I agree it may be an exercise in crass shabbiness to excoriate other people's beliefs and values in public, it has to be taken into account that in the context of blasphemy, asking a reasonable, polite question may also be prohibited, no matter what language is used, or even if the question is not even of much importance on the scales they themselves use. The form of the blasphemy is of little or no importance, if offence will be taken in principle anyway, independently of every other consideration. And if certain groups, be they religious or secular, want to talk about their message in a very public way, then surely it is a bit much, as the English of a certain discreet class cleverly likes to say, for them to complain if I, whoever I am, speak in public as well. And to believe otherwise - that certain people have privileged or exclusive speaking roles as human beings - is to subscribe to the first principle of fascism. This last word has now taken on many of the trappings of cheap insult in Europe, and in a qualifying form, functions in many ways like a curse, but this should not blind us to the fact that attitudes to freedom of thought and expression are a very efficient and embarrassing test, both for classic fascism and for nascent fascism, including in personal relationships. I might tentatively propose that it would, at least, be sensible scientifically to assume that embryonic fascism is the default position - and not happy news for students soon to go into their twenties - and that it would be good science to give evidence which would show where this assumption sometimes does not or may not, apply. It might also be included in the brave and daring curriculum of the new, very brave and sometime naïve, discipline of peace studies.

We all usually decide, implicitly at least, that we have prior rights with regard to ideas, attitudes and values, and with regard to communication, and in the twin cultures of Britain and Ireland you will now find more intellectual diffidence and humility among the various Christian clergy than you would in my tribe, the journalists, academics and intellectuals, in that rank order. But you will find that those of us who belong to one or more branches of this holy trinity, can be quite articulate experts in the tactics of *hide,* if that does not seem a little like contradiction. We can be adept at not being explicit, in contrast with classic religious blasphemy, about expressing what cannot be said, and, almost more importantly, what cannot be the subject for analysis; predictably there are those, and not only journalists, who now make a living out of *saying the seeming unsayable*, something which also marked the beginnings of journalism in English as we know it in the early seventeenth century in London and Dublin, for example (and which is still alive and well in the popular, sometimes lurid print media in London, and in a paler version in Dublin). Blasphemy of the religious type, however, if only because it often delights in its hauteur about its public right and duty to be explicit, still has a lot to teach us about what precisely prompts the accusation of blasphemy.

The fact that vulgar language or ribald images are sometimes used, especially but not only in modern religious blasphemy, may only be an additional element, even a distraction and a side show, and is not necessarily the core of the issue. It is what is said is the real problem for those who have appointed themselves the vicars of their god, not, ultimately, how something is expressed (a peculiar expression may of course be used as the hook to wage a counter attack). Empirically, this is how they have always reacted, although sometimes the very fact that someone has the audacity to say anything at all in what a group considers its exclusive domain may in itself be the elemental blasphemy; or it may just make the situation worse. And on a purely emotional level, I can understand too, if the Orwells explodes in exasperated despair, with a story of inhuman humans and human animals, when faced with the absolute and morbid logic of an ideology, religious or secular, which brooks no question. Especially, for example, when it has always regarded and still does regard, women as not properly human - there are a lot of phrases which echo these last three words - and also has a savage history in its treatment of what is regarded as dissent, including shades of mass slaughter, and especially if a religion or an ideology, also uses and demands the right to use the language of scientific and intellectual exchange to enhance its standing.

A particular religion may cry blasphemy if you depict one

of its reputed sacred personages engaged in unseemly behaviour, but I may also be accused and sentenced without trial if I talk as a scholar about a linguistic or semiotic aspect of the teachings or sacred texts of this religion, be it in translation or the original, or about certain historical and contemporary incidents, or about the behaviour of some of the founders and the officials of this religion. The most superficial analysis of the semiotics of blasphemy will tell you that the only universal, practical and relevant rule is that you are to say nothing which relates or has any relevance to, the teachings of the religion or religious denomination, other than what this religion explicitly says - including what it says about what can be said - at a particular time, which itself can be the pivotal, and most difficult element, and not only for an outsider (who may want to come back with *but in the 1790s or the 1990s something completely different was said*, or some such). Those of us who were the last generation in Europe educated in the Classical tradition learned early in life about how religious and secular institutions protect themselves; we were the beneficiaries of the very first cultures to leave prolific accounts of their religions and politics, in Greek and Latin, and in conceptual, linguistic forms which would substantively and sometimes entirely, instruct our very ways of thinking and talking and writing, in every register of life. It is relevant as well to note that the Christian religious tradition, and not only my particularly Catholic one in Ireland, was sometimes obsessed with mediating the *Good Book* and the related semite cultures in minute, sometimes obsessive detail, which was often in direct contrast to our exposure to those aspects of the Graeco-Roman cultures which dealt with - in all kinds of forms, including poetry, and sculpture and sometimes even the ceramic tiles used in some public baths, including those with restricted, elite male membership - forms of behaviour which were regarded as taboo and sometimes gravely sinful (and which were also sometimes a great laugh when we were fifteen or sixteen).

WE ARE NOW in the domain of ideological or moral choice, but also in the more complex domain of semiotics. Everyone, artist or not, has the right to write and to rewrite stories - story, here, has no hint of the meaning which sometimes attaches to the term, as something which is superficial or suspect etc., in some way - unless you accept a preordained and arbitrary statute that certain people can proclaim that they have an absolute prerogative on stories of all kinds. And that they have as well, a comprehensive copyright on expression - including what nobody has ever said - and every form of expression, because only they, as the *incarnation* of truth and reality, have, and are, absolute truth.* My not very humble advice is learn and get used to this *talk*, as we all have to do, or else there will only be an inadequate understanding of blasphemy, or a totally erroneous one, which can in itself also be very dangerous in many contexts. In practice, we are all sometimes capable of working with these oxymoronically tinted assumptions, but we normally find practical solutions to the problem because we do not often make such explicit and authoritative demands as those who also make explicit the sanctions which can follow in the wake of blasphemy (they always claim, after all, to be the agents, in every sense, of their god, which, in their eyes, is very explicit, plain talking). But, very importantly and relevantly, it is also to be noted that usually we do not have to make threats, because the implicit rules about what is to be said, and especially, what cannot be said, work perfectly. They are not only shared meaning, but also meaning which is accepted, in practice. In addition, those who engage in a very public condemnation are usually those in a particular institution which claims to have a particular relationship with some special authority, supernatural or secular. There will also be a selective series of texts which are used as a source of knowledge and wisdom and the leader or leaders of the institution will believe that only they can give an authoritative interpretation of these texts, and in a translation which is hardly an accurate rendering of the original, inspired text, if such a text survives. I mention elsewhere that I was gifted a very easy relationship with language and languages, which means that checking translations is sometimes, at least, not a very onerous task. This, I always add, has nothing to do with being particularly intelligent, which I am not; it is a professional judgment based on years of experience teaching in universities in very different cultures which also had very different standards of second level education that also had distinct influence on standards of entrants at third level. I have always had students who were so obviously more intelligent than I am, that it would have been impossible to think that I was the *King of the Castle.*

*(Note: I have put incarnation, above, in italics, because I did not stress adequately in the original text all those years ago that talk about blasphemy is difficult and sometimes impossible for those who have never had a real experience of religion. They do not have the cognitive tools, and may regard, for example, the blindingly beautiful concept of incarnation which is central to Christianity as nonsensical, because when such a term can have no potential reference for those outside that particular, albeit very large, religious circle, it cannot make any sense, at best. The ignorant and very hurtful term such as nonsense, may also be cavalierly bandied about. Maybe, subconsciously, I did not want to alienate any more than I have already, but now, alienation has been born again and is out and about everywhere, because of the ever new Internet and social media, in particular. In a solemn and very grave sense, we are now a one world like we

have never been before, for good or ill, and sometimes continuing to pretend there are borders as in the old world, physical or in terms of communication, is sad, and potentially dangerous fantasy. Nation states however are still sometimes more anxious about physical borders than ever, and are staging popular referenda about protecting borders in some of the now free, former satellite colonies of Russia in its Soviet Union phase, but the Internet seems to be winning the battle - and the small number of mostly American companies which dominate the Internet totally - which mirrors a globalization that had been with us in one form or another for centuries, but it was somewhat undercover, because, at least partly, it did not have a name.

Early on in doing research on the symbolic violence against the Irish by the foreign ragtag which later evolved in part, into the English, I suggested that it was the advent of writing in popular culture which did the real damage. When stories are sealed in language - and some of these writings in manuscript in the 12th, 13th and 14th centuries, had a very extensive readership, geographically, as Irish writing in theology also had then in parts of the mainland of Europe - they sometime attract an aura of permanence which can also carry a certain prestige, but which does not necessarily happen in oral stories which may also morph quite substantively. Semiotics has noted with great interest and admiration, that the miracle of the written medium in all kinds of forms, is finding a very welcome home, in all kinds of ways, in electronic media. When a great writer nowadays amends a novel after a few years, this is now heralded as news, and not just to readers of contemporary writing or literary critics).

IT IS easy to sit here looking out on the galloping white horses of the Irish Sea and over the horizon of the city with its two tall chimneys to the bizarrely named *Sugar Loaf Mountain* and talk as an intellectual about blasphemy. I have to pinch myself to remember that if I read what I am writing now when I was in my late teens at university, I would have regarded the writer as strange - *strange* was a very common expression where I grew up and it referred to ways of thinking, speaking and behaviour, just one, or two or all three - if not quite an ally of the devil. My version of my own religion, which was, in general, a gentle and loving belief, would have me pray for the poor misguided fool that he would see the light. I would not have called for physical punishment, but I might not have disagreed with those who thought they had a sacred moral duty to make sure that such a person should never get a job as a teacher or a journalist, for example, and if he had had such a job, that he should be dismissed. I would have considered this as perfectly normal, which was itself a very common expression at the time, for some reason. I would of course, have been upset if he had a dependent family but this would not have affected my thinking about the decision to dismiss such a person. In trying to understand blasphemy, be it religious or ideological, it is critical to make every effort to appreciate every last iota of the emotional import. And sometimes it is necessary to stand on the other side, on the side of the believer, which is easy for me, and easy for me to say, because I was such an absolute and what many now would consider an extreme, believer. I am not embarrassed I was such a believer or to admit it either. I have a very tender, loving respect for the many people of my home town who practiced a religion that was happy and generous and loving and full of good will, and who were, in the main, probably more open and tolerant than I was in my late teens. But maybe it was also because of the severe intellectual demarcation lines and the sometime rabidity that was the norm then, that I now also have a special and often very unwelcome eye for such blasphemous tactics outside the realm of religion; reading the map within religion is like meeting old friends from a long time ago. Intellectuals, for example, and universities, my place of work, give me constant and sometimes too many, uncomfortable examples, but the usual boring semiotic rule applies here too, I am no different, I am ordinary and normal. I first wrote I am the norm, but this might be misunderstood or thought presumptuous in an essay on religious blasphemy, and Irish culture sometimes looks very closely and suspiciously at anyone who says anything about himself or herself which might be regarded as self-praise, and not because of *Learn of Me, for I am meek and lowly of heart* which Christ advised [2].

In some important areas of our lives, we must be able to appreciate both ideational meanings and those which have intense emotional import or else we may understand nothing, or we may misunderstand everything by confusing two registers of meaning which can cause all kinds of confusion and danger. In parts of today's Western world we may be very generous about safeguarding what is important to us in our secular, everyday lives, but we may be correspondingly sparing in our understanding of those who say their religion has been and is, the subject of blasphemy, including racist type blasphemy, and especially now in parts of the so-called West, if this religion is Islam, and in particular the Islam of the current political power in Sunni or Shia countries which now sometimes seem to make every effort to disagree with each other about everything.

(Note: The last paragraphs were written before Daesh, ISIS, ISIL, IS, became part of the daily news everywhere because of the various campaigns of total violence, but, more importantly in the longer term, because of the espousal of the absolute semiotic, We are, We are meaning, the model presented and used throughout all of the these essays on identity. I am, I am meaning is also found in many different, very early manuscripts in various languages, both secular and religious, and not only in the three related monotheistic religions. There is the usual - usual to an Irish person who has had to live since the early 1970s with what to call those who have an ideology which espouses constitutional change by violent means and sometimes violence with no limit of any kind, in Great Britain and Northern Ireland, and, in practice, the Republic of Ireland as well - battle, but one which regularly threatens to go to every extreme about what language to use in the first sentence in this Note, to refer to the comparatively new group in Syria and Iraq, with some world leaders using the acronym Daesh, which, it is thought, does not give credence to the group.

The group itself is deadly serious about what it is to be called and, predictably, the sensitivity is of the life and death kind, and there is no sometimes qualifier between is and of in this last phrase. It originally called itself al-Dawla al-Islamiya fil Iraq wa al-Sham, the Islamic State in Iraq and Syria, but changed the name a few years later to Islamic State, because they thought it was being misunderstood, which I never really understood; my reading of what they were trying to do was that they thought it was time for a change, as Madison Avenue sometimes advises its clients. They had used Al-Sham to refer to territories from the Caliph period in the seventh century of our era - and which, it might be noted, is not their way of referring to time - and this also included, for example, Egypt, and what is now called Anatolia, and, to add to the complication, certain foreigners also want to restrict it to modern-day Syria. English in particular suffers from a very extreme form of acronymitis because of the dominance of American English in film and music and in world-wide popular culture in general. Names and language can cause terrible damage - if you are not conscious of this from your own culture, read Translations, the play which has this as its theme and which is set in a particular period in Irish colonial history by Brian Friel - but nations which are not directly involved may think this is immature, and sometimes much worse. Everyone is highly sensitive, of course, about names, but about names that refer to themselves particularly. Names are us, and are an essential part of the weave of our identity - elsewhere I wrote that sometimes names are us, and I am my name, and even my name is my identity, in a desperate attempt to talk about names which are attributed to us as individuals and members of a group - whether we like it or not.

In another essay, I tell the story of my only journey into physical violence, outside hurling, when I was not yet four and in my first days in school. My hair was prone to curl floppily, and when another boy - it is some seventy years ago I still know his name and the house where he lived - called me curly, which I knew would be my permanent nickname in school unless I did something dramatic, I clocked him. The slang verb is from our popular slang noun for face. Another essay goes on a tour of the names which were used about those who wanted constitutional change in the Irish and British isles, but those pages are for the very brave. Other essays also go on a linguistic safari as semiotics must, no matter how boring and tedious it may be for people who are not blessed with a somewhat obsessive gene for forensic linguistics. But this is another example of how horrible semiotics can be, everyone engages in such forensics when what is at issue is important emotionally, as it may be in certain emotional relationships. But we all know, the great and the good, and also those of us who have no such public name, that language is the master of all, and always has been, and often to the chagrin of the said great ones. Semiotics follows the language trails wherever they go, and also all the many other communication paths which do not use verbal language).

In our Western culture, we often behave in a perfectly

contradictory fashion with regard to emotional meaning. We often regard it as childish, to give just one example, when it is life itself, for all of us, at every age. But there is also a deeply sexist, prejudicial attitude which can have extremely dangerous consequences for all of us, that emotional meaning is not very *manly*, and is more properly the domain of women (I would sometimes add in class *Tell that to the bomber who will blow you to kingdom come*, if you survive). The abusive and virulent implications of this apartheid sometimes seem to have no limit, and are sometimes, even in Christianity itself, hostile to the religion of Jesus Christ. Yet, in what we regard as the most important areas of our lives we insist, in practice, that emotional meaning is the foundation for everything that matters most, which tells us better than anything else, how we live our lives far beyond what is often deemed the extremes of absurdity which Beckett exploited in Waiting for Godot, and Wilde did in *The Ballad of Reading Gaol*, his awful last *will and testament*. Confusion about the rational and emotional aspects of meaning will often guarantee that dialogue is hardly possible, and also, that communication will most likely generate mistrust and anger. In addition, the situation can only be made worse if I insist on applying criteria of rational meaning when I examine the meaning which is important to you, emotionally, but not do the same in my own case. The same applies in any group context but now some of the potential consequences are taking on the aspects of nightmare, including in the context of both secular and religious blasphemy, and especially when the secular and the religious are seen as one, as can happen in the *parti pris* politics of America, and not just in the case of the wider regions of the Middle-East and North Africa.

WHILE I AM BEWILDERED by the absence of any studies on the complex and very important phenomenon of the implicit secular blasphemies in our Western cultures, I am still fascinated by the tangible arrogance and intellectual insolence of what is sometimes classic religious blasphemy. In this midnight court of blasphemy, for example, you, the blasphemer, are impeached, and that it your lot. You are not consulted, you are the defendant, and that is the unhappy end of the story, for you. You have no more relevance. You are accused, but in this special forum, to be accused is to be guilty, guilty of the crime for which there is no forgiveness. God, the Almighty and Merciful of my youth, is all forgiving but those who have decided with bountiful arrogance that they are His representatives on earth, judge what can be forgiven and what cannot be forgiven in this life or the hereafter, which, objectively, in terms of theology, defines themselves as superior to God, if only because they, human beings like you and me, abrogate this power to themselves which sails very close to saying they are God. This mode of thinking has been and still is, found primarily in certain strands of Christianity and Islam which feature clear hierarchical structures, in terms of general power, but also in terms of sovereignty and control in the contexts of doctrine and teaching. Again, however, it is to be remembered that similar and sometimes even more extreme hierocracies will be found in some contemporary social and political contexts, and always, also, with the male as dominant, or even as solely dominant, as in certain strands and denominations of religion, and not just one religion, or just the monotheistic, related religions which had their origin in the regions of *the two rivers.**

  *(Note: I originally wrote The male stalks the world of violence all those years ago, but I deleted it in case it became a distraction to what was the core of the discussion of blasphemy. I have always been somewhat of a slow learner in certain quite

important contexts, and this was one of them, and an unforgive-able one. The male has always stalked blasphemy as well, but saying this may still be read as feminist, and all that this word sometimes says, rather than what it is, a boring statistic with mortal consequences, as the next paragraph below, also says as well. But now - we are in the closing stages of the second decade of the third millennium - there are also maniacal elements loose on the world stage, and they are all male. Maybe I find it easy to understand, because I am a very ordinary male, and a tribal one at that, with no illusions about the male or the male tribe, including about our little vanities which have almost never featured properly in writing. I am not going to add and which is primarily done by the male. That would breach all the rules of decorum).

You cannot, you are not allowed to, enter into a discussion with those who purport, officially, to know the mind of God and who now bring down the wrath of blasphemy on your head. You could not, by definition and decree, be an intermediary between man and God; this is the patrimony they have bestowed on themselves, and they, and only they, know and can know, the mind of God. Putting yourself on a level with God is a very special - I first wrote pure, but deleted it as an oxymoron and inappropriate - form of blasphemy and figures prominently and in various ways as absolute *sin* in the *Sacred Books* of the three related, monotheistic religions, but that can never form part of their thinking which ultimately denies that God is the God of Divine Love. The brazen arrogance means they decide who God loves - they make decisions for Almighty God, and just writing this now, invokes the feelings of horror and fear I would have had when I was sixteen - which means they never have to consider, even to wonder, if God the Merciful would forgive the person or persons accused of blasphemy. They may also want you to confess and admit your crime before you are punished, but that is purely to reinforce their very banal human feeling of being right, and has nothing to do with the logic of blasphemy itself. When you are accused of blasphemy, the trial is over, the sentence is already handed down. The self-appointed accuser is the jury and the judge, and it is his sacred and bounden duty, and that of his allies and minions, to decide if he wants to police all thought. This is ordained by the god they have created and continually recreate in their own image, and if this logic which attaches itself to blasphemy is followed to the bitter end, and it can be a very bitter end, he has no choice. It is not in his giving, as it were, to forgive you, you must be condemned. He must punish you, he must protect the innocent, the way the shepherd protects his sheep from you, the rapacious and savage wolf, or else his story disappears into the thin air.

IN WHAT MIGHT BE CALLED traditional blasphemy - in the world that is blasphemy, however, mistakes are not allowed, which, in itself, becomes a very acute problem if you are never absolutely sure what will be regarded as blasphemy - some might even take this phrase as a blasphemous insult in itself. Which itself is a warning about the acute sensitivity which can envelop the whole field of of blasphemy where there may be no difference between the accusation and the trial. The accusation is the trial - it is important to keep in mind, if I can be so forward, this happens in other spheres of life as well - which is very clever semiotics because no further argument or proof is now needed; and retraction is not possible either, with rare exceptions. And if you are prudent, you should not initiate a discussion with those who have declared you guilty in such cases. All you are doing is giving them the opportunity to accuse you of repeating the heinous crime and the chance, maybe again, to list lots of other charges against you, including historical ones, especially if you are or if you are regarded as, rightly or wrongly, a member of a traditional religious group or sub-group of some kind. The whole question of ascription - referring to me as Irish in an international context, for example, or Irish and Catholic in these islands, or *white*, and then on this basis, I am assigned meaning, including whole bundles of meanings over which I may have no control and which I may reject - is critical in any understanding of blasphemy, and like any major aspect of our lives which tortures reality and meaning, talking about it may also be extremely difficult. This means, in turn, that trying to avoid using tortuous language may also be correspondingly tiresome, and impossible. But the problems do not end there. You will be accused of adding to the blasphemy every time you open your mouth when, if you try to explain or defend your original words, you are reprising the evil, which may cause more intense fury, if this is possible. The accuser works, *par excellence*, with a very sophisticated and inclusive semiotic attitude to behaviour. The principle the prosecutor works with in this instance says that talking and writing are (forms of) behaviour, and to talk or to write or to make images of some kind, is consequently, the *sin of blasphemy*, when you say or write or portray, something they disapprove of. They also ascribe to the practical and highly refined semiotic model we all use, implicitly, in various ways and in different circumstances, that thinking, feeling, talking, is behaviour; they are meaningful behaviour in the same way as we all regard physical action as behaviour. And, sometimes, of course, feeling etc. can be regarded by all of us as somehow a more reliable indication of authentic reality, and not only when it is to our advantage.

(Note: I had not been brave enough to say when the main body of the text was written some twenty plus years ago, that if you or your people have not been regarded or treated negatively, or both together, in recent history, it will probably be impossible to appreciate what blasphemy is, with the result that most of what is said in this last paragraph - Note, in the main text - will not available to you, in any real sense. Emotionally generated meaning may be closed in varying degrees, if you are not or have not been, involved in some way in that particular world of meaning; saying this, however, sometimes gives me the uneasy feeling that I am in danger of being a semiotic racist, that some people are not able to understand certain things in any adequate way. I am not talking about sensitivity or any kind of inability to appreciate meaning, I also say elsewhere, for example, in the same vein, that it is impossible for the male - years of personal and now very embarrassing experience, lie behind this sentence - to appreciate in any adequate way the surfeit of sexism which is arraigned against the female in all societies, including how women can semiotically experience safety in public spaces very differently from most adult males. It can be awkward to have a discussion in a seminar in any country about the various cultural and structural forms and types of sexism which are found in various countries without the different arguments becoming very acrimonious and sometimes very angry, if a particular society or group of countries are said, for example, to have made multiple forms of such symbolic violence their emblematic identity. The discussion is also very useful to illustrate that discussing violence in various societies and cultures can itself be regarded as violence, and even a very vicious, destructive and damaging form of symbolic violence, which itself gives violence a certain ironic protection. Students of second or third generation immigrant backgrounds, of course, may sit and smile if the discussion is about the country they are living in now).

The way meaning is assigned in conventional blasphemy is often highly complex. The symbolic crime, *sin*, is apportioned, firstly, to the thing in itself, be it a word, phrase, sentence, poem, book, image, film, whatever. Secondly, to the person, people, groups who create, express etc. the blasphemy. And thirdly, by very dangerous extension - this is not a universal - with potential destruction without limit, to the racial, ethnic, linguistic, religious, or cultural group, *the sinner*, the individual or group transgressor, is deemed to belong to. And now, as usual in the fields where blasphemy is found, we are deep in the semiotic thickets again. Deemed to belong to can mean everyone travelling in any car, bus, train, plane, just as everyone from any particular group, or worse, anyone living in a region, country, continent, can be eligible as a candidate for elimination, as (if they were) a plague; which also means that if this includes people from the same background as those ordering and carrying out the violence, this is no different from any other type of pestilence where *the healthy* may be exterminated sometimes as well in such a sweep.

I was going to apologise to those whose cultural heritage does not give them any help in understanding and appreciating terms such as *sin* and *sinner* as those who live and have lived such an intimate religious experience.* But the impatient teacher also prompts me to say stop lagging behind. And anyway it is much too late. The tensions now escalating internationally around religious identity and blasphemy leave no alternative to understanding, or, at least, making a very sincere and serious effort to understand such terms in their totality; it is not as if we were not here before, when Communism, in the form of the Soviet Union, and the *West*, in the form of the United States, for example, were on the brink of mutual destruction and also the annihilation of the rest of us caught in the middle and on the sidelines, and everywhere else, which, of course, had no real relevance of any kind to those engaged in the particular conflict. The inner teacher who also has a limitless talent for the boring is also not able to make any allowances anymore for the type of primordial prejudice which might say that there is nothing to understand in the type of primitive thinking which itself generates endless accusations of blasphemy. To think like this is a gross form of misanthropy and one which may also have significant elements of racism that has no specific name. It is part of being human to understand, and that includes understanding us in all our awkward diversity, including, as here, how we think and assign meaning and value. It is not politic to say again here, that if you look a little under the surface we all follow the same patterns in assigning meaning. Sanctions may differ hugely, but some sanctions which are structural, in the context of gender, race, pigmentation, and many more such examples, can seriously hurt an individual or group, small or large, including destroying every chance of potential development; and sometimes forever, in practice.

*(Note: When it is said that their cultural heritage does not give them any help in understanding and appreciating terms such as sin and sinner, this has now assumed serious proportions with potential and very grave consequences because of the profound ideational changes in many areas of Western cultures since the above paragraph was a part of endless drafts for lectures, some twenty five, thirty years ago. Most of those now under forty in Western Europe and not just Ireland, are not able to have any real understanding, because sin does not have any existence in their semiotic world except, at best, as a mild, casual metaphor whose original roots are unknown, and a brief dictionary explanation which cannot do justice to emotional meaning may convince them anyway, that it was all primitive nonsense, or, worse, completely insane. When I say in the middle of this last paragraph above, it is not as if we were not here before, this refers to the very long history of violence, including before our era, which had religion and identity as its driving force and

which would be mentioned elsewhere in class. The constant thread in all the lectures and Notes was always violence is easy, identity is the problem. One time, in desperation at my failure to communicate, I even listed those who might easily have destroyed large parts of the world. I was also conscious that it was easier for someone from a small island lost out in the Atlantic in the south of Ireland near the wonderful islands, the Blaskets and the Skelligs which I have known in all kinds of ways since I was very young, to talk in this way about those from the major powers. Island people are not always burdened by the complexes about identity which are often the norm in large societies and great nations. It is sometimes easy for us to see their grandiose foibles for what they are, and because they are sometimes so enormous, we can happily avoid seeing our own little frailties. We used to use all kind of such phrases to indicate that any wrongdoing we might do was really of no consequence, as if this could also influence any potential sanction).

Semiotics indicates better than anything else that we are all equal because we assign meaning in the same and very similar ways, and any attitude which is predicated on the prejudice of superiority and which implicitly says, in practice, *There is nothing to understand*, and, *This is primitive beyond belief*, is on a very dangerous road. And plain wrong and silly. I will always be the first to rush to say there may be very little to understand, in the sense that what is being said is something a child learns very well at a very young age, but the same child knows how important it is as well, including how violence may be the next move, especially symbolic violence. Ignorance about how people assign meaning, and worse, condescension about how people think, including children - and also ignorance about how children learn language and assign meaning and think, which are the magical trinity of this our world and also the source of what is the foundation of the model used in these essays to explain violence, which says that we all assign patterns of meaning in the same and similar ways - are twin recipes for understanding nothing in the world of meaning. They have also often proved, historically, to be one move and sometimes no move, away from violence without limit. The meanings in the angry and dangerous discourse which is traditional blasphemy, must be understood in their own context and not haughtily dismissed as *beneath contempt* and understanding, if we are not to go back to the very dark days of genocidal destruction generated by religious identities going rogue, again, and imploding and exploding in different strands of the monotheistic religious cultures, in both internal and external circumstances.*

*(Note: This last paragraph was not written in the immediate past, so to speak. Not appreciating adequately that simple is not simplistic has also sometimes hindered us in understanding the gravity of meaning. The phrases the very dark days and identities going rogue in this last sentence in the main text have much more relevant and poignant meaning now because groups, sub-groups, individuals now have given themselves the license to punish whoever they decide is the blasphemer or, more alarmingly, whoever belongs to a group which is deemed, in principle, to be a blasphemer. The attribution of such collective guilt is as old as our first records in many different places and cultures).

ALL OF THESE essays follow the lead of the overall title, *Violence is easy, identity is the problem.* Unfortunately, I was not clever enough to say as well in a few words, that while identity can be very complex, it may also be very simple, and in the farthest limits of simplicity, as sometimes happens in the world of blasphemy when identity is pared back to the bone, as expressed in the formula *I am right, you are wrong*. Which may be said by an illiterate individual or group without any education about or to, a highly educated individual or group, or indeed, vice versa. The world of blasphemy is good for humility and teaches us like no other that learning, being or not being literate, numerate and educated, may have no bearing on being able to predict where the accusation of blasphemy will come from, or the severity of the charge, or whether there will be retribution, or even the level and intensity of violence, symbolic and physical. Despondency and sometimes even despair often come to my door when I realise that some of the most educated people in the world now do not seem to have learned the lesson that was dramatically on offer in the 1930s and '40s - it is not now part of the Kant notion of *common sense* among the under '50s that 1945 saw the first and so far, the only use of the nuclear option - that the seeming sophisticated and unsophisticated, are perfect, bound twins, when it comes to the *I am right, you are wrong* game in the world of blasphemy, be it religious or secular.*

*(Note: What is said in the last few sentences above is exacerbated now, because the explosion of access to education has also seen the birth of a new age of a sometime ideational nudity, where those under forty in the West sometimes have no context for anything which might serve as the basis for understanding how religion has gone rogue, again, in other places, especially since the beginning of the new millennium, and that religion goes rogue in a continuous pattern because certain people - ordinary human beings like me, you can decide for yourself - go on the I am right, you are wrong track, and stay on it, usually forever. In large tranches of America religion is a primary and dynamic part of identity and this itself has also created a very large area of no understanding, and worse, within the West as a whole, with the result that America is now sometimes dismissed

as strange and primitive and even deviant, and sometimes much worse).

The idea that certain groups were *beyond redemption* was still a sometime part of the rambling portmanteau of the religion when I was growing up, but in the popular culture of my upbringing in West Cork, there was also another implicit, parallel, almost polar current, which happily ignored this and was summed up in the popular imprecation *God is good*. It was also never far from the lips either, of a few of the priestly guardians in the parishes who sometimes seemed to have a more *laissez faire* attitude to and also probably a certain degree of ignorance about parts of the current dogmatic theology in Ireland then, which was not in rude intellectual health and was more in the style of short answers to set questions. But whatever the reality in detail, it is a good reminder that hiding underneath an apparent cloak of religious absoluteness, there may be another world which survives in the context of a peculiar lack of explicitness, which is purposeful, objectively, but which does not necessarily have to be subject to analysis and exposure, and conflict. The phrase *God is good* commonly heard in Ireland carries the richest possible spectrum of meanings. It is a statement of theological fact, that God, the Almighty, is good, that God does not condemn lightly, and in what was my religions culture, it was also an acknowledgment that we are nothing without God and a declaration of hope but also a prayer to God, to help us *in our hour of need,* and to forgive us and our departed loved ones, our weaknesses - which were always acknowledged as real, even by the *saints* among us - and which was also implied in the other everyday confessional prayer *Help us, O God,* because without His help there was *not much hope* for any of us, which was our way of saying *no hope* without any of its raw absoluteness.

The real religion, semiotically, of the people of that Ireland, was complex and had none of the racist cliché of the simple peasant kind, and was based on the belief that we all need redemption by God, that the relationship between *man* and God is one of love, and that our Saviour Jesus Christ was the messenger and channel of this *good news*: we knew all these three central parts of our faith, of course, in our own way, but no less worthy or valued because of this. This benign, popular religious culture - strikingly beautiful in its simplicity and as such, tellingly similar to many of the most profound scientific models - survived despite the Catholic Church going on what would prove to be a very successful campaign to establish a theocracy in the newly independent Ireland. And despite some politicians and members of various secular elites also joining them - and also sometimes *drinking the drop down* and behaving any way they liked in private - and sitting with the religious hierarchy at national celebrations of every kind, including the All-Ireland finals of our very popular national games in the iconic Croke Park at the end of summer. *The People of God* retained the primary element of our traditional religious culture - *God loves us* - which could sometimes be very different from the official, hierarchical religion which frequently and very explicitly told us in all kinds of ways, that it regarded control as its reason for existence and that nothing less than total obedience was expected from us. The accusation of blasphemy was always there in the wings as a weapon of choice for what would be regarded in any way, as dissonance. We accepted absolute religious governance without question and also retained our absolute belief in the goodness of God which told us that we and our loved ones, would always be together with Him, in Heaven.

(Note: It is years since this last difficult and rambling paragraph was written, and I have decided to leave it as is, as an accurate - and as accurate as any such very wide, social and cultural summary can be, if that does not seem too boastful -

picture of both our religion and the official religion, but also of how we regarded the latter. It would be wrong to dismiss the second last sentence just above as the product of sentimental memory, this is hard talk anthropology from someone who has always been bordering on the ridiculous in trying to educate himself across a very wide intellectual range and who also cannot write very well).

A PROFOUND APOLOGY for not being less clumsy in trying to explain what was blasphemy in practice by introducing very different ways of talking about being and existence, but, again, unfortunately, this is the default for understanding the key concept underlying blasphemy which constitutes the basis for the behaviour of those who accuse others of blasphemy. For the person who accuses you of blasphemy, *you are a blasphemy, your existence is a blasphemy, your very being is a blasphemy*. I remember when I first saw the English title of Jean-Paul Sartre's *L'Être et le néant: Essai d'ontologie phénoménologique* - Being and Nothingness: An Essay on Phenomenological Ontology - I said to myself *this* is not going to get *too many laughs* in the elegant spires England. And I only meant the *L'Être* or the *le néant* part, and not the second *phenomenological ontology* part which would have coined some choice not very scholastic quips at *High Table* in Oxbridge and the much lower tables in the public houses in Oxford and Cambridge. In Catholic intellectual culture, it would not have been unusual to say, despite, sometimes, being expressed in more circumlocutious or scurrilous terms, *your religion is a blasphemy*. Religion in this context here, could and often did mean denomination or sect of the religion, but also religious practices unworthy of being regarded as part of a religion, as such. Or, *Your nation is a blas-*

phemy might make an appearance, especially to refer to England which had this quaint form of theocracy which might have been dreamed up by one of my many English heroes, Lewis Carroll. Those who make such accusations of blasphemy are very partial to the grandiloquent *pronunciamento* style of oratory beloved by Shakespeare in his Roman plays. But even though it would not commonly be said explicitly *Your very being is a blasphemy* - and which can easily lead on to *and you should be treated as such* - this very *Catholic philosophy* way of talking is crucial to understanding blasphemy. There was an expression which featured the same existential type construction in our demotic English with a very secular meaning, *He's a right walking idiot* which would also sometimes feature a proper taboo word as a very intense modifier bullying the noun. *Walking* cleverly carries the idea that it is a part of him, that it is a permanent feature; the expression says *the person is an idiot*, with the copula being used as the equivalent of = in simple arithmetic, that he embodies idiocy, that he is the prototype of an idiot etc. Some of us had to use *hard words* and big words to appear clever, but the language of the street could use more down to earth ways to do the same thing, and sometimes did it rather well, and even better.

But maybe an expression of the type *Your country is a sewer* is more accessible than the usual *blasphemy* talk. This, for example, is the way meaning, sometimes, often, in practice, was assigned, implicitly, explicitly, in many different types of European colonialism in the last half a millennium, including by the Anglo-Saxon cultures themselves, to what were countries, regions, cultures, and to those who shared a certain pigmentation etc. We probably all know something, at least, of the staggering violence and destruction which ensued, and which still ensues, and whose legacies will never end, in the aftermath of such semiotic constructions generated by colonialism, and which were made real and lasting, in an act of real demonic magic, if I could break my own rule about using such metaphors from religion, for effect.*

*(Note: The last sentence should have included the following as the reason why will never end was included. Some colonised countries adopted the colonial philosophy from their masters - some of the Irish who went to America are a relevant example, and I am talking particularly about the Catholic Irish, and not those who regarded themselves and who were not regarded, as Irish in the same way as the so-called indigenous, Catholic Irish - and became very adept at imposing it on others. I did not include it then, because every attempt at qualifying the background of the Irish ended in ruins, as this Note has also done now. But I will add that, at least, this serves as another example of how language can fail in talking about all kinds of symbolic violence and not just blasphemy).

IN MANY CULTURES, in different periods of history and especially Western history, and in particular in the Catholic tradition and the intellectual cultures influenced by Catholicism, speaking, writing and thinking were (regarded as) behaviour, and just like any other type of behaviour were capable of being sinful and blasphemous. But this type of thinking was not confined to religion. The supposed philosophical type belief in freedom of thought and expression often found in certain segments of Western cultures is more a child of some of the intellectual traditions influenced by certain naïve strands of Protestantism, and is not found in such an adorned state, for example, in Christian cultures in the Orthodox and Catholic traditions; this may make it more difficult for some to understand the idea which regards thinking and language as behaviour, because it is not part of an explicit, normal way of thinking in the majority of the English speaking cultures. But *explicit*, as usual, is the key here. In semiotics, if you probe a little, you will see that we all - this is the magical *everyone*, and everyone begins quite early in life - believe, implicitly, that thinking and language are regarded as forms of behaviour, and very important forms at that, and sometimes they are a matter of life and death. Read the great writers, including the young ones, and the poets everywhere of every age who work hard at their trade; they all know better than I do; and they know how to write as well, which is why they deserve to be called writers.

We all equally regard that a person's very existence, her or his very physical being, is meaningful, and, hence, communicative, which can mean that the very fact that I am regarded as belonging to a particular *group* (*white*, *Christian*, whatever) can be an anathema, a blasphemy, independently of whether I believe in or practice a religion, but also independently of whether if I say or do anything which could be even remotely considered to be blasphemous. I, by just the very fact of existing, am communicative, so that, someone, some group, may assign the tag blasphemous to me. When I was young, we used the existential expression *You're a right walking idiot* when we were particularly annoyed at a friend's stupidity, which is from the same field as the phrase immediately before this, *just the very fact of existing*. I was not given a choice, I was regarded as passive in this quite clever and popular game of cognitive fascism, and nothing that I may say or do, makes any difference. This is not a paragraph from the canon of the literature of intellectual pestilence and despair, this is semiotics which lives very firmly in our real lives, and which shows how we assign meaning, including how we assign meaning to each other. And which can result in *you are an abomination* being formally and automatically applied to me and maybe to you too, if you are in their sights, by people who may not even know of our actual existence, which takes meaning and existence into the far regions of surreal, but very real, if I or my loved one or child is threatened or killed, randomly. Except that, to add yet another layer of complexity which makes it virtually impossible for me to explain and not only complex to understand, all of this is perfectly simple for the person or group defining me, who may not be able to read or write and who may or may not have a job, a job which requires no peculiar knowledge or skill set, or who may have multiple university degrees and what is regarded as a very prestigious job. But there is nothing particularly random about choosing me, I am an abomination, in principle, and can be treated abominably, I am not part of a world where morality applies, and worse, or could apply, and I can be treated immorally, as moral is sequenced in terms of meaning by whoever is defining me. It is not just that my existence has no value or importance, in a very real sense, it does not matter if I exist or not, but if I do happen to exist, my existence can be arbitrarily and randomly negated. I am and belong to a category entitled to nothing and not just to any moral rights, as moral is understood by the group defining me; entitled to nothing is the automatic, logical accompaniment to my existence and those who are bundled with me. I might as well not be or have ever been. This was the same model of assigning meaning which said in a particular context, that the category human was not to be attributed to a designated group or sub-group, and in a certain timeframe this became the driving force behind the killing of all those deemed not human in the Holocaust.

Some people will not be impressed and will brand the last paragraph as nonsense and the last sentence may bring a variety of accusations, but one of the prevailing ideas running through this essay is that avoiding hard talk about violence has often given it yet another hiding place, as if it needed help from anyone. Certain groups did not regard my people as properly human - properly is a very important qualifier here - and I am not talking only about millennial *olden days*. I am also including the whole of the twentieth century when the classic logic of symbolic violence was used again and again no matter what the peculiar circumstances, when people regarded themselves as particularly superior and precious (and not just in comparison with us). I never accepted their logic and frame of reference which I knew was silly and stupid even as a boy, but I knew it also made no sense. It could have no existence - young people have limited experience of the world but you would need to be very silly to think that the young do not have antennae which can detect no sense - which is why it was not given any consideration of any minimal kind. But what I will say next will probably irk many more people. Semiotics as the study of meaning wherever it is found, could only come from the Catholic tradition which also assigned meaning to thoughts and attitudes and feelings and emotions. The priest would ask quite casually, *Any bad thoughts my child* - he would ask those who had no idea what it could mean and also those who had never had any such experience but were beginning to wonder what all this talk was about - which was confusing and embarrassing for an eight or ten year-old, not to mention a seventeen year-old, but which would turn out to be wonderful practical experience *in situ*, as it were, for a semiotic leech like me. Thoughts were behaviour - well they are, what else are they, you think them, you do them, I say them *sotto voce* to myself, and sometimes so intensely they might as well be out loud - and could be regarded just as sinful as any other type of action. In the same way the very abstract, ideological and naïve emphasis on freedom of thought and expression could not come from such a tradition (and I have now added even more people to the queue taking umbrage). When I use the word naïve here, I mean intellectually immature, because such a belief has no necessary link with the reality of our lives, and could not have. No respectable intellectual properly reared in the Catholic tradition could resist asking those who strenuously advocate freedom of thought and expression very awkward questions about where this freedom exists, and whether it guarantees freedom from sanction in emotional relationships, and in contexts where I have worked, for example. In the case of the latter, I am not talking only about sanction from the university authorities, for example - I have worked in very different ideological and religious cultures - but also from certain academic colleagues, including a varied list of implicit sanctions from those who may hoist a liberal sail in public. But if you prefer to stay with the Protestant tradition, or any other analogous religious or ideological tradition, you will have, at least, to pretend to cross over the line and (do your best to) be a good Catholic, intellectually, if you are to understand blasphemy. I know I have now pushed the boat way out too far out to sea where a regular compass does not work, but if you want to row in semiotic waters, the best thing to do is to take instruction and do your best to become a Catholic, if only for a while. But you can also go inside yourself and find your inner Catholic, which is in all of us, and give it a little space to blossom.

If we work with the principle of language as behaviour, then this introduces the possibility of guilt and blame, so that if, for example, I say something which is *not to be said*, then this means I can be called a blasphemer, and regarded and treated as such, with all the consequences this can attract. We, of course, work all the time implicitly with the idea that speaking and writing are forms of behaviour, but because these rules are contextual and not explicit, we seem to have great difficulty in understanding in a consistent way, the idea that language and thinking are behaviour, and in appreciating that we behave all the time with this as a working conceptual framework. I am talking semiotics not metaphysics, in case you were wondering if I had had a relapse and gone completely native in a Catholic hinterland. I am not saying that ontologically, *thinking and language* are behaviour, as it is sometimes popularly understood and where it refers to overt action which is perceptible. But I am saying that we often regard and treat them as behaviour, in other words, that, semiotically, they are behaviour, in terms of meaning (which is the field where I work). Talking, for example, is what we do usually when we are together, it is what we do together, but we have not done well when we use the term *communicate* for everything, if only because content sometimes has no relevance in itself, which a teacher should say only when he is alone in the forest trying to prove one way or another if a falling leaf make a sound even when nobody is listening (or something like that). Thinking and talking are the primary forms of behaviour we engage in when we are together and which we use, for instance, in the developmental stage of our relationships, all of our relationships, and not just intimate rela-tionships. Frequently, it is the only form of behaviour, and sometimes relationships can founder because of language, which we all know to our cost, including *platonic* relationships. In a similar way, to give another example, if our lover or partner broods mentally in some form or other on someone else, you and I will probably be disturbed emotionally because we regard what our lover/partner, husband/wife, is engaged in mentally, as behaviour; it is because we do not regard it as ethereal and insubstantial and outside the framework of behavior, that it may be very threatening to our identity, with its sometime need for the idea and feeling of exclusiveness, but also security in certain contexts.

If we, and that is all of us, regard words, spoken or written, as behaviour, at least sometimes, then it is predictable that blasphemy has traditionally regarded writing or speaking, not only as a form of behaviour and hence subject to moral judgment, and sanction, but also as a constituent part of the person, which may again, be too much of a Catholic way of talking. It is an intrinsic part of them, it is them - what I call the existential trap, but I always cringe a little when I say it, when I know that one of the budding comedians in the class is brain mouthing *pretentious twat* in some form, or some language, if it is a bilingual context, and I happen to be lecturing in English to students whose first language is not English - and hence subject to censure. I hesitate in such an essay, to give the example of what can be erotic stimulation, when a still photograph may be more relevant than actual physical behaviour. The great pornographers are great semioticians, and always have been, in classical India, Greece, Rome, China, Japan, for instance, but less so, somewhat strangely, in the more Protestant regions of Northern Europe and the Anglo-Saxon and the so-called Celtic worlds in Ireland and Scotland which are not Catholic.

Those with a particular sensitivity to or revulsion against, a Catholic intellectual tradition, may not know that the inner language we use which is not voiced (out loud), and mental images, have also always come under the aegis of behavior and have been prolifically regarded in certain periods as mortally sinful. This can include blasphemy, and, in a nightmare scenario worthy of Dante at his most extreme and obscene, such imputed inner blasphemy, has indeed been subject to suspicion and sanction, including torture and death, in secular worlds such as Stalinism and many other so-called Communist or Marxist contexts spawned by the Soviet Union and its early Communist satellites, and not only in a religious *milieu*. In any objective context, the fascists were right when they decreed in practice, that thoughts imputed to you could bring terrible misfortune, for instance, in Communism. This sometimes ended in total absurdity, however, when *you might think such thoughts in the future* leads to torturing you so that you can somehow see into the future and confess this future as reality - and not just potential reality which might happen - and then execute you on the basis of this confession. This was something never imagined even in any religious eschatolgy as far as I know, and not just in the monotheistic religions which are my culture of origin and my education and experience. It is also relevant to realise that this internal language is what we do, when we are alone, which is why it was of such interest to the moral custodians in the Catholic tradition; they wanted your soul, your mind, your feelings, not just your body, which also often attracted pejorative descriptive terminology (despite the teaching that we would all be reunited on the Last Day with these very same bodies in Heaven). It is not regarded in our usual way of thinking either, that this inner language is a constant, in the sense that we cannot, normally, be in a state when we are not using this internal language. It is our behaviour with ourselves when we are alone, awake or asleep, and the latter is sometimes regarded as such, in certain schools of psychology and psychiatry. Those who have a blanket intellectual prejudice against the Catholic tradition may find a linguistic argument a little less unpalatable.

Language is the primary behavior we engage in when we are together, when, for instance, in the first stage of communicating personal interest of an intimate kind, and it is not a difficult move from accepting language as behavior to accepting inner language as behavior.* There is no acceptance in anything said here about others sanctioning such behavior, be it a lover or a partner, that is a moral issue, to be answered by you, me, as individuals. But semiotics does not permit us to behave like grasshoppers arbitrarily assigning meaning and categories of meaning to suit ourselves, which we all know and sometimes too well, to our cost. Meaning is the ultimate dictatorship, going alone in the worlds of meaning can also be regarded as an indication of mental imbalance, or, very, very rarely, and usually only after a time lapse, as genius, and even then, there may persist a suspicion of *peculiar*, or one of its infinite number of less salubrious cousins in English.

*(Note: In the original text I was going to say that Sartre was also very Catholic - I thought it might distract from what I was trying to say above - and not just when he talked, Joyce style, about bodily fluids such as the infamous le visqueux, and that you would never find that kind of thing, as we would say when we grab peculiar phrases from our neighbour when we want English to do something subtle with a hint of sarcasm. You would never find the equivalent of slimy in the sober German of Husserl and Heidegger).

WHEN YOU HAVE BLASPHEMED, your words are a blasphemy and your person an aberration, because your words are you and you are your words. As the incarnation of blasphemy, you embody the crime, and this is why the disavowal is not accepted, just as it may not be either in a secular context, in Kangaroo political courts, for instance, or in highly charged emotional relationships. If all of this is dismissed as *mumbo jumbo*, there will be no understanding of these last examples, including what may be the very distressing and sometimes calamitous examples from our personal lives. If religious blasphemy is not understood as a sin incorporated in the blasphemer, it may be difficult to understand why your accusers may believe that saying sorry changes nothing because the deed cannot be undone.* Saying they are not even human because they think like this, is much worse than the usual shoddy intellectualism, if this is the way we all think, and act, analogously, which it is; specious argument is specious no matter where it comes from, including me, and you. Nobody gets a free semiotic *passe partout*, specious is specious in religion and also in all of life. The deed is you - this is not just some out of world figure of speech - and the two cannot be separated; it can also be *sine die* and extend to the afterlife which puts every-thing in a much more highly charged context. The blasphemy is in the bones in the same way as the inelegant Latin *ius in re inhaerit ossibus usufructarii* has it, when it refers to the legal doctrine that *the right in something clings to the bones of the one having the use or enjoyment of something*, but here it is the sin, the crime, which attaches itself leech like, to the person. It was part of our Catholic culture to say and say openly, I am a sinner (in the sense that this is integral to who we are, which was some-times not too different from *we are inherently evil*, which was an extreme form of heresy). In some circumstances, when someone was regarded as a blasphemer or guilty, for instance, of being evil in a context outside formal religion, even their bones were also sometimes burned to ashes so that no remnant of this person remained, because their physical body also was blasphe-mous or evil, which itself was bad theology from a Christian point of view which teaches that life is eternal. Every child knew when I was growing up that fire cannot negate the eternal or the body, with which we are united again on the Last Day. This was also an endless source of rather cruel fun for us in the middle period in our younger youth when we innocently thought we were the lords of funny, which we were, of course, until, after a few short years, we had to leave that happy world, and never to return.

*(Note: The recent manifestation of the particular type of Islamic fundamentalism which espouses total violence is now the example par excellence, but this might as well be another

planet in Ireland. Absolutist - we sometimes had fundamentalist analogues as well - ways of thinking in the Irish Catholic tradition were already on the wane when the above was written in the late '80s and '90s - I did not know how quickly - which meant that as far as some students were concerned, I might as well have been talking about stitching patterns in early Chinese tapestries, which I am told are extremely complex. The terrible danger now in talking about violence and religious fundamentalism is that it may also stoke and reinforce racism of the most extreme type, if it leads to they are all like that, even implicitly, and it may also be a waste of time, saying, for example, that Muslims, including babies and little children, are often the first victims of such fundamentalism).

You should not be surprised, when you blaspheme, if people think that you have become, that you are, this very sin against god - their god, of course - in your own person. We are now in territory where semiotics seems to have wormed its way into ontology, where meaning is of the same quality of existence as any other reality, and there is no easy distinction between you and your words and their meaning. The words, the blasphemy, are you, and no new words can change this. And, again, a health warning, this is semiotic talk, and, of course, a philosopher may and must sometimes, indulge also in very different and maybe more insightful talk, but saying you were talking philosophically, will not do you much good either, if you are accused of blasphemy; it is much worse than saying you were talking semiotically, which nobody pretends to understand. The zealots of god will be happy if you recant and repent, this is a good example for others and a testimony to and a justification of, the truth of their teaching. In most religious contexts, however, this has no relevance, if they so decide. Your deed once done cannot be undone and hence cannot be forgiven which is as heretical as heretical can be in terms of Jesus Christ who forgave even those who were his closest followers and who betrayed him. He forgave them in an easy, gentle manner which was given to us when we were very young as the model for our behaviour with others: that Christ forgives us no matter what wrong we do was also the nucleus and focal point of our joyous faith. But for the zealots, wherever they come from, blasphemy will still have to be punished even if you confess your wrongdoing, and for some, this punishment has always been death in the form of execution and often preceded by some spectacular form of theatrical torture, whether this was a dramatic concomitant to disavowal, or as the earthly punishment exacted by the men of god as their own sanction, which, of course, to follow the thread of blasphemy to the very end, is itself the most grievous blasphemy against Almighty God, which was one of the ways we talked about our Creator.

Their behaviour functions as a way of indicating that while god, theoretically, rules over life and death, they, in practice, are the rulers of life on earth and can prolong it even in a staged and miserable fashion, to reflect their imperious image of themselves, or they can dispatch whoever they name immediately to everlasting punishment; their eyes were also always focused on the future so the idea of *discouraging others* as the French cleverly say, was always present. Such men of god take themselves and everything to do with themselves, but especially their own importance and righteousness, very seriously and solemnly - even when their own behaviour in any number of ways, was hardly a model of virtue - which can hardly be a surprise, when they blasphemously usurp the power and status of God Himself. Nor are they ever diffident either, about going beyond the powers of the Almighty, which may be the most important factor in any semiotic consideration of many forms of such blasphemy.* Such blasphemous expressions of extravagant self-indulgence and excess, increased exponentially in certain periods of Christianity and Islam, and coincided with particular periods of troubled or triumphalist identity, and sometimes both together. Which itself, analogously, is especially worthy of note because it is common also in other contexts of violence, including in very everyday situations in our own lives. To put yourself in the place of God is blasphemous and the gravest of sins. It is the sin attributed to Lucifer, for example, which was used as the ultimate example of the sin of pride in my religious upbringing which also told us that angels were the pinnacle of God's creation. Our religious tradition used stories to illustrate this *blasphemy of blasphemies* to ensure that there was no confusion about such a sin. The campaign was so successful that any such thoughts about being greater than God were so beyond absurdity that when I saw the Luciferian absolutism of the plague of dictators who took unto themselves the trappings of gods and scarred the landscape of my young adulthood - look again at the Communist leaders who would also later hone a particularly cruel and inhuman kind of fascism in East Germany, especially from 1971 onwards, as if the human world had learned nothing from Stalin, Hitler, Mao etc. in the previous half century - they also became icons of stupid ridiculousness, which is the ultimate revenge semiotics brings down on all our heads when we indulge in stupidity and not just that level of pretentious and ludicrous asininity.

*They may, for instance, declare that sexual behaviour of every kind, be it same sex or other sex, and accompanied by the most grievous violence, including ultimate violence, with those regraded as *outsiders,* is not sinful; outsiders here also means non-human, whenever necessary. It would be easy to slip into way of thinking which regards this as non-human, but if humans do something, semiotics does not and cannot, discriminate ,and calls this human behaviour as well, whatever it is.

SOME OF YOU may want to say that people who scream religious blasphemer like this at others are primitive and uncivilised, more of you may want to shout at me, but it is irrelevant. I am only trying to explain in a series of essays which wants to provide an explanation for violence what semiotics is and how people - the eternal and ubiquitous you and me - organise their world when violence and identity is the primary focus; those who shout loudest always get attention because they can also easily move on to threatening everyone, and especially now when communications in its widest sense, including when dramatic action communicates very forcibly, is becoming more and more relevant. And the mean, unwelcome lesson in semiotics is that we all indulge in the same and similar ploys, which is all very unpleasant and very unwelcome, I am sure. But, and I cannot put it in any less cruel way, it comes with being human. Most of us, for example, and this is my semiotic litmus test, will subscribe fully to the idea that language is behaviour, and a very important form of behaviour, if we find that certain words from someone we love are directed at another. They are not just words anymore. No distinction will now be made which will regard words as having some kind of disembodied and irrelevant existence, and, in the same vein, it will not be much different with regard to desires and certain ideas, and maybe much worse.

We are all very clear, and not just implicitly, about these rules and the practical consequences of such rules, and especially when they are breached, including the sanctions which can be imposed. And ditto in many religious contexts, you should, at least, have some idea about what you are doing when you say or write things which others regard as blasphemy; it seems unworthy somehow, to protest later, that you did not think that anyone could ever think or would interpret, what you say as blasphemy. The book, <u>Satanic Verses</u>, is, comparatively, not very good blasphemy, if it were to be judged according to the ruthless criteria of some of my mentors, Swift and Joyce for example, but it is blasphemous. I could imagine someone with even a modest talent for sarcasm suggesting there might be a hint in the title. Anyone who thinks otherwise does not have a rudimentary understanding of Islam, or religion, or blasphemy, or of elementary anthropology or semiotics. If a publisher asked me if it was blasphemous - this translates as *whether it was likely to be regarded as blasphemous* by certain groups in the Muslim world at large - I would have said yes, absolutely, which is saying nothing, one way or another about publishing the manuscript, or author intention, or about the writer's right to write his book, or about the rights of those who call it blasphemy. If something similar was published in 1958 when we were finishing school, we would have regarded it as blasphemous. That is the way semiotics *operates*, as the Americans cleverly semiotically say, that is the rule. Those who think that this or that is blasphemy against their religion make the call, that is how blasphemy and lots of other things work. Saying this is not how it should be, is another very different epistemological world.

This is not terribly different than if I am asked in court as an expert witness in language and semiotics the meaning of *consent* in a case of sexual assault, or the meaning of derogatory terms in our English such as *gombeen man* and *sleeveen* in a libel case brought by an Irish government minister against a journalist. This is not a Solomon scenario, this is simple, humble semiotics which tries to say what meaning is commonly assigned to *x* or *y*. We have all sometimes felt very foolish when we said to a loved one, *I didn't mean it*, especially when we know, even as the words are fumbling out of our mouth and falling over each other, that we are only exacerbating the situation and making everything worse, and also making a bigger fool of ourselves. Semiotics is simple, I sometimes wish it were not so simple, I might then be able to think, the odd time at least, that I am quite clever, at least for a little time, maybe even *a big little*, which I used to say endearingly when I was small (and which I remember because someone laughed at me). It is not about sinister black holes which stifle the escape of light, it is about how you and I assign meaning, and there is always plenty of light to be able to see what is happening, unless you want to feign inability to see, for some reason, maybe even subconsciously. Or unless you do not want to see, as I mentioned somewhere about Swift's very rude Polite Conversations when I was adapting the language of the *Good Book* for effect. Consent is not (regarded as) the absence of an explicit negative, nobody thinks this unless they have a peculiar angle to suit themselves, but nobody thinks either, that we cannot express consent in ways other than verbal language.

The author and most of his defenders did not seem to know much about how meaning works, or much about religion either, or anything very much about meaning, except grandiose ideas about freedom of speech which may have no real reference and no bearing on anything in your life and mine, except in limited and very well-defined contexts. Many of them did not seem to know much about anything to do with meaning as it sometimes operates inconveniently in the real world, if truth were told, despite their public standing as journalists and intellectuals. The big guns from the Arctic Circle to the southern rocks on the islands off the coast of Sicily and from Galway to Prague, and maybe even far beyond, to the Sea of Okhotsk, may be hauled out against me now, but leave your pistols at home and your pikes in the thatch, and *enter into dialogue*, as the dogs in the street in Ireland now say as part of the *discourse* about terrorism which every now and then seems to be choking the life of the nation in so many different ways, including when the most grue-some violence is said to be done in my name by one group which has never asked my opinion. With my very Catholic background, I am a little cautious of things always being done in my Irish name by people who never talk to me or ask my permis-sion in any of the many ways we can ask permission. And if you want to call me names and have me removed from your civilized society, politely, of course, you are now rowing in the same boat as those with scatter guns at the ready and who scream blas-phemy and take aim at everything and everyone who says anything they do not like. I learned *hard talk* and scurrility in a good school, in Irish and English, and the latter in two often very distinct registers, Irish English and English English. My scurrility register in Irish has unfortunately never been as prolific as my English varieties, and the reason I always give is false and mildly boastful that *we were better than that* (the real reason was that the spoken Irish I learned very fluently in school had been cleansed by the linguistic police acting *in loco Eccle-siae* before it came to us, but I did manage later to fill in a lot of the missing words, but I never really felt at total ease with them). All three can be devilishly vicious and remorseless when it comes to *savage discourse* which means I am never at a terrible disadvantage, so to speak, if it comes to *name calling*, and not only when the person calling me out is unilingual and knows only one type of English. You might not know that the English version can be particularly vicious because it may feature a very polite restrained front, as my nearest neighbours can do like no other. My early fascination with the ultimate game that is language, which includes a whole variety of accents in English, ensured that gormless chauvinism could never interfere with my love affair for the magnificent glory of English English. I could recite pages of Shakespeare by heart from the age of eleven and twelve; there was nothing elitist or intellectual about it whatsoever, it was just that *he was the real king of England*. I had a teacher when I was eleven who did Shakespeare with us when we should have doing spelling lessons or tables or some such - and I did not care what most of it meant, it was *sound talk* and all magic, and some of it very bloodthirsty as well which made it even more exciting for an eleven and twelve year-old. But most importantly, I was lucky. I would later learn, and again from the best, that we all play games most foul when we appropriate meaning in certain contexts, and of all the writers in the world, Swift and Joyce are not the teachers you should ever read if you want to wallow in any form of pious indignation or *faux* innocence and naivety.

I had never studied any of them when I was in school - in English classes in second-level school, we did poets and Shakespeare and little or no prose, which I would now also recommend to the inspectors general - or read anything they wrote. I had never heard of them. I was not the intellectual type but I was so not intellectual, I would not have even been able to play the part when I was coming out of my teens, if I had known that was something you could pretend to be. I came across banks of very loud posers in my first week in university in Dublin - they were always standing in small groups in the corridors, talking loudly and always laughing even more loudly - who were funny in a kind of comedy of manners way when people want to draw attention to themselves by guffawing in public. This was all new to me, Cork's special brand of withering humour would give short shrift to anyone who had to shout and bray like a donkey to draw attention to himself in public: *making a show of yourself* would not win any respect where we came from but we also knew our Latin rather well, of course, and what *infra dignitatem* meant. I would find out later these particular groups were from expensive, private Catholic schools in the capital and had already been in training for quite a number of years to be the bulwark of Catholic Ireland. It was much later I stumbled across Swift and Joyce and they quickly became my mentors when I was floundering around looking for help in trying to understand semiotics, and going nowhere very slowly - it was so slow I had no idea how slowly I was not making progress - and how we construct our various worlds of meaning, but especially the semiotics of violence and the particular worlds of meaning where violence lives. The two of them talked hard talk which I had never come across before and were perfect for someone who was ready to go hard thinking for the first time in his life about how we construct and manipulate meaning.

Swift and Beckett were also not the type who take up *les causes celebres* of freedom of expression, and for some reason I also had an aversion to this kind of talk from quite early on in the university. I already knew quite well that while you are engaged in theatrical shenanigans, there are endless cases every day in the world and sometimes at home, where freedom of expression is denied, because it is of no interest or importance to anyone; and that sometimes freedom of expression is even being denied in the institutions where the most important actors on the international stage live and work. But when I say that the message of semiotics is sometimes unacceptable, I accept that aspect of semiotics also, no matter how unwelcome it may be, emotionally and intellectually, especially for someone who lectures in the university on semiotics (which is always easy in practice, when examples are the original low hanging fruit, and when theory is easily accessible in the examples). I must acknowledge this is how the allocation of meaning works, including when it says *this or that* meaning or this or that part of semiotics is unacceptable. Semiotics is the savage discipline - if I may use one of the most favoured adjectival qualifiers in the long annals of symbolic violence in Europe - and, even worse, it also sometimes turns back mercilessly on itself. But, ironically, that is the easy part, but only relatively, however. I must also personally accept, in the sense of acknowledge, that this is how the assignment of meaning works, which is the difficult, sometimes impossible part, and acceptance here does not in any way signal moral approval. I have to acknowledge, for instance, that a Serb may be tried in an international court for crimes against humanity, and condemned, and that fellow academics who are now *international political gurus of great standing*, whose government, when they were its official consultants, had responsibility for the wholesale use of chemical weapons in an offensive war across three sovereign countries, countless deaths, appalling injuries, and genetic devastation for future generations, can now shuffle into a television studio like large cuddly bears, and then adopt guru like *personae* and drone on uninterrupted about whatever *international situation* is now in vogue. If you heard just the disembodied voices you could easily think it was a resurrected James Joyce doing a sardonic party piece after a couple of gorgonzola sandwiches and a few glasses of Burgundy in a hostelry on Duke Street. Joyce, when he was just simple James Joyce and another contestant like any other, won a prize at a most prestige music festivals for his aural talent, and would do the grave, funereal accent perfectly.

I must also accept, as given, semiotically, however, that if I say anything about the way the Serb is comparatively treated, I will, at best, be ignored, with the eyes of those who do not want to listen, not to mention hear, becoming glazed over, at best, and that is those who are *near and dear*. I was lucky to be a teacher, I learned about *glazed over* early in life. It took me a little longer to accept that family and friends too, indulge in dumb glazing as well, but it has not completely stopped me indulging myself, yet, and continuing the pursuit of meaning wherever it goes and wherever it takes me; but I still sometimes find talking about violence difficult, not because the violence shocks me, but because it happens. It can still be very difficult even after all these years to say, and this is just one example from the United Nations, that x and y can, in practice, do anything they like with impunity but z must always be condemned. It is just that if violence committed by x will not receive comment or can be ignored, and sometimes it is violence with no limits, I have no idea how to navigate in those waters. You might note as well, apropos of *I have to accept that a Serb* just above, that I carry no flag for what a peculiar section of Serbia did in the Balkans in the final years of the second millennium, and when the term genocide was theatrically used again and not just by the press this time, to describe what was done publicly in front of the world's media. Genocide in that Europe was when a particular group which is defined by religion, is to be completely destroyed. There was never genocide against my people, for instance, there was sometimes wholesale slaughter and destruction, and we were often regarded as not human or not properly human - the distinction could be a very fine one - but there was never any decision made to kill us all because we were Irish.

MEANING CAN BE joy and suffering when it is emotionally intense. We all know this, and very well indeed, from when we very young, but, in practice, we are not able to understand or appreciate such meaning when it is not on our own emotional agenda in some way. And to continue the analogy used above. The sweet words and promises spoken by your lover to another which can destroy you, may only be sweet nothings in your mouth, if you say them to another, but you will decide the meaning and also whether the additional tag of important will be added to the base meaning, if someone else says them. In the various worlds of meaning, your lover's fleeting whisper which disappears into thin air and then disappears forever once it is said, may linger on forever and poison your mind and your whole self, including what was your identity. The various ways we assign meaning must be taken into account in any essay on violence, which has to deal in the normal way with meaning and how we explicitly and implicitly assign meaning in the multiple domains of violence; this includes taking account of a model which deals with the different ways we assign meaning to suit ourselves, depending on the circumstances. For instance, it will have to indicate that purpose and intention is only one layer, and that the text itself and the interpretation and effect have to be taken into account too. The model has to cope, for example, when I am on some campaign or other and want to deny any intention of causing harm or damage which is a direct consequence of my particular actions. Or, when it is convenient, we may want to pretend that meaning is purely intellectual, and we may want or have to, ignore that communication, information and meaning, are of emotional import, and that meaning is particularly important to us when it is emotional. You do not have to be travelling for very long on the road studying violence when you find out that talking about violence, and especially about violence and identity, can itself cause terrible hurt. Blasphemy often has a habit of wanting to come top of many of the lists which travel down the roads, big and small, of identity and violence.

Writers of great literature have always been my guides in trying to understand the whole gamut of meaning - which is all a little ironic seeing that I never studied them formally in school except for four Shakespeare plays for four national exams at second level - and especially emotional meaning. They explore meaning everywhere, in every corner, under every clichéd bushel, and have no talent for playing the role of semiotic virgins, unless that too is a literary gambit. And they, of all people, do not have the right to hide behind the nonsense of saying that only they can decide, *a priori*, that what they write means this or that, only, or whether it is blasphemy, or could be regarded as blasphemous. The reader buys the book and pays the bills, and we will have our say too, whether you, dear writer, like it nor not. You are gifted like none of us are, and reveal meaning like no one else, but it stops there, you do not have exclusive rights on saying *this means this, that means that* - nobody does, which is what caused all the trouble in the story of the fallen angels - unless you too dear writer have a trace of the fascist gene which is not uncommon in the various worlds of meaning, or an inordinate fondness for lording over meaning, which can also afflict all of us, as we who are also teachers know too well. Semiotics is ruthless, it respects nobody or anything, because of who or what they are, as the *Good Book* might say. Of all the early books, the *Bible* can sometimes be a friend of the humble and the humbled, and is especially cruel when it talks about us when we have *notions above our station. Notions* in this sense of ideas which were just that and which had no basis in the real world about your identity and worth, was very popular in our English when I was growing up - and which have nothing to do with the reality of who we are. But it is particularly dismissive and often to the point of rudeness, of those of us who set ourselves up as idols, of whatever kind, and it reserves the ultimate condemnation for those who like to lord it over meaning; you may not know that indulging in such lordship often gives a feeling of great power. Plato, a writer of genius and master semiotician, along with Socrates, his seeming mentor and idol, knew that writers of literature work with a much more sophisticated model of meaning than philosophers and social scientists, which is why he did not want poets and dramatists having any role in his new political Republic. And those rulers who implicitly follow the same ideational map and put his uncompromising proposals and their conclusions into practice in different centuries and cultures, are faithful followers of the illustrious Athenian and his muse, despite not knowing his name.

Officials of certain religions and political ideologies have a third eye which watches out exclusively for blasphemy and favour closed models which impose meaning, and only vary in their attitudes to rigidity and the range of sanctions for non-acceptance and criticism; sometimes, of course, there is change in content, even radical change, but the principle remains intact, and rigidity becomes an integral part of whatever is the current doctrine. They are in the business of painting the canvas of life and their image of the world and sometimes a life after death as well, and do not like others outside their very small inner circle daubing their pictures; this always includes the *ordinary* person. You will know that most primary forms of Communism such as those found in the earlier forms of the Russian and Chinese varieties, would also have no truck with intellectuals, creative writers, artists, composers etc., unless they served their own, strict purpose, which could be a very ominous phrase in that peculiar world. Such Communisms were particularly dismissive of writers who might be regarded as challenging their message, and that was sometimes a very broad brush. The absolutists among them - and there is always a constant drift towards abso-lutism in all such closed systems, religious or secular - did not want anyone to paint any picture, of any kind, or say or write any word, other than what they say or ordain.* *They burn books, don't they* is not a historical cliché, they are still burning every-thing, and if it is not online and flammable - endless people and institutions and states hate online with a special venom and the latter two now also have scores of minions whose purpose in life is to *block access* - they build more jails, and take out the hammer, the rack, the crusher, the bullet and the bomb for those who speak and write the books. The pattern has a long history and is always the same, no matter what the historical period or the peculiar culture, which also means that prediction does not tax the imagination; the more absolute it is, also means that it is not, has never been, and can never be, creative, even in the forms repression take which may go back millennia.

*(Note: The earlier forms of Chinese and Russian Communism referred to in this last paragraph, have now changed radically, and a select few are allowed to flaunt their standing and even their extravagance, but especially in Russia where the culture of control has moved to a more traditional oligarchy of one, without having the embarrassment of having to talk about ideology, as in the old days).

A CLOSED SYSTEM of meaning is called closed because it is closed, and this is not an attempt at a smart quip, it is a simple statement of what it is, structurally. And, in periods when there is intense introspective focus on identity and on the system itself, as sometimes happens in religions and certain secular ideologies, other elements are also created and linked together in a daisy chain model; the accretion of constituents, similar to the shift towards absolutism mentioned above in the last paragraph, could take on a life of its own at certain times, in Irish Catholicism, for instance, in the twentieth century, almost immediately after independence, and, as also mentioned above, in the early Communism of Russia and China, which can also sometimes implode in some form as well. A sometime obsession with adding more and more components in such systems also means inevitably, adopting ideas and values and practices which do not necessarily have anything intrinsically to do with or which are even complimentary with, what were regarded as the initial, fundamental ideas and values. Sometimes there is a clash which itself can generate terrible confusion. In both Ireland and Russia and Ireland at almost exactly the same time - the revolutions were ten months and some fifteen days apart, respectively - multiple and sometime, endless accretions became the order of the day, which prompts the idea that this is somehow inevitable whenever the idea of control itself become the primary dynamic, no matter what the size of the country or place where the revolution or radical political upheaval takes place, or even sometimes the ideology.* Leaders and their bureaucracies may also blindly introduce contradictions - unrest and mutiny are always busy and confused and noisy - which cause semiotic and psychological chaos for the citizenry. In Ireland when I was growing up, for instance, the rules which had been introduced about fasting from food and liquids from the first second of the day Holy Communion was to be received, would be a perfect case-study in a first year easy introduction to psychology and psychiatry, but it could not now even figure in a historical book of absurdities because it could not have any trace of credibility even in Ireland; in a similar way, the jokes which were rampant in all of Communist Eastern Europe from nineteen fifty onwards died in ninety eighty nine. When more and more provisions were added in such top-down Communist systems, it was difficult to jettison any item in the chain explicitly, in case it gave the impression that the system as a whole, was unstable, or worse; instability can easily cause confusion for those expected to know the rules, all the rules, including what rules are especially applicable at a particular time. In Communism, the confusion often ended very badly if some people were not always sure what rules were operative or even relevant. In Ireland, when the fall came, some people began the process of jettisoning the religion as a whole, a larger group exploited a cultural Irish gene, kept what they liked and deleted the rest. Others, and primarily women, decided *we hold what we have*; they may also set up forms of Irish Catholicism which will have little in common in terms of hierarchical control with what it was ten years ago - Irish culture has not yet lost all of its traditional matriarchal heritage - unless the Vatican makes a virtue out of necessity and changes its policy of exclusive male rule and priesthood. Any such change, however, is highly unlikely, and English, for some reason, has a lot of popular and sometimes quite vulgar, expressions for volunteering for your own demise.

*(Note: Some people will take umbrage at the mention of the Russian and the revolution on a little island out in the Atlantic in the same sentence, but semiotics will make a fool of you if you insist on using crude measures. Some of my actor friends were addicted to telling jokes about the Communist regime in Romania, but they were all the same and all equally awful which is not surprising; there is a limit to how many different jokes can be created about one topic and particularly when the topic is always enmeshed in violence and potential violence. But I resurrected an old friend from my childhood and offered up my pain as reparation for my sins, and laughed as heartily and insincerely as any modest actor could. The only lesson in anything like the Russian Revolution, and a bloody long revolution it was, is to avoid anything remotely similar happening ever again, but in the late '40s and early '50s, the misery was again brutally visited on many other countries as well. Stalin was brutalized by the war, any normal leader would, if had had to fight every hour for the survival of his own country for seven or eight years, and being brutal was now the only way Stalin knew how to rule. Violent revolutions have a baleful record of having harmful and sometimes malignant streams a century later, as has happened to some extent, in small, in my own country where the three main political parties still have blood ties of many kinds with what happened after we got our

independence a hundred years ago and which left a haunting spectre of unfinished business. Some of the former Russian colonies in Eastern Europe now seem to be in a state of permanent rehearsal for old style, top down rule which is abhorrent to the major states in the EU which themselves also have certain similar legacy issues, so to speak, and which have been zealously kept at bay for the most part.

P.S. You have to love the English language, who else on God's earth would fashion an expression such as take umbrage, in the first line above).

Semiotics is a simple soul, as the Greek dramatists and Plato and Socrates, the twinned *genii* of semiotics, showed us. Cicero too, and not only for reminding us of *the divine spark of genius* which often lies hidden because of our very practical struggles in life, and Swift too, for warning us, in particular, of the dangers lurking in the myths of identity, in terms of species identity and also national identity. It might be noted the creative genius for writing is a common thread in all those mentioned just above in this paragraph, even though Swift also indulged rather a lot in bawdy and obscene vitriol, and not just for *a man of the cloth* (but maybe some the Greeks and Latins mentioned just above, also did, when they were just talking). In the early days when I was discovering Swift and marking his place in the development of semiotics, I was always baffled by the *which comes first question*, and whether talent for expression and its nurturing, is the *sine qua non* for people being able to explore and, in particular, develop their own thinking and especially in certain areas, or whether it was sheer brilliance. I eventually came down a little more on the talent for expression in writing, but I changed that later, not, however, with any great surety.

PLATO ALSO SET out an extremely pernicious and seductive agenda when he linked knowledge and goodness, which has important consequences in some of the other essays on violence. Some years ago in an international seminar on racism and the media, I heard educated and clever people echo Plato when they proposed that symbolic violence of the racist variety is a product of ignorance and that the state should use the education system to teach children about other cultures and religions, so that they would respect and appreciate them, which brought on an attack of intellectual hyperventilation and *déja vu*. It is (almost) a form of analogous racism in itself to say that some of the most crass symbolic violence on the basis of gender, has often come from the most highly educated males, including members of the ordained and professed religious, and especially those of the highest prestige among them. In the realm of violence, ignorance and foolish arrogance frighten me, and when it is well-intentioned and not just naïve, it can also be even more alarming. European thinking has often been blighted by pretending to ourselves that meaning is part of reason, when we all know in the very ordinary, everyday lives we live and have to live, this is grandiose nonsense of a very special kind. Meaning is primarily and extensively emotional, for everyone - and everyone means everyone, which always seems to irk *lots of the everyones* - except in the minutest aspects of our lives, and then often, when it is not of much importance. Consequently, for example, it is useless defending yourself with what you think are rational words against blasphemy. This is a category mistake of the worst order, and category mistake comes top of every historical list for deadly consequences. Rationality, however it might be defined, is hardly ever in play - this is comparative numbers talk - and the only option you have, is to follow the example of Swift who would exploit every play in every possible game, including using the most demotic language possible, and would urge his foes, which also often meant those he put in the box marked enemy, to jump in the Liffey and swim with the rest of the rats. He knew very well that using language like this was no different than the feral rats fighting in the dirty Liffey, and he himself could be very generous in the range of abusive language he used, and not just because it came from the quill of a professed man of religion.* It can be easy or, rather, difficult not to, to slip into linguistic impropriety in talking about the most appalling violence which language can inflict on individuals and groups of every kind, and sometimes I find myself beginning to echo the very violence of the original language, as if nothing else is adequate to talk about such violence.

* I once said in a seminar can you imagine what the good cleric would have written if he had had access to a laptop.

Swift was without peer in exposing blasphemy, but he was also a serial blasphemer himself who explicitly and crudely exploited the structure and logic of blasphemy. He knew that when people accuse you of such a heinous crime, this is a signal that you are not involved in an exchange of views, which may seem obvious but is often forgotten. He knew that the other part of the quotation may contain the phrase sins that cry to Heaven, if those who shout and threaten you, see themselves as guardians of the name and person of god, whoever or whatever their god may be, and whatever the particular time frame, place, and theology, both doctrinal and moral. Your accuser, the arbiter, judge, censor, who has declared you guilty, has also appointed himself the angel of revenge for a god who needs posturing prelates and their foot-soldiers, to feel his pain and to exact revenge on his behalf, as if God the Almighty, was not capable of such power, if He so wished. In the language Swift used to describe those who would accuse him, whoever they might be, including all the clichés of the great and the good, not to mention the other, even more superior, group, the high and the mighty, he did not bother with any of the usual polite conventions, which sometimes often seem to fail anyway because of some hypocritical social contract. He was also much too good a theologian to think he was an avenging angel seeking justice on behalf of God, although I am not sure whether he or his colleague, the Reverend Sheridan, were or would be regarded as, theologians in any usual sense of the word in a more exacting religious mileau. His God was certainly not some weak, helpless figurehead. He also knew very well that those who accuse you of blasphemy think they can do anything they like, including what have been and are, the most barbaric and inhuman acts in god's name; and which are not always different from the kind of criminal behaviour which would also be regarded as exhibiting symptoms of severe psychosis, if carried out by an individual in a personal context. When violence of every kind is or is deemed to be, carried out in the Name of God Himself, this is the ultimate form of blasphemy. To put yourself in the place of God, to behave as if you were God, is, to ape a popular Latin type construction, the blasphemy of all blas-phemies, and, in comparison, every other form of behaviour, traditionally called or described as, blasphemy, should be reas-signed a different and lesser degree of meaning, and a new terminology. To consider yourself greater than the Almighty is *sui generis* and beyond common or garden blasphemy. You are also guilty of the most extreme charge of bizarre and ridiculous anthropomorphism, talking about God as if He were a *mere* man like yourself. P.S. I felt my fingers tensing when I wrote *in the Name of God Himself* nine or ten lines above.

(NOTE: When I first wrote this essay as class notes, I deliber-ately avoided taking a tour of how blasphemy is talked about in the Bible, because I wanted to concentrate on what it means and how it operates from a semiotic point of view, now. I also avoided dealing with how legions of parti pris theologians and religious commentators of all kinds would talk about blasphemy in the context of the three monotheistic religions, which often seem to have had more than just a special interest in blasphemy, but especially in the case of the two later ones. In certain periods, discussions among the commentators acquired all the hallmarks of an obsession, especially when intra-religious denominations, large and small, would erupt and accuse others of blasphemy; which could include, for instance, saying that a particular group is not a religion, or is an antireligion, which has a certain Nietzschean touch about it, and long before he and a host of others in the German language family, cast a suspicious eye on certain ideas current at the time. And all the while inter-religious blasphemy might also flare up, or indeed the intra-religious variety, and go into a period of seeming calm, and then horribly blow up again, and sometimes in a way which might have a potential end of time feeling about it. When there is a predication or an assumption of absolute truth which is made explicit in all kinds of ways, there is no humble page which talks about probability or a margin of error.

Error, no matter what the field in question, often has a simple absoluteness about it, and there is no There's something in what you say there now, I have to admit, when there is no being a little right or a little wrong (despite the magical sound of these nine word). It is suggested elsewhere in this essay that a breakdown in language - and language does occasionally exhibit the symptoms of a breakdown in the context of the group, large or small, as it also sometimes can in the case of an individual or a couple or family - has caused endless problems within Christianity and Islam, when there is a sometime assumption, often of the very explicit, that x is the religion and y is not. In so far as possible, the term denomination is now being avoided in what is being said here: x, or y, regards itself, and it alone, as the religion, and using the term denomination can attract the accusation of blasphemer, from x or y. This is no net, high wire semiotics again, and may be fraught with danger, from everywhere and everyone - including now in Ireland from those who are in every other context, mild-mannered and extremely polite - but it is the example of examples of the labyrinthine complications and sometime brutal, blunt danger, when accusations of blasphemy are made against others, be they individuals or groups.

This paragraph now, is a kind of inter-scriptum between paragraphs in this peculiar Note, to illustrate a few aspects of this last paragraph, and which would put in train a deduction of marks in an undergraduate student thesis. When I was growing up, we quietly regarded our Catholic Church as the real religion and the other Protestant Churches in the town as not. We did not hate them in any way - they were all the same, which tells its own story, we merged them all together, they were not us, and we did not know, which also means it could not matter what their differences might be, because it could have no relevance, no reference, in cruel semantic terms - or ever bear them ill will in any form and would never have condoned the slightest violence against them. If they were putting themselves in danger in terms of the next life, this was their choice, which they could change anytime, by converting to Catholicism, which sounds cold and clinical now that I have written it, but it is a valid description of what was our casual reality then. A wary religious politeness was also the norm in this system of social and cultural apartheid in Ireland when I was growing up. It began to fade a little in the 1960s --a wag would add you wouldn't want to be hurrying things like that now, would you - but not in Northern Ireland, where constitutional discrimination and structural racism against Catholics was the default. If you think this was particularly bizarre, semiotics, again rudely, will tell bizarrities of every kind, are not rare, and not only when religion and variants of religious ascription, are key components of identity, as nationality can also sometimes be, and race, ethnicity, colour etc.

P.S. There would be rejoicing when someone converted, a kind of Biblical joy that the lost sheep had come home, but this was also tinged with triumphal chauvinism, because converting said we were right. Converted was in one direction, and I cannot imagine what would have been the shock in the town if a Catholic became a Protestant. It gives inconceivable a very eerie literal meaning.

We are now again, in a period of crisis and Islam is imploding. Any x against any y, and within x and within y. Tens of millions are displaced in all kinds of ways, and many are literally, fleeing for their lives to other Muslim countries which cannot cope, and also to Europe which is now living with the trauma of terrorism from splinter groups within Islam and from lone actors within Europe whose lack of prestige identity in the new country where they are immigrants, can now be blamed on Western discrimination against Islam. These Muslim factions have for some thirty years now, declared Jihad against the enemy in some form or another, where the enemy is defined by a particular Islamic group, large of small, as another group, be it all those who are not Muslim, or all of Islam except itself. This has happened in the past, in Christianity too, but I might suggest that some of the elements found now within Islam are substantively different in kind; not because of the ideological and conceptual framework in play, but because of instant global communications and the access to weaponry of every kind suitable for urban warfare, by every group, and not just by traditional nation states. Every kind of weaponry is what it says, and the only real caveat now because of the sometime tendency of certain states to go rogue, is portability and means of delivery, in the case of chemical and nuclear. Two of the three superpowers also take positions against each other again, very openly, in the Middle East particularly, with Russia sometimes seeming to want to go rogue at every opportunity, in its quest to return to what it regards as the glory days of its Soviet and imperial past. Russia is the teenager whose ego was grievously hurt when he was fifteen, but he is eighteen now and wants revenge against all those who humiliated him some thirty years ago at the turn of the 1990s (and not just America which always has the honour of being first among equals). Nor does the West understand that Soviet Communism worked with the principle that outsiders do not have any right to the truth, and when untruths are told, they are sometimes told without too much effort being made to give even a semblance of minimal plausibility. I mentioned elsewhere that when I worked in the university in the very closed Communist Romania, I had difficulty in the first year coming to terms cognitively with a world where what is said may not have to have any relationship of any minimal kind, with reality, any reality, but the people had no other option other than accepting this as their permanent reality which has to be accommodated, including repeating verbatim what is said, except within a trust group, which itself could also have a very relative meaning as well because of the somewhat peculiar obsession of the regime in Romania to try and make everyone an informer.

Islam is at war with itself in all kinds of different ways and contexts - but this is country versus country war, not the type of so-called civil war which happens within a country, and which happened in Ireland immediately after independence, for example, when you could have son against father and brother against brother - and Europe is not sure what it is now or what it wants to be; it thought it did, especially in the '80s, or at least what it could be, but that is now ebbing away somewhat. Parts of the West also feel particularly under siege from particular groups within Islam, and at the same time parts of the continent are entering into a post-religious phase, with the largest denomination within Christianity also seeking to redefine its damaged identity as well. National, cultural and religious identities are also being defined by any x, which may, for example, bundle my identity into one generic category, the enemy, which can mean assigning a religion to me, and a racial type identity, as Western, for example, and a whole set of cultural traits, whether I am of that religion or not etc. And you could add one more etc., to make sure that all bases are covered. For those who define me in such a way, I have no say in my identity either as an individual or a member of a particular national grouping which in my case, is Irish. This is a form of violence with no boundaries, and is sometimes the ultimate form of all forms of violence which has always plagued the world in different ways since the first written records.

P.S. In one of the essays written in what now seem the salad days of the 1980s, I mentioned briefly and not with much grace, in a lecture in an Arab university that it would not do, so to speak, to herd me into a coloniser pen, seeing that all of the tropes, including the symbolic, were beginning to be forged some eight centuries ago on the backs of my people in Ireland which was long before they got special attention. The whole island of Ireland was made a colony by our nearest neighbours who would also, a few centuries after that, begin their long, fateful journey to becoming not only the world's supreme coloniser in history, but also the lord and master of the two largest countries in the world.* Some of these same symbolic conceits were still active in America until quite recently, among the descendants of those who broke away in rebellion from the mother ship in London in the late eighteenth century. They retained, however, the colonist tropes of symbolic violence which their ancestors had brought with them from the mother country, including those whose origins were the lowest classes of the day in England. It is ironic, but an irony which has also done inestimable damage, that the newly free, revolutionary America, adopted the patterns to define its superiority which were modelled on and sometimes taken holus bolus from, an England of the late seventeenth and eighteenth centuries. The monarchy might now be gone and a seeming radical democratic model of representation might be adopted, but it retained its highly prejudicial religious point of view, which is why it is being mentioned here in an essay on blasphemy. The simple I am, You are not model which originally drove these class notes and essays in the 1980s, was operational in that America, and would be used to exclude in a variety of ways, including when religious ascription was in play. Even now, nearly two and a half centuries later, the ethnic and religious background of candidates for the Vice-Presidency can be noted - as it would be in discussions in the American media if the two candidates for the Vice-Presidency in Iraq were from Sunni and Kurdish backgrounds - and if one of the candidates, and a fortiori, both running for the Presidency was Irish and Catholic, this would be well noted, and repeated.

*(Note: London is now trying to extricate itself out of the European Union, and the regulations which will operate between England and the remaining twenty seven, are beginning to assume a dramatic, out of all proportions, role in the discussions about London's withdrawal: it is a model of ridiculousness but it is small and easy to study and a perfect case study of what can happen when identity is in play and being manipulated by anyone and everyone, including, predictably, by a disproportionate plethora of creative writers of genius with international reputations. The majority of countries in the

eastern and south eastern parts of the EU, do not know much or care, about Ireland and its peculiar border - and the majority of their populations know nothing whatsoever about the little island out in the Atlantic which is less than five per cent of the Union - but those who are managing England's withdrawal on behalf of the remaining twenty seven countries do not seem to be very well disposed to showing London any special good will because the problem is now also seen more and more as London playing games to get ever more favourable withdrawal terms: seen more is a very powerful semiotic phrase, and as in all contexts where relationships are significant, it can assume an all-powerful meaning. There is, however, another problem lurking there as well, England is also going through an identity crisis which was masked in the last twenty years particularly, by London being part of a large, somewhat politically significant, economic Union for decades. Now that it wants to sever the ties with the European Union, the other Union, with Scotland and Wales, is becoming more and more tendentious. Those in Northern Ireland who do not want to be in union with the Republic in the south of the island, are now a pawn and we, the older generations who were born in the late '30s, '40s and '50s, do not want to see the other Irish in Northern Ireland humiliated and forced to do anything politically, but there is also another factor, and a very significant one it is. Young Ireland is an open minded, culturally diverse, highly educated country with hundreds of thousands of European immigrants and tens and tens of thousands more from India, Africa and the Middle East, and this Ireland can make a somewhat new country again and this time one which does not have to force others to toe the line, any line.

Because London is at war with itself - Scotland and Wales seem to be happy enough to stay on the sidelines and not go on to the actual field of play - and in the absence of any major personality, those who want to be The weyward sisters are involved in open battle which is all very sad when you think of what England has contributed to world culture. And in the absence of getting revenge in mainland Europe, the political entity that is Northern Ireland is going to be kicked around like a rag ball to spite the European Union and my own little country will be collateral damage. The big beasts in London are going to have to appear to win something, and they are leading the line against vassalage - from Middle English via Old French via Medieval Latin etc. - and satrapy - from Old Persian etc. God love them, my grandmothers would say, and God save us from them a lot of older people would still say today in Ireland. Males in their early fifties are often stricken with the idea that maybe this is not quite the last chance saloon, but their last chance to make a mark, and there are gaggles of them in the Lower House in Westminster at present. I too have often worked very hard to make a mark, any mark, but I decided reasonably early in life not to bother hiding it or being embarrassed about it.

When these essays began their life in the mid-1980s, I had no idea that the world would again suddenly rush to provide me with endless example of the second half of the overall title - identity is the problem - in the first decade and a half of the third millennium. The reality, however, is that I did not need more examples of symbolic violence in essays about semiotics, because violence is easy, the first half of the essays' title, and the patterns of such violence which, predictably, border on the simplistic, were established a long time ago, a very, very long time ago, everywhere. The do anything they like behaviour in the name of their god mentioned earlier in this Note about the Muslim on Muslim violence, in Syria and parts of Iraq, to give just two examples from an ever expanding list, may include for instance, acts of the most extreme violent forms of sexual behaviour, including rape against adults and children, of both sexes, and also torture and execution. But these recent devotees of religion now absolve such behaviour, or rather, change the usual meaning of such behaviour, because those deemed to be blasphemers, are blasphemers because of the identity which has been assigned to them: this is an identity assigned by those who are inflicting such violence, including male and female rape, and one which someone or some group being defined like this, may obviously not accept. The identity assigned may also be only on the basis of a perceived, generic cultural identity and not be religion specific, in any explicit, particular way, which also expands the assignation of blasphemy beyond religious identity per se, to include cultural identity, in its most expansive sense, which, it is to be noted as well, has always been the case, and happened in Ireland, as mentioned earlier, in the first decades after independence.

In general terms, for instance, someone or some group may be glossed as white or western, and either one of those identities can be deemed to be sufficient to define an individual or a group, as belonging to the category of blasphemer, a classification which can then be chosen to be the subject of whatever violence they choose, including the most appallingly cruel, haphazard death. But that is only the beginning, and just saying this is only the beginning is itself a most awful obscenity. What are normally regarded by the perpetrators, and also all religions and cultures, as violent and obscene acts, can be and are all the time, inflicted on those defined as blasphemers, including children: but they are not (deemed to be) sexual behaviour, as this is now understood in their peculiar strain of religious ascription. I first wrote sex has now been made a fetish in a way never witnessed before in history, but of course this is not the first time, and I wrote that in a pathetic, stupid attempt to give the awfulness some absolute standing. Those abused sexually - and there are no sexual limits or boundaries of any kind, and any kind means any kind - are not human, which means that this is not haram, it is not forbidden. But it also does not even come under any rubric which would define bestiality as haram, which means that because those violated have no standing of any kind, they are neither animal or human. Human beings have always been treated abominably and all kinds of groups for all kinds of reasons, have been regarded as not meeting all the requirements necessary for being defined as human. My people, for example, were deemed not to meet the requirements, but the supposed reasons for being defined as human can profitably be seen as a distinct field of semiotics in itself, if only because it is a system of assigning meaning which arbitrarily goes into total freefall, but this also as you might expect, also has a rider which often makes an appearance in semiotics. Freefall in the context of how meaning is assigned, has never been unusual when a group, including, proportionately, a miniscule one, regards itself as the absolute arbiter of meaning, as happened in the region which bequeathed to the world the term democracy. But it has to be remembered as well that ways of thinking which are based on linear models, horizontal or vertical, are sometimes not of much use in semiotics. A circle pays a better dividend here, because the same and similar patterns of assigning meaning keep going round and round, and particular meanings alight here and there in what may seem very different contexts, in terms of time or place or culture in its widest possible sense.

In the example given in this last paragraph, the sexual behaviour may also be regarded as a duty, which is an additional factor in transforming its meaning in the eyes of the perpetrators and one which removes it from the category of the forbidden. Having sex outside marriage now is not haram - is not a mortal sin, in Catholic talk - if the woman is haram. I will take responsibility, again, for the awkward writing - I am getting lost sometimes in a sea of qualifiers and modifiers because when identity is in play, generalizations and sweeping statements may, in practice, be worse than saying nothing - but, also, if someone wants to say that what is talked about in this last paragraph has nothing to do with true religion, that is a theological and philosophical discussion, and not semiotics. Semiotics is interested in religion when it is used to define identity and this, for example, may also exclude me, for instance, because I am defined in all kinds of ways which may also involve whole varieties of violence, as an outsider, and all that this word can mean. Throughout history, defining others negatively is not unusual, defining others as not properly human, as not fulfilling all the conditions of choice, for being human, is not unusual either. It was quite common in many colonial contexts and not only when practiced by various European countries in colonies outside Europe in various continents. Nor is regarding and treating whole categories of people as not human unusual. Massacring and attempting to exterminate them, is not unusual either. The body of the essays were mostly written in the last two decades of the century which had witnessed numerous historical obscenities in Europe, East and West, and also in Asia, and not just when Communism was imposed in the country with the largest population on earth and which also has a most extraordinary culturally developed history. The twentieth century is also the century of my majority and is what it was, and does not care one iota if I like it or not, or you, which sounds rude, but is not meant to be. But on a very basic human level, no one at the turn of the third decade of the third millennium should be shocked about what is said about the last century in this Note.

It is an indulgence, which is itself a shocking thing to say, to be shocked, for example, about the sexual, when those used and abused for sex, are also tortured and butchered in the most cruel ways imaginable, before, during and after the rape, be it against children, male and female, or adults, male and female: shocked makes me ask if we are also not facing up to the reality of what we humans do, and my childish religion always told me that it is a sin to think you are better than others. All I am doing is reading how meaning is assigned in real books, as were, when reality goes beyond fiction and imagination, when violence and intended human cruelty is in full play. We also now seem to be in a very different phase again when there are no boundaries, and Muslim countries are allied with Christian countries in destroying Muslims, but not vice versa, which, I might suggest, also tells its own story, but one which might be told with great caution. Violence is easy and can destroy everything, including when talking about it can seem to take me over the border of violence as well, if comparisons are inevitably made, and must be made, if there is to be any minimal understanding).

I LEARNED about semiotic extremism with no boundaries and no limits from Swift who sometimes and very deliberately, never bothered with ifs and buts or on the one hand or the other one, or about anything else much in that vein. Deliberately is included in this last sentence, because Swift did not want any respect wharsoever shown to those who were his targets. Which meant he also had no illusions about blasphemy either, whether about what it is and even more importantly, about those who regard themselves as the guardians of a particular religious or secular truth and who use blasphemy as the weapon of choice against anyone who challenges or seems to challenge, their truth and whatever they regard as their absolute rights. I also learned from Swift - and this is probably more important than anything else because this is where the detail of his thinking about blasphemy is found - about the various forms of blasphemy to be used if you want to do battle against blasphemy and blasphemers. This is peculiar to Swift and was never always a key part of the general strategy used by others who wrote about blasphemy; he could go to war against blasphemy itself with the best, but how he countered blasphemy, including what he would say against those who used blasphemy and who also accused others of blasphemy, became his hallmark. He knew and knew that he had to understand like any good general should, the stratagem and the endless machinations employed in the war, because he made it his trademark to indulge in the accusation of blasphemy himself, including in its most extreme forms, when it suited him, but, as you might predict from a clergyman in that age, never the sexual, which would make him very vulnerable and open to ribaldry of every kind, which was a popular pastime for those who wrote a particular type of popular journalism then.* He used the tactic not only against those who had already accused him of blasphemy, but also in anticipation against anyone who might do so in the future, a pattern of behaviour also found in those who accuse and not just those who seem to become addicted to accusing, others of blasphemy. In another place, I called those who manipulate time in this way *time movers*, which was already embarrassing for its gaucheness before I even attached the *s* to *mover*, but there seems to be no expression for such gamesmanship, despite its popularity in many different fields of life throughout history. This last two word expression is another awful cliché, but it proves itself useful and valid when applied to those who have always manipulated the idea of time. It is also found - which tells its own story - across many very different cultures, languages, and historical periods.

*The title of his 1714 An argument against abolishing Christianity might be the banner introducing a satirical progamme on English television three centuries later.

He also wrote, like no other, about how meaning goes to the extreme, and sometimes every extreme, with no limits whatsoever, which, again, was used by Joyce to write a pilgrim's progress about us, all of us human beings, and our no progress, and our seeming to stand still, and also our going backwards like no one had ever done before. In Swift, meaning going beyond any and every boundary, could include the ultimate form of secular blasphemy, when being human - the ultimate, precious, minimal meaning - is denied to some group or other. In that paradigm, no blame, no negative moral charge of any kind is applicable to the perpetrator, no matter what is done to those who are denied their human identity, and, consequently, their rights, including what might sometimes seem the most inconsequential. This can include depriving people of the means to live, even minimally - the accusation he made against those who had stripped the bound duo *Irish and Catholic*, because they were Irish and Catholic, of everything, including the land which provided food - and which exposes an individual to starvation and the Irish people as a whole, to casual extermination, because they, the blasphemers, had stolen the power of the divine, and given the power of life and death to themselves. They decide, in their self-assigned role as creator and gods of meaning, including in the crucial context of reference, when and how the term human is applicable. But especially, in this context, when it is denied to some group or groups, so that no matter how these people are treated, no matter what is done to them, including depriving them of the means to live, it is not (regarded as) immoral, it is not murder, and not only is it not sinful, it may even be deemed a religious obligation and moral duty, a six word phrase which has brought great happiness to the world and damage without limit in every age.*

*It is tedious to read *it is not (regarded as)*, but we often go seamlessly from *it is*, to *regarded as*, whenever it suits us. But the move has wreaked every type of violence and also violence with no limits whatsoever, in the history of every culture and related groups of cultures.

***

SWIFT AND JOYCE knowingly and deliberately blasphemed and did not bother denying what they were doing which differentiates them from many religionists who blaspheme incessantly and outrageously. Nor did they defend themselves against it, which is the usual reaction, because entering into a discussion with their accusers would be to give such people the respect of acknowledgment; they also stripped blasphemy back to its core, and deprived it of all its many hiding places. Swift would sometimes repeat the blasphemy, and add more foul language, but when he and Joyce refused to accept the logic and epistemology underlying the accusation of blasphemy - including the ways of thinking and the content of such thinking - they were also rejecting the very possibility of being guilty, which itself is the most definitive statement of intent. In their eyes, to defend oneself would be to play this serious and sometimes very violent game according to both the mind-set of and the rules and the peculiar logic used by, the accuser, and, equally importantly, it would define you as the victim. Entering a discussion when someone calls you a blasphemer validates his point of view, and again, in the same tedious, boring cycle, it is always a *he*. Swift and Joyce would not accept the logical parameters of this scenario any more than they would waste their time trying to have a rational or indeed any discussion with someone who mouths nonsensities continuously because of a seeming linguistic tic. In the deadly script that is blasphemy, to attempt conciliation - maybe because you (want to) think of yourself *as a decent person*, and sophisticated and educated and rational etc., in a benign attempt to assuage those who profess offence, anguish, anger etc., with excuses and pleas such as *I didn't, don't, mean to cause any hurt* - will be taken as an admission of weakness and error. Even if there is no express admission of error, for instance, on your part, all it will do is reinforce the accusers' sense of rightness and righteousness, which is a formidable combination which uses *right-* as a kind of special five letter prefix.* Some will say the Swift and Joyce attitude adds fuel to the fire and sends the fool further and all other such expressions, but this is an essay on the semiotics of violence which uses blasphemy as a case-study, and reconciliation etc. is beyond its scope. Which is just as well, because when the block is semiotic it will always stand fast, if some group or other always marks everything they say as absolute. In a religious context, absolute belongs in the realm of the divine, and change is a divine prerogative.

*(Note: This is a rider to what was written some twenty five years ago. Rightness is being right, and in this context this includes being always right. Righteousness adds the idea of virtue, and being right flows from being virtuous. This was serious semiotics, because it could also create the idea that this is why you or I can be and are allowed to be, violent. Halfway through the last paragraph, I marked he in italics which some may find tedious and worse, but we still find it impossible to acknowledge in any minimal way, that the male identity has caused violence without limit, and change is infinitesimal and often transitory; to call this pessimism, however, is a moral judgment. The final sentence in this last paragraph read like a platitude when I said it to myself again after all this time, but maybe it is as good a reminder as anything else of the awful banality when human beings, in an act of pure blasphemy, regard themselves as absolute. I repeat again, that in the very gentle and loving religion of my childhood, we knew that God created us

out of love and we would live forever in this love, in Heaven, with Him and our loved ones, after we died. And if anyone thinks this is now a little boy dreaming, we also knew very well that we also lived in a parallel religion that could use a stick and a strap without bothering too much about excess, and which could be hard and cruel in all kinds of other ways as well which have no place in a sentence which comes after one which says God created us out of love).

Joyce and Swift were always acutely conscious of why they were writing blasphemy. This was ultimate war and when language was chosen as the weapon of choice, language was and would have to be, pushed to its limits and often beyond, which means that Joyce in particular, often flirted with seeming nonsense in the effort to expose all of meaning (we all indulge in seeming nonsense of course, but there are rules here too which provide legitimation when needed). The two Dubliners were also merciless and scurrilous in all kinds of ways when they went after and hunted down without let or hindrance, both the secular and religious blasphemy created by others. They would also figuratively and repeatedly spike those who denounced or who might denounce them as well, which gives their writing on blasphemy an extra dimension in depth and scope. They are both also great story tellers and knew far better than those who accuse others of blasphemy, that imagination has always been the source of all great stories. Note Swift's seeming simple move to tell childlike stories with an allegorical gloss where we are the animals, and the animals are the victims, and Joyce's gentle short stories and his fascination with theatre - including managing one in Dublin before he took up permanent residence on the continent - which has been the public place for telling stories for millennia. In their own blasphemous texts, their poisoned arrows were not aimed at God or His true religion, they were fired at those who have perverted God and human life and society, with their stories which are written and told in the name of their religion and which have also brought and continue to bring, danger and sometimes endless disaster to countless people. For Swift and Joyce, to recant would have been a lie, a metaphysical lie, a denial of the existence of reality, an act of irrationality and immorality against themselves, and ultimately, an act of cowardice. Those who blaspheme are denying the right of others to say anything and to decide what truth means, and Swift and Joyce who regarded themselves, and in different ways, as supreme intellectual players, would not allow anyone to arrogate to themselves the exclusive right to exploit the very concept of blasphemy any way they wished to silence and punish others. Both of them and again in different ways, often wandered across the boundaries of the seeming religious and secular which is itself a very dangerous game, as the history of the three monotheistic religions especially tells us, and often in a very graphic way. The bound sanction of *silence and punish* is itself a useful model in exploring the history of blasphemy in what often seem to be quite different religious cultures, and not just in those cultures where there is no separation or only a partial separation of the religious and the political.

BLASPHEMY WAS CHOSEN as a topic in a series of essays on violence to illustrate that identity is the most complex and difficult factor in any explanation for violence, and also to illustrate the idea of *game* which is also useful in understanding violence. In our traditional ways of thinking in Europe we have not always kept it explicitly in mind that game is a very complex notion, and nothing seems to have changed, despite the fact that those who actually fight wars now brazenly and honestly call their preparations war games. Nor have we made much progress either in understanding that blasphemy too is a war game, and that the violence which is a consequence of blasphemy and which may be inflicted on the world in all kinds of ways, small and large, and sometimes very large and dramatic, may have no boundaries. If you are of a sensitive disposition or if you like to think of yourself as a person of delicate manners, you may apologize for the unintended hurt you have caused when (those regarded as) blasphemers are sanctioned, as happened in Ireland when a person's employment and a whole, extended family's future, could be in danger; such sanctions could always have an absolute scope and the apology may be just a *lie*, of the hypocritical, *wanting to have it both ways* variety. Swift the ordained cleric and Joyce the layman who might also have been a more informed theologian than the cleric, knew as well as anybody, that the *Good Book* has very harsh words for those on that very long hypocritical list. Elsewhere I mentioned that nothing seemed to anger the Son of God like our hypocrisy, and which has never seemed to get the attention it deserves from the great thinkers despite the fact that it has always been part of the staple diet of creative writers everywhere.

(Note: Many of the under-35s now in Europe have very low or even no religious sensibilities, and no points of reference to understand blasphemy, or the Swift and Joyce talk about blasphemy, in any remotely adequate way. Which means, for example, they will hardly understand anything of what is happening now between various Muslim branches and factions, and if it is mentioned it may be dismissed as stupid and crazy and a whole host of analogous terms in the different European languages.* It is also a terrible waste that many of those from within the religion and who come from the great Islamic intellectual traditions and who might contribute to the discussion and help those of us outside Islam, have not and are not allowed to have, a voice. But, and in all kinds of ways, it is a devoir humain, and we do not have the right not to understand the conflict - it is also very much in our own interest when various ISIL type groups and lone rangers are already in residence in the West and other places around the world, waiting to wreak serious harm - which is flooding Europe with haunted refugees who are often repeatedly running away again from war, but this time they are also coming into a Europe which often does not want them, for all kinds of complex reasons; the whole affair has been exacerbated further by people from sub-Saharan Africa also joining the caravans and trying to enter Europe also as refugees fleeing from war. A number of countries are also now in conflict with others in the EU about the refugee problem and this is already changing the Union in a whole variety of ways, and may push it to very fundamental change, and possibly breaking point. I might say the centre cannot hold, I never need an excuse to steal from Yeats, but the Union never had a centre, which is not any kind of smart comment; it was a very clever way of talking to give us reason to be ambitious about cooperating with each other, including keeping the peace, as it were. It also had considerable success until the prophet Yeats had his way again.

*One time I said that using terms such as denomination and sect is fraught with danger of every kind and will earn you a rebuke or much worse. The only problem was that fraught seems to have been slipping away gradually from the language and the first question was about fraught which was obviously more interesting than branches of ideologies and religions that I was talking about in the seminar on symbolic violence. But at least it gave me another opportunity to say that in the Catholic religion of my young life, the assumption was that our belief and practice was a religion and Protestant groups in our town such as the Church of Ireland and the Methodists, for example, were not. This brought retorts of prejudice and worse, but it was also an easy entry to the general semiotic reality that we usually assume - and, in certain contexts, this morphs to always - that what we do is valid and what others do may have little or no validity, or worse, and that a liberal attitude covers only a minute fraction of life as lived which was, as usual, not terribly well received either.

P.S. For years and years, my mother had a visit from a neighbour every day of the week except Sunday, my Mother was Catholic, the five minute walk away neighbour was Protestant. There was never any mention of religion or any mention of anything which might have any connection of any remote kind, with religion. Going to funerals was an absolute social obligation, but not if the deceased was of the other religion. Being present at a Protestant funeral service was regarded as an occasion of sin by the Catholic Hierarchy and priesthood, and while my mother might take care of a dying Protestant neighbour for night after night, for example, and maybe also prepare the body for burial, there was no question of her going to the funeral. I left Ireland in the very end of the '6os and when I came back to Ireland in 1980, people who were ten years younger than me went regularly to Sunday service in the Methodist Church because there were very few from that Church left in the town and surrounding countryside. It was a pity that no studies were done in that Ireland about how absolute mental transformation and radical social change can happen in the proverbial overnight, it is too late now).

BECAUSE WE USUALLY, at least implicitly, gloss our meaning as true or absolutely true, semiotics needs to be interested also in how we flag meaning in this peculiar way. Indeed it would be important to ask whether, in practice, the default system in all communication is that what I say or hear or read or write is true, unless there is an explicit indication to the contrary, and especially in the areas of what I say and write. This whole question about how and when we implicitly assign the gloss of truth is very relevant to the whole of communication and not only to blasphemy and ultimately to violence, which is a central question in all of these current essays on the various facets of identity. The question has haunted me for quite some time and it is beginning to become clearer every day that I do not have the ability to deal with it, other than to point out its importance; and it is in this regard that those who scoff at the idea of the possibility of truth make such fools of themselves when they apply their maxim to everyone and everything except themselves and their *dicta*. The peculiar logic people in England used in the first half of this century - *Note, The twentieth century* - was sometimes a little too generous to themselves. And also in some of the other old ways of talking, saying *I do not have the ability* just above in this last sentence, would prompt a particular friend of mine of some years, to say what else could I expect when I made the likes of Swift and Joyce my mentors.

Swift was sometimes obsessed with truth, and also reality, and when he committed blasphemy, his arrows were mortally directed at those who have taken unto themselves the right to call themselves the divine shadows of God on earth. *Woe to you Scribes and Pharisees, impostors* he told them, you have no right to lord it over others, or to make up rules and doctrine on God's behalf. Swift came from a distinguished creative and intellectual family tradition and also a most extraordinary cultural and linguistic heritage which always seems to need a new language to describe its genius adequately. He was an eminent divine and the Dean of St Patrick's Cathedral in Dublin. He was also a clergyman who did all the day to day work, celebrating Church services and preaching and officiating at marriages, baptisms, and funerals in a major parish in the second city of a burgeoning

Empire; and he was also a highly educated intellectual besotted with the pursuit of truth which he often masked by using very unecclesiastical language outside the confines of the Church. It would now be regarded as peculiar, but he obviously regarded his writing as extra-curricular, as it were, as he also sometimes seemed to view other aspects of his life as well. But in his clerical world, he was in the perfect position to understand blasphemy, and when he was not using satire, he often behaved like *any good Catholic* would and used the tactic of the *disputatio* of the medieval schoolmen. But this was not the random *quodlibetica disputatio* where everyone could contribute, or, at least, where the impression of everyone freely contributing could be given, which is my favouite story in the history of ideas, if only because of its sheer arrogance. This was the magisterial master talking. He first demolished the opposition by indulging in multiple forms of the most extreme blasphemy, sometimes in language most foul, against certain religions and denominations of religions and ideologies. Then he might revert to being *the medieval schoolman* again and put together a whole panoply of dogmas and principles of a religious, political, and linguistic nature, which were to his liking. His attack on secular blasphemy in Gulliver's Travels created what might be regarded as the satire of all satires, and the vitriol still sometimes directed at him ever since by his own religious denomination in England and Ireland for writing such a *travelogue*, has never ceased. The blasphemy he exposed does not come more grand than the bombastic, ridiculous and false ideas we have created for millennia about ourselves, and our place in the hierarchy of creation. Swift also went back to the original Greek tradition of that most extraordinary fifth century in the classical era, but now his text takes the place of *the curses* hurled by actors dressed as satyrs. In Gulliver, he also plays with the interchange of animal and human shapes in the manner of the Greek and

Roman tradition of satyrs and fauns. Swift would have known well the sexual overtones of both, in the literature of the two cultures, where the Latin seemed to be determined to counter the Greeks, and particularly in this field.*

* Maria Edgeworth who was born a few years after Swift's death wrote what she said was a continuation of Swift's own work. Her *Essay on Irish Bulls* is the first major work ever written on symbolic violence, and which is still, strangely, not recognised internationally as such.

In Ulysses, Joyce would match Swift in the manic business of *savage indignation*. He denounced anything and everything in the best of the European and Irish traditions that took his fancy, but his blasphemy knew no bounds when he railed like an Old Testament prophet - but never ever, against the religion of God - against the religion created by the *insane* in His misappropriated name. To deny those who have appointed themselves the priests of God, either to create a religion or to decide what religion is, or to be the ultimate arbiters and guardsmen of religion and morality, would be regarded by some religionists as the most insidious blasphemy of all. Swift and Joyce - with their intimate knowledge of religion and a wide variety of Western intellectual traditions and languages, and their blinding literary talents and range of styles - were in the classic and often very precarious position of gamekeepers turned poachers. Swift attacked false prophets to promote his own religion, Joyce was more the epitome of the highly educated, intellectual Catholic who broke from the particular religion where sometimes nothing seemed to be outside its scope, to become the universal anarchist who said a plague on all your houses. When it suited him, of course, as you might expect from any proper well-educated Irish Catholic anarchist with, what might be routinely said in a different Irish context of the time, an aspiring eye for *the purple* of the clerical aristocracy

But neither of the two of them were remotely confused by what they were doing, which makes them very different from most of those who have been talking about blasphemy recently in Western societies and who sometimes seem to be confused about what model of meaning they are using, or what such a model could mean. These last six words may be taken as the height of arrogance, but naivety is particularly frightening when the potential for blasphemy driven violence has never been so universal - with pictures on television and on the front pages of every newspaper, of books being burned again almost nonchalantly, on the streets of capital cities in Europe - because information became globalized with infinite implications for semiotics and for how meaning will be assigned in every corner of our lives, especially the ones which were hiding in dark corners. This is the spectre of universalism in a world where the individual, from a very young age, will be ever more alone and isolated and informed and socialized by electronic communication, but one which gives the impression that we are (all part of) a community. This newness, however, refers only to the new global, easily accessed channels of information, but the memes and themes are the same, which is why an understanding of blasphemy is all the more important because of the continuous and permanent threat of violence which it always generates and because now, the world's stage is more and more visible to ever more and more people.

Both Swift and Joyce saw that language itself was the battleground for the religionists and the ideologists, and both were more than willing to engage the enemy, not just those in some green and pleasant land but in any and every sewer as well, if necessary, which gives them both a very unusual advantage as did their command of so many different registers of language and their routine unwillingness not to be bound by the usual linguistic rules, including its decrees on propriety. Sometimes, despite their education and seemingly limitless creative and linguistic talents, they often remind me of two *gurriers* (the local substitute uses a hard, stressed plosive in the first syllable, for the insipid somewhat standard *low-life*) going around Dublin *looking for fight* (another very regular phrase in our Irish English when I was growing up) wherever they find it, which may seem to be trivializing the violence which accusations of blasphemy can generate: but just because religion is a serious subject, this does not mean that those who advocate and inflict the extremes of violence in its name, are any different from and should be talked about differently, from thugs fighting on O'Connell Bridge or further down the river on the day of a horse fair in Smithfield. *Violence is* notoriously *easy* to explain, *identity is* always *the problem*, including now when anyone can take a phrase, an idea, an image, and use it and abuse it, to form or reform his identity, as mentioned just above.

The two Dubliners were obsessed with identity and obsessively conscious of the logic of the accusation of blasphemy which is why they both went to war with no holds barred against the accusation, and sometimes against any potential accusation. Blasphemy says you are wrong, by definition, when you are accused. This is the meaning of the accusation, and both of them will tell you very quickly, one way or another, to say this is not fair is pathetic and of no relevance; the language they use will be more graphic, of course, because they will always let you know one way or another, that they always use whatever is the appropriate language for the occasion. Nor can you say you did not mean what they think you meant, if you are accused of blasphemy. Can you imagine James Joyce pleading innocence and ignorance about the disgusting scene in the early pages of Ulysses when he tells a story about a funeral in Glasnevin cemetery, a place of rest not much more than ten minutes down the hill on the bike from where I work. Or the repugnant scene at Mass in the beautiful church I passed yesterday on Dominic Street, or the pages where Swift told the English that they had reduced Ireland to such a hell for the Catholic Irish they might as well break every other taboo as well, and fatten up their children and eat them as a substitute for veal. Imagine the horror and furore if that were said today where people are now being made destitute in parts of the Middle East and deliberately starved and where their children are being treated worse than ragdolls on a scrap heap. The two of them will tell you that you only add insult to injury and fuel to the fire and every other cliché - both were rather addicted to using the cliché when they made a fool of language - when you plead that you are a decent human being and did not intend to insult or hurt anybody, when you mince and pince and deny you meant to offend anybody when you blasphemed.

The high priests who accuse anyone and everyone of blasphemy - they change robotic like all the time, as if there were a secret plot to take it in turn - and their minions, decide what you mean, that is the crowning presumption in the logic of blasphemy. We are all imprisoned in the battle field that is semiotics when blasphemy appears, and the fight is for meaning, and sometimes it is to the death, and not just figuratively, as is now being shown on television every day in every country unless government censors switch the screen to a dubbed *Tom and Jerry*. You do not need a blow by blow account of every major battle fought in the name of meaning, and the list of the vast casualties which resulted from such violence, even in the context of a small little country like my own. *Resulted* is in the past tense - violence makes its own rules even with the often draconian rules of language, and is desperately being used here in a kind of continuous past, present and future mode as well - but this does not mean it is still not going on in this small island. They decide what hurts them, and what hurts the sometime legions of their followers, in the past, now, and in the future. They have assumed the persona of Cronus who was jealous of his father, the ruler of the universe, and have also made themselves the lords of time. It is a waste - it will also be taken as an insult and be dangerous as well - telling them there is no need to be hurt, if they really understood your intentions (really is very popular in this world, it means if you, whoever you are, would just agree). Or, the unkindest cut of all, if they understood their own religion properly, or, even worse, and not just in the case of so-called fundamentalists, if they understood that their interpretation of their own religion was plain wrong. Or, as we intellectuals say, if they understood the function of the writer or artist or intellectual in society. You might as well Whistle in the Dark, as Tom Murphy called his play which shows (the morphological and syntactical structure of) language breaking down on the page as a reflection of what happens when violence comes on stage and becomes part of who we are in life.

(Note: Joyce was like a scout for a movie and located blasphemy, and everything else that took his fancy, here, there and everywhere in everyday Dublin. In the second last paragraph, there is mention of a Church on Dominick Street which had its own Joycean history. The government planners who were part of London's overreach in the second city of the empire, had stipulated that no entrance to a new heretical place of worship could face onto the street - it was bad enough having a blasphemous edifice a few streets over from the centre of Dublin - but this was somehow not noticed during the construction in the mid-nineteenth century some twenty years before Joyce was born, and gives his blasphemy in Ulysses a reality which is still raw and shocking, even when it is a line or two I have known for years. There is no chauvinism at play here, I do not know any masters of semiotics, and not just in the explosive area of blasphemy, who combine an intimate knowledge of religion and the history of ideas, and very graphic, recreated real place and space, with intellectual brilliance, more trenchantly and incisively than Swift and Joyce, or who exhibit more malignantly and obscenely, the ultimate Irish battle cry *Fàg an bealach,* Leave the field - I will not play by your rules. They could write a little as well, as faux modesty says it, and switch styles at will, and also often use the very switching of styles on the same page to communicate more dramatically - Joyce would do it sometimes in the same sentence - and sometimes more blasphemously as well. In addition, concepts such as abusive and wicked should be applied to many other ideas as well, and not only to certain matters sexual and religious. But extending the idea of blasphemous to ideas sometimes found both on the street and also among the intellectual elite, and also their refusal to play conventional, polite games in their writing, has meant that Swift and Joyce have been largely excluded from what is regarded as the usual intellectual canon. Thinking in the European tradition of the Romance languages has not always been well served - and the world of violence is no exception - by the tradition of using highly stylised registers in certain types of exclusive writing and not availing of all the lexical resources of language in communication.

It would make an important study in itself, in terms of the semiotics of control, how such an elitist, homogenous system of communication has been achieved in what may seem to be quite different cultures, including those which might also have regarded radicalism, in terms of content, as an explicit badge of honour and respect. Nor does anybody know yet what is going to be the effect of the kinds of writing which are now social media, but especially because of the particular style which favors a practice of a reduced range of syntax and lexis, where one syllable, for example, can breach the stringent rule governing length and where the brevity rule means that the

overall piece is sometimes hardly more than what was sometimes a decent catch phrase in Dublin in the first decades of the
twentieth century. Even talk about extending the length
modestly, is now world news. At least, we need to ask if we are
entering a revolutionary phase in social evolution where objective, implicit censorship has become a consequence of the way
we communicate, if only because the primary mode of communication is the very novel, brief, cropped mode and length which
was first exhibited in various styles of texting used in the early
years of the new millennium. This is not my inner fossil talking.
I love the crazy experiments with writing a poem, a novel etc. as
a tweet. Nor is it the barbarians are at the gate quip, it is a
comment on homogeneity in communications and the race to
brevity and abbreviation, which will have consequences for all
kinds of new forms of blasphemy in the secular and religious
worlds. Everyone now is able to react instantaneously and
simultaneously to everything and also become a blasphemer and
an anti-blasphemer, and sometimes one that also uses blasphemy in retaliation, in an infinite, very vicious circular maze,
where everyone, everywhere, can actively participate, and take
offence, in every language. Reaction to one single tweet can now
run into thousands in a day or two, which introduces the nightmare of a twelve year-old in one country gravely insulting the
sensibilities and beliefs of a fifty two year-old in another country
on the other side of the world - without realising what he has
done - and the electronic world becomes an inferno in half an
hour, and with violence on the streets on the same day).

THOSE WHO CALL you a blasphemer are hurt and sometimes,
very deeply hurt. The pain is real and genuine, but because
displacement lies at the heart of blasphemy, the distress is self-

induced, which is not an uncommon phenomenon in the fields of play and life which are of high and sometimes supreme, emotional value. Those who deem that their god, their religion, in any of various ways, have been blasphemed, have taken unto themselves the powers which are properly attributed to God, in the theological and religious sense. They are now the word and truth and goodness, or the avenger, and whatever other virtues and traits they may have bestowed on their god and which, critically, they have appropriated to themselves, sometimes implicitly, and at other times, brazenly and explicitly. It is this transference of meaning and identity - which is a good description and even definition of the ultimate blasphemy in the three monotheistic religions - which gives them the right to decide when they are hurt and how they are hurt. And to decide what punishment they can exact, which depends on their popular or particular sectional support, and, or, their access to *armies* of enforcement, formal and informal. Transposing themselves semiotically, to the divine plane, gives them (the impression of) almighty power over what everyone else can say and think and do, and most importantly, not say and not think and not do. *Everyone* here is a very big word, and means everyone, in the past, present and future. Being *in loco dei*, as in the analogous, secular, sometime legal phrase *in loco parentis*, gives them this total power - it means they have assumed this power to themselves - including, ultimately, the power of life and death and also destiny in the hereafter, over anyone who breaches their commandments, and many more than the ten listed in the *Decalogue*, including those which can hardly be expressed in any form. But in this strange convoluted semiotic world of meaning that is blasphemy, expression here can include the ideational, which has no limits, and which takes us into a very dense semiotic jungle, which in personal contexts might be given a sometime psychotic tag. This is the purpose of the exercise, and it is pointless saying nobody should have this power.

This is a complex way of marshalling and managing ideas and meaning, and it would be of no benefit to be supercilious about the intellectual sophistication of those who behave like this, unless you are prepared to be open and candid about what you think and to keep keep saying what you want to say and what you think needs to be said, and to protect yourself if necessary. If violence and, or, the threat of violence, is the mode and language of communication chosen by your accuser, you have two choices, raise a virtual white flag and never say anything they do not want said, or, refuse to do this; it would be prudent to assess the whole range of potential consequences, if the latter is chosen. Sometimes, however, it may be difficult or impossible to know in every single context what is not to be said, when the topics go walkabout and wander into what you may think has nothing specifically to do with what seems to be their religion or religious denomination, or when it is something which is part and parcel of what you regard as your culture, and what you regard as your rights within your culture. In some contexts, if you yield one iota when they cry blasphemy, and this can include a willingness to discuss the problem in what is regarded in polite circles as a calm, rational way, they have won, and not just that they will think they have won. Semiotics never fails to warn us in case we forget, that thinking is behaviour and part of reality. Which is why I say they have won, and what you may think is of no relevance; in the world of blasphemy, you might add whatsoever you like to the no relevance world, including yourself.

There can be no understanding of blasphemy unless it is understood that those who accuse you of blasphemy are god on earth, and their actions are the actions of god. The more usual way of saying this might be that they regard themselves as carrying out the wishes of god or some such expression, but what is being said is categorical and unequivocal, and the *regard themselves* expression, does not, may not, convey the absoluteness of how they may regard themselves, and the consequent absoluteness of such a blasphemy. I will take responsibility for my failings in how I write, at this stage, the accumulated evidence hardly leaves me with a lot of options, but not in this and the last paragraph. When ways of thinking and behaviour go beyond what language can cope with, as it does when they become god and take the place of god, and when they act as god, including saying things which our mental world cannot cope with, then there is absolute breakdown between them and us. Psychiatry might comment on when identities of such imagination and fantasy are assumed, except that it too has consistently failed us in never consistently paying adequate attention to group think of any kind. There are contexts, for example, when someone from a group will defend the action of other members and those outside will shake their heads in disbelief when the seeming indefensible is defended as if there was really nothing to defend. Political experts on Northern Ireland and the Middle East will have their say about everything including the violence, but this is usually different in kind from professionals also looking at the violence and the various groups of people involved in the violence from a more detached, even clinical point of view.

It might not be the best place to say - which is why I am also somewhat lamely moving to a new paragraph - that the endgame might sometimes seem to be that you adopt their religion, or the particular denomination of their religion, but this may also be impossible, if only because denominations may split into further variants, for example. It may also be unacceptable to them because you are ultimately unacceptable for multiple reasons, including that you are regarded as not properly human because of your deviant religious beliefs and blasphemous practices - many other people are sometimes not regarded as properly human because of gender, physiognomy, colour etc. - which is something that has always haunted the history of violence. Some might also add, for example, that you have left the human world and joined the world of Satan. I was brought up in a religion and a particular denomination of the religion that was Irish Catholicism, which was often positive and joyful. I also learned - we would sometimes operate very cleverly on two different tracks which never meet - that boundaries are very clearly marked, and that the sanctions, be they religious, and social, legal and civil, for going beyond the demarcation lines can be absolute. Those who might shout blasphemer at me now, are saying that (what they regard as) their religion and the rules and practices of their religion now, are absolute and sacrosanct. We are all at one time or another, tied in all kinds of ways to an assumption, at least implicit, that there is a bedrock of rationality in human behaviour, but in certain areas which assume very high levels of emotional meaning, and not only in relationships and religion, there may, ultimately, be only one rule which has two closely tied parts, *I am, You are not*, which transfers in the context of a group, to *We are, You are not*. If someone or some group puts me eternally in the negative sector, that is how I am defined, and in certain religious contexts, this is for all eternity as well. They, for some reason, also insist that I am eternal, whether I like their idea of my eternal fate or not, or whether I agree with them about even what eternal might or could mean. Which is as stark an example as any of the absoluteness of meaning, and not just its absolute importance.

This is how category models sometimes work, and we have created a perfect dilemma for ourselves and often unfettered disaster, by the simple fallacy of always using a *common noun* for religion itself, and then also for different kinds of religion,

Jewry, Christianity, Islam, to name just the three related monotheistic religions. Some religions do not regard other religions as religions, which is putting it mildly and vaguely, and sometimes grossly inaccurately. In addition, some in Northern Ireland, for example, did not regard the loving religion of my childhood as a religion, and, similarly, some Sunni Muslims do not regard Shia'a Islam as a religion. Sometimes, the negativity may extend to saying a particular other religion is not a religion, or worse, and may use terms such as heretical and blasphemous, or that it is the antithesis of religion, and the same language may be used also for a peculiar denomination of a religion. The next part, mentioned briefly elsewhere, which flows from all this, is that, based on the beliefs of what is regarded as a religion, in the context of the Christian religion, for example, there is no Christian religion, because there are only disparate shards, which, on the basis of a generally accepted simple logic, that there are, potentially, endless groups saying they are the religion, and that the others are not, and that there is somehow a core religion which is Christianity. This has been the situation in Christianity almost from the beginning two thousand years ago, but you would want to be very brave or extremely foolish to say what such a core might be or that Catholicism, for instance, is the Christian religion and all the others claiming a Christian heritage are fraudulent, or worse, and the negative list is very long. I am giving Christianity as an example, and am not saying this is exclusive to Catholicism etc. The Pope and the Hierarchy in the Catholic religion believed and said, for example, that other Christian denominations were in error, and we followed faithfully as we did in so much else, and believed that also.

The next line in this logical exercise is that therefore, there is no religion, which will be regarded as blasphemy by everyone, in every religion. But saying there is no religion is not just a bald statement, it is just that the language and how it is commonly used by many religious leaders, says this.

I am not saying this, which is why this last sentence is being isolated and given the status of being a paragraph in itself.

Sometimes when a Christian or Muslim group is attacked in some way from outside the religion, by those who profess another religion or none, this can often have the effect of uniting all or most Christians or Muslims, as the case may be, for a period, which means the religion becomes whole in some way, for this, usually very brief, period. There are also waves of ecumenism, especially among certain Christian factions now, but in an essay I published some years ago on symbolic violence - and which now seems a very long lifetime ago - it was proposed that such ecumenism works best when the various groups are less intense and insistent about claiming they are right and less strident about saying that others are wrong; and also that ecumenism may work best when there is an implicit agreement to say nothing very much; and, thirdly, denominational strife may decrease or disappear, at least for a period, when the whole religion itself, Christianity, for example, feels it is under siege in some form, which can include physical attack. But the ultimate dilemma which has plagued religion is the sometime insistence about making everything explicit. Sometimes the level of detail may cross over to what would be regarded as obsessive, in many other contexts in life, and very dangerous in personal relation-ships, as we all know, when it is the turn of the other party, as it were, to insist on such detail. And there is also something else that can haunt my life and your life at any time when what we have assumed to be absolute may be challenged and declared a blasphemy in the world of some particular religion or some peculiar religious denomination, and then the circle of violence may also ensue.

Reality is not a Socrates type dialogue in any circumstance -

his were a pedagogical device, and might more properly be called unilogues, and a mode of argument and *disputation* which certain medieval theologians used as well - and blasphemy is no exception; sometimes just an indication of a readiness to talk may be interpreted as a sign of weakness and guilt and you will be expected to retract. You may not even know what exactly is to be redacted, and redacted to nothing, if you do not have any real competence in their religion or denomination or their religious culture and the peculiar logic of how they talk about their religion, not to mention their language and the peculiar variation of their language which can take on a very particular importance in various forms of Arabic, for example. Especially if they keep an open agenda where anything and everything may be added on their side which is always the case with groups within a religion which talk loudly and carry *big sticks*: *big* and *stick* can be literal or metaphorical, and when both are in operation at the same time, this may generate unlimited power and violence. The operative word here is talk. There is no intention to discuss anything openly, because there is no possibility of compromise or change. This is the land of absolutism, and it is often not known in the West, or is just conveniently ignored, that we all have absolutist parts of our lives and, furthermore, that many aspects of life as we know it, would be impossible without them. This is what the logic of their position entails, and the best you can hope for is that recantation and apology will suffice, and you will not suffer loss of position or physical including terminal, injury, or that people you have never heard of but who are regarded as your people may not suffer either, as often happens when race or religious ascription and identity are in play.

Appropriating the power of God includes the right to punish who they regard as blasphemers and the enemies of their god. This of course makes no necessary or consistent sense in the context of a Christian theology based on the scriptures of the New Testament, but this has never been a hindrance to those who ascribe absolute power to themselves, especially the power of the Almighty. Certain Christians too, for example, have borrowed and will appropriate as their linguistic prerogative the bloodthirsty language of the Book of Judith from the *Old Testament*, when heavy ordnance is required. Translations of the Bible which use beautifully crafted archaic language can also provide an impression of power and solemnity compared with contemporary variants, especially those in some variants of American English which always try to match colloquial speech, as if writing could ever match what is thought to be, spoken language. They have carefully arranged the world of meaning in which they operate which may often include saying they have a religious obligation to strike down the blasphemer - at least metaphorically, but the use of this last word should not lead us to think that in the worlds which are violence, metaphor always pales in comparison with the physical - and that they would be failing in their solemn duty if they did not obey this sacred trust. In other words, and very ominous words they are, it would be sinful, which is a perfect example of how they will move from one plane of reality to another, whenever they choose, including, as here, the eschatological. Some might be tempted to chide me for using the term *reality* and *eschatology* in the same sentence, but this is semiotics; we all use such terms in multiple ways, and it has no relevance if your realities are different from or better than, those of others, as far as I am concerned. It is not my problem, which is not the usual abrupt, caustic phrase that be used on the *mean streets* of New York, it just cannot be my problem, that is just the way the world (of meaning) is, and you living in *the real world*, or choosing not to, is something I can do nothing whatsoever about. They may stretch the story to say they are not at liberty to forgive the blasphemer, because only their god can forgive such a sin, but they may also work at the same time with the supplementary and contradictory theological principle, that god does not excuse or absolve such a sin; only they can know this because in the *real* world, which is our world, they behave as if they are the mind of god, which is as blasphemous as blasphemy can get. And this has always been so in each of the three monotheistic religions, and not just the two later ones, which sometimes seem to have what might generally be regarded - including sometimes by themselves - as not always having *a very healthy attitude* to violence, both symbolic and physical [3].

They also frequently seem to have a particular need to defend themselves against blasphemy with all the might they can muster - clichés of all kinds, especially metaphors of warfare, including centuries old terms such as muster, easily find a welcome home in this world - if and when it strikes at the very foundation of their complex chains of command and their various claims for authority. They will stretch any story and to infinity if necessary, to defend their position, and in this world, time is all time which may seem a very complex idea, but in these contexts, it can be common both among the illiterate and the highly educated. This can often include the idea that the sin of blasphemy can be only expiated by the death of the blasphemer, which is a very worldly punishment for those who make divine proclamations. But the belief that blasphemy dies, and can only die, with the death of the blasphemer, is just another optional entry in a system predicated on the assumption of absoluteness, including absolute truth and power. This also can mean, however, in those religions which believe in individual eternal life that the blasphemer carries the mark also after he dies, in whatever way this happens, natural or not, which makes the worldly death of the blasphemer a mere ideational vanity: giving an example of identity even the great psychologists never talked about, including those of staggering imagination and creativity, who did not (seem to) know or care, what *limits* means or could mean. They have assumed the omnipotent and supernatural power of perfect knowledge and truth which negates your position, whatever it may be and however it may be articulated. This is what gives them *carte blanche* to say and do anything they like.

They are almighty, which also skirts the borders of blasphemy, but this is also often exhibited by their partiality for expressions such as *the power over life and death*. Which can, for example, extend to the practice of punishing a child in the womb by death, because blasphemy may also extend to *genetic pollution* which as you might already know or imagine, can also have a very broad meaning - and a history in a few short years in the 1940s and '40s which might have brought Europe and half of the rest of the world to an end - and ultimately, it can mean whatever they say it means. And again, moving from one plane of reality to another, whatever they say it means can come into play, for instance, even when the woman had originally been raped by a member of the group which has assigned unto itself a label such as *righteous*; and, to introduce another semiotic twist, the sexual intercourse is not regarded as *sinful* or *haram*, as intercourse outside marriage would be and which would be absolutely forbidden, and, in many contexts, punishable by a very violent death. In this instance - and another example which may not be accessible to the vast majority of people in the *West*, of how meaning can be construed - the woman's *negativity* is regarded as transferring *holus bolus* to the child in the womb, as if the male had had no genetic contribution. And if the child is allowed to be born, she or he may not be accorded the rights of being human, and sometimes seems with consequences I could never write about. But violence can also extend beyond death in this world, and the graves of those whose very person was regarded as a blasphemy can be violated, with headstones broken and sometimes bones dug up and scattered everywhere, including tombs and crypts and catacombs many hundreds of years old, and not only in the regions of *the two rivers* where our three related monotheistic religions have their origin.

In the context of many Christian denominations, being authoritative and all-powerful was and sometimes still is, the meaning they have assigned to themselves on earth; this may contains nothing of the Christian theology of incarnation or the vulnerability of Christ, the Son of God, when He assumed human form and lived and died in our world, for us. Absolutism is the default, *the natural state of things*, which is now difficult or impossible to understand in many parts of *the West* - except in comparatively large sections of America - where the general assumption is that any such top down, absolute, social or cultural model is primitive and belongs in history (when it is convenient, as the next example cruelly illustrates). Interdenominational violence in Norther Ireland changed fundamentally in little more than a decade, but desecration of graves sometimes still happens, as it does against Jewish graves in France and other places in Europe, and not just in *the notorious Balkans*. In other parts of the world, little or nothing has changed, and in large swathes of America, crosses may still burned or lighted, to use the phrase sometimes favoured by certain white Christian groups as an act of symbolic violence against people of colour who are also Christian and who may also have quite similar denominational beliefs as the arsonists. This practice had been taken to America originally by Scots Protestants and then also Protestants of Scots origin from Northern Ireland. Catholics, predictably, and not just those of Irish origin, would also sometimes have been subject to the same peculiar violence until very recently. But there is also an addendum which is impossible to talk about without causing rancour. The Irish of Scots origin would have been and would been regarded as, belonging to the lower social economic classes, who often seek to identify a group lower than them, and in America the Catholic Irish played this role.*

*This persisted into the closing decade of the twentieth century, and anyone looking to understand American politics at the turn of the millennium might remember that the Democratic Party had always been the party of the otherwise unwanted, the Jews, Irish and Italians. You will note that Blacks and Hispanics are not even on the list of the unwanted, despite the latter sharing a religious faith with two of the chosen members of the rather unholy alliance that is still the Democrats. Semiotics will never be a great success in academia if it always insists on always coming first in the long list of the politically incorrect.

(Note: These last fifteen lines sentences will be read as prejudice talking in many places. So maybe it is time to say again that in my youth we also believed and this was an easy belief, that Heaven could not be the eternal destiny of those who had had the opportunity to know about and understand our Catholic faith and then rejected it. I also decided not to say this in the original text in case it might be a distraction, but in the religious culture which was my youth, there was also an underlying thread of thought, that a child born out of wedlock was significantly different, which meant that the child was not - did not fulfill the usual conditions for being regarded as - part of the community in the normal way, unless the child had been taken at birth from its mother and given to another family, including somewhere outside ireland. Which could also mean that the child was not entitled to all the usual rights which were the expectation in the culture, including the religious culture, but also in crucial contexts, the law of the land as well. This is a good example of a voodoo type culture, in Ireland, but it shows better than any description of mine could ever do, what can happen to a people, including my people - and, I will always say, we are good people - when meaning is created in a society like this, but also how language also has to be put on the rack as well, when the meaning has to be articulated explicitly.

But, in case, someone might add that the responsibility for all of this lies at the door of the Church, I remarked elsewhere in another Note, that during the revolution and fight for freedom whose centenary was marked a couple of years ago in 2016 - and which I also personally marked by assembling the traditional Irish white stones of remembrance in a small traditional cairn or mound, and also in lines - there was the ritual of priests shriving those who were going out to kill soldiers of the Crown, even though the sometime rogue Bishop in my own diocese of Cork who seems to have adopted the identity of a traditional Irish chieftain from six or seven centuries before this, had declared that all those taking part in the revolution - which might mean in Catholic semiotic territory, all those who supported it as well, and not just those who ordered the attack or who took up the gun - were committing a mortal sin and were excommunicated without ceremony, from the Catholic Church. Their excommunication might also have been virtual and would not include any ceremony of the bells, books and candles type for each guilty individual, but bishops like this in Ireland assumed all power to themselves including committing those who supported such violence to Hell and eternal damnation, in principle (which would also include priests who also carried the gun in some manner). You could never say that the Irish did not absolutely exploit the limits of semiotics and the assignment of meaning, but this also included numerous virtual worlds. This might not be the best place to say this but such thinking and behaviour are often regarded in our other worlds as indications of serious mental disturbance.

P.S. I have no idea where to begin thinking about why we had such gross disobedience in my own diocese when two such contrary systems operated in such a tandem. Killing representatives of the Crown was regarded by some, including what we still call God fearing people - which is still our expression for good, faithful Christians - as different in kind and not just in degree, and was not necessarily regarded as murder, but to call this gross hypocrisy is lazy thinking which will get you zero in my term semiotics test.

Killing could be glossed as not a sin, but just in case it might somehow turn out be a sin, in the eyes of God, when you died - which means it would carry the sanction of Hell for all eternity - it was shriven even though it might not have even happened yet, but the sin of becoming pregnant outside marriage, for example, was and was regarded as, fundamentally different in that Ireland, and the pregnant woman could also be deprived of certain basic human and legal, rights as well. When eschatology of any kind - and there are also powerful secular variants - enters a culture, any culture, this may also introduce very diverse ways of thinking which do not match what is usually regarded as reality, or, maybe saying that it introduces another, parallel, and sometimes contradictory reality, is a better way of saying it. This is a universal rule in anthropology, but saying this may also prompt a reaction which breaches the rules of polite academic discussion from those with a seeming congenital aversion to any such universality talk, which is hardly surprising, when it can sometimes throw a very unflattering light on all of us).

THIS IS a semiotic essay and not a paper on religion and we all know, albeit in different contexts, that there are forms of secular blasphemy which can compete with the most extreme forms of religious prejudice and blasphemy and which can extend to the very disturbing and multiple areas of the non-verbal. There were periods in various Communist regimes, for example, in a seventy year period in this final century of the second millennium, where your existence was a blasphemy, which resulted in the displacement, punishment, torture, rape, and slaughter of tens and tens of millions, on the perceived basis of social class, education, ethnicity, race, religion, mental ability and mental health, physical ability, physiognomy etc. etc. And also frequently, serendipity, which sometimes seemed to come in waves, out of the blue, like a tsunami, similar to the cultures created by the Greeks and many others throughout history which feature *monsters* of every kind. In Russian Communism and its progeny in China, for example, this was just another feature among many of a general metaphysic of brute realism. My best friend serendipity is also a reminder that there is a danger of straying into a grave fallacy without realising it, if you assume blindly that there is anything which would normally be regarded as rational in the endless specious reasons given for violence which follows in the wake of blasphemy, of whatever kind. It is barbarous to engage in comparisons in contexts when induced famine alone resulted, for example, in the deaths of millions, but, in any count, the numbers for the punishment which follows on from what is perceived as religious blasphemy pale into insignificance, statistically - no matter how this is calculated - when compared with the figures for secular blasphemy, in just that seventy year window alone. If only because of wars first stoked in Europe and exercised everywhere, including places known before only to a few and whose languages and dialects are still unknown, or dead, or dying rapidly. The scale and seemingly never ending pattern of this destruction in the long history of violence in the world, had as one of its principles, a semiotic construction first developed as an ideology in Europe which used ideational patterns from a Christian eschatology and which had originated in the regions of *the two rivers* in the *Middle East*. And to complete the circle that no Dante could imagine, this secular ideology had militant atheism as one of its signal principles which, in turn resulted in the imprisonment and death of millions of Buddhists, Christians and those from many other religions as well, including those which had originated in the indigenous and autochthonous cultures themselves. But the advocates of such Communism which made anti-colonialism a primary value, do not seem to have noticed, and if they did, it was never duly acknowledged in any minimal form. No, that is completely wrong, if someone had said that they had had *a bad dream* and had seen it happening in their sleep, that would mean immediate death, and also penury and misfortune for the person's misfortunate family.

(Note: You will be aware that Russia went from a particular Christianity in the 1910s to a Communism which had militant atheism as a primary value - and which killed we will never know how many on their new crossless altar - and then also to a rejection of this some seventy years later and the adoption of an amalgam of what had been Italian, Spanish, Portuguese and German fascism in various periods in the twentieth century and which can also flamboyantly flaunt the full grandeur of traditional Russian Orthodoxy. I sometimes feel I should thank somebody for presenting me with real examples which nobody could ever fashion in their imagination without worried friends nodding empathetically behind their back. P.S. We have no idea what have been the social, psychological effects of Russia moving from one political system to another, and can never know because such questions are not asked, I am not even sure there is any consciousness that it might be important for the health of a society to ask such questions. We have seen the disquiet in Spain, to give one example, when extremely difficult, awkward and often very brave, questions were beginning to be asked decades after fascism moved to democracy. The break with the Church in Ireland in the '90s is quite different because a significant segment of the population concentrated on a part of the culture which had never been relinquished. I call it 'the happy quotient' which was evident, to give one example, in very popular, sometime fanatic, competitive games down to the almost micro geographical level, and which is a phenomenon unique to Ireland. Sometimes it seems there is a determination to be happy, which can also have a very dark side when alcohol is notoriously abused).

SEMIOTICS SOMETIMES LIVES in very dark places, and none more dark than when *one world only* became a reality because of the violence everywhere in that seventy years; violence, of course, flourished as it always does, when ideational blasphemy takes root. The ideational in the secular world sometimes surpassed religion in fascism of every national colour in countries such as Germany, Spain, Italy, Serbia, Croatia etc., and not only in Communism. Religious blasphemy, however, is primary as a semiotic case-study in violence, because religion can use a more varied palette of meaning, including when the whole world is seen as one world and there are no borders between the secular and the religious and life after death and rewards and punishments in that *after-life* are also an intrinsic part of the whole, and when absolute may be attached as a rider to every belief and every action. But the example from religion is also important because those who accuse you of blasphemy in religious contexts, may continue stoking the emotional flames and never stop complaining of the anguish you cause. In the secular world, those who accuse you of blasphemy do not care one jot about what you think or feel and may casually deprive you of everything, and just as easily use mass murder as well, options not usually available to those who accuse you of religious blasphemy, if only because they now may lack the concomitant secular *fire-power*, as it were. Which will change in the future, if religion becomes the absolute ideology within more nations, as has already been happening, and not just in small, in parts of Islam, including those states which are regarded internationally as *third* and *fourth world* countries in terms of development and democracy, but which also have or are on the road to having, nuclear capability, or other forms of mass violence and destruction which can be delivered electronically. The citizenry may starve but the fatherland will have the bomb, as is happening now also in certain countries which have retained traditional Communism.

(Note: There is no claim for genius or prophecy, but these last sentences are becoming truer every day, as I would hear the adults say about anything and everything when I was small. I avoided naming the countries twenty years ago when most of the above was being written for class notes).

The religionists will also often switch back and forth from theology to psychology to anthropology, history, whatever, whenever it suits them; almost all major campaigns of revolution and protest, and not only those against blasphemy, are led by an educated elite, which can primarily mean a religious education in some contexts. And if you think it is not acceptable to tell people they are not being vilified and degraded, there is also another problem. In our everyday way of thinking, only a fool tells others they are not hurt or that they only think they are offended, not to mention telling a person he or she should not be aggrieved; and it sounds bombastic and extraordinarily pompous to tell people they do not have the right to be hurt. The last nine words sound so imperious they almost seem like bad grammar. They are hurt, and this can be wholly genuine and extremely distressing. To understand how those who accuse you of blasphemy assign meaning, it is necessary to see blasphemy from a semiotic and then also, a psycho-semiotic perspective, otherwise you run the risk of making a fool of yourself by arrogantly proclaiming that these people are insincere. Or that their pain and sadness is not real. Or that they do not have the right to feel like this. Or that they are uneducated and ignorant or challenged in all kinds of ways. Or mentally deranged. Or that they do not understand religion or that they have a totally erroneous idea of religion. Pomposity and ridiculousness are not the prerogative of any person or group, including my peculiar intellectual and academic tribes, and even if I work in a university where students and staff in all kinds of departments may be much more intelligent than I am in all kinds of ways, it can still be easy to fall into the trap of assuming everything I say and write is valuable and valid. I have always had a very intense work ethic and I think one of the reasons for trying to educate myself is to compensate for my comparative lack of ability. I did this too when I was a teenager playing hurling and when some of my teammates were born *with a hurley in their hand*. Ir was not that I ever thought in both intellectual life and in hurling, that I could ever be the best, I just wanted to be good enough to be able to play with them in the same field.

It is a constant refrain in these essays - which is putting it gently - that we have generated a dreadful intellectual problem for ourselves, all of us, in practice, and not only in the so-called *West*, by working with an assumption that meaning which is generated by feeling, may sometimes be of low standing and merit, despite being the most important aspect of all our lives: and this fallacy may easily be exacerbated much further, when it is extended to say that *they*, whoever the relevant *they* are, operate entirely irrationally, because their emotions and feelings generate the meanings they use to live their lives. The phrase commonly used is *govern how they think*, which itself works on the implicit assumption that reason, whatever it might be, is the driving force behind what and how we think. When there is film of riots and protests about blasphemy and screaming mobs engaging in the most awesome violence of every kind, it would be easy to slide into racism of various kinds and colours, and forget that in certain periods in Europe - and we are not just talking about locked away, safe in the past, ancient history - accusations of religious blasphemy were made, and grave sanctions were often meted out by and to, the most highly educated elite of the day. We cannot have already forgotten our very recent histories in the *West* when sanctions without limit, and often without limits of any kind whatsoever, were also meted out for secular blasphemy, to millions. Rationality of the most minimal type, however we might regard it, quickly vanishes in the world of blasphemy, as it often does in semiotics, and not only when it goes to rest or even to die, in the very dark places. When I was small I was afraid of the dark until I forced myself when I was sixteen to make *there is nothing there* part of my instinctive way of thinking; just as well I had no idea that I would spend my life learning about the dark places where violence unlimited lives and all the other dark places we create.

(Note: Some cultures make stoic an emblem in their culture, and it might be a breach of manners to ask if the foundation of this sometime obsession, sometime phobia, is driven by fear of chaos if we move beyond the comfort zone of the rational. As if the rational which has sometimes given us violence unlimited is all that wonderful and safe. But I live in semiotics, and will, as well, always be in front of everyone humbly holding on to one of the ribbons on the banner which proclaims Emotional meaning is an almighty mess, and underneath in much smaller letters and in brackets, but blame us, not God).

I allude only indirectly and in passing to secular blasphemy because it is usually more reticent and usually even more hypocritical than its religious twin - I will studiously avoid states which use variants of the secular and religious combined - and not only because those who make accusations of religious blasphemy often glory in being explicit about everything, including the most grotesque forms of sanction: nobody can be explicit about everything all the time, is an absolute rule, and the only exceptions are comedians and then only for a brief few minutes, or someone who is quite unbalanced in some way. Those who make the charge of religious blasphemy are acting on God's behalf, that is their story, as Irish cleverly says in a kind of ritual all of itself; and some stories can carry a very solemn message, as every culture knows, be it among the Ibo in West Africa, or among the monks who used to live on the Sceilg, or the islanders who lived next door, as it were, on the Great Blasket off the same south-west coast of Ireland. This is how they have constructed their identity and for this reason their pain may know no bounds. Their anger and the sanction visited on the blasphemer reflects, in their eyes, the fact that it is the Person of God Himself who has been abused and violated. His pain is their pain, their pain is His pain. There is no point in telling them God cannot be hurt by man, that such anthropomorphism is often very bad theology, except in terms of certain streams of Christianity, and then only in the context of God, in the mystical person of Jesus Christ, when He assumed the form of man, in that very particular context bound by place and time. Which is a long list of qualifications, but it also needs to be added that it is a complete waste of time telling them, if they are indulging in such discourse, be they of some Christian denomination or not, that to say God is hurt by what we say is blasphemy, and that we talk like this because this is how we talk about everyone, and not just about them in particular. People who make accusations of blasphemy hear, but to listen would give (who they say is) the blasphemer a role in the discussion, which could be a further blasphemy in their eyes, and which might also infect them as well. Nor would it be politic, and it may also be on the extreme end of dangerous to tell them, gently or haughtily, that a lot of their ideas about God and themselves, are theologically ridiculous, and blasphemous. It is always too late to tell them that if they would just think about it, they would not feel such anguish; once you are deemed to have blasphemed, you have had your say, and more than your say, in their eyes. If you have already blasphemed, you are too late, and it is also usually too late to say anything, about anything. It is too late for everything, except an *end game* of some kind, if those who accuse you also have the power. Blasphemy is not a toy genie, you cannot take it out of the bottle whenever you like and then put it back again with the cork on. Blasphemy is sometimes the monster we learned about in the old stories, and like many of these mutants, it becomes more incensed when it smells and tastes blood.

FINDING out what is regarded as taboo and blasphemy - in the secular and religious worlds - is a quick and useful way to learn about many different aspects of how meaning is assigned in a culture. In some contexts it may also be the most useful because it may see things which are veiled or completely hidden, but we might be careful not to fall into the trap of thinking that if some people in a society such as my own, does not now think that depicting a religious figure as a sexual human being is a matter for grave scandal and offence, that this is a sign of a tolerant and liberal group of people. It just means that for them, it is not blasphemy now (which itself sounds very pompous). It might have been an absolute blasphemy in the very, very recent past, but that world of meaning no longer exists, because significant erosion and cultural change can now happen very quickly in the case of particular segments of religious belief and values, for example, in contemporary Ireland in ten- or even five-year periods, especially in the fifteen to thirty five age-group.* The self-appointed praetorian guard of a particular religion or religious denomination must, first of all, have the support of a large section of the people, and not only the over-fifties, and then the mainstream media, and a significant number of powerful people and institutions, if they are to make effective accusations against what is blasphemous or against those who are (regarded as) blasphemers; there is always the possibility, of course, that certain people, especially from outside, may take it upon themselves to punish what they find blasphemous, in any part of the world.

*(Note: Intellectuals never envisaged this happening, and not just that it would happen overnight, but if you want to wait for us to say mea culpa, I had no idea, I never saw it coming, you do not know that in this type of context, we are great believers in the American folk philosophy of moving on and not dwelling on the past when it concerns ourselves. And another good and unwelcome example of how we all manipulate the meaning of time, to suit ourselves).

If you make such charges of blasphemy without a serious level of patronage among the people in a society, you will be ignored, or regarded as irrelevant or a bore, if you go on about it; or you will be ridiculed as a buffoon, or maybe prosecuted by the secular authority. In Ireland, in recent years, the hierarchy of the Catholic Church has been working on the double principle of, *Hear no evil, See no evil,* because of what sometimes seems the incessant floods of publicity now given to the sexual perversities of some of the celibate clergy, the priests and religious brothers, bishops, archbishops and cardinals, including some of the Irish-born clerical diaspora and clerics of Irish origin in other countries. But it is to be noted as well that while the numbers of offenders was often in comparative, statistical terms, miniscule, it is the lies and the hypocrisy of the official Church which fed the blaze. This is not the bonfires of the vanities of 1497, this is the rage sparked by the kind of lies and hypocrisy often condemned by Christ Himself long before the Savonarolas in their various guises came amongst us. We are in the main a tolerant, happy people, but complaining about politicians in the *they're all the same* mode is a cultural twitch which can sometimes turn into a spasm, and now the Church has also been given this role as well, but in a much more intense and sustained way. This was the Church which had been our whole life when we had been reduced to nothing after the 1600s in particular. *The untruth* and *the sinful behaviour* of the Official Church drove this popular, religious revolution in Catholic Ireland in the 1990s and they too were now also dismissed with the same well-worn *they're all the same.* But this now also had a touch of the absolute and extreme about it, as did our belief after the bishopric began to claw back their power in the last decades of the nineteenth century. It was our Church and when I was growing up in the '40s and '50s, it could not have been more respected or deeply loved, in any way. When I was a young boy, people would be fasting from midnight on Saturday to receive Holy Communion on the Sunday morning, as the rule was then, and I knew people who would walk long miles and often on *poor roads* every Sunday to Mass. Many of us knew fields which had been taken from our own people because they would not betray the faith, which was to betray Christ Himself who had died that we would live. *The people of God* - us, we were His people - were deeply hurt when it was revealed that the Church in this world was a lie, that it had blasphemed against God and against the Church founded by Jesus, the Son of Mary. But also against us, the children of God. Many people turned against the Church because the sometime arrogance and lack of ordinary good manners which a few might have sometimes shown, could now also become an issue; we might have been more forgiving in the spirit of *aren't we all just human* but forgiveness now also seemed to be in short supply.

While Ireland may remain Christian and vibrantly so in some ways, that official, bureaucratic Church will never be seen again - some priests will also add and it should never again - and will never recover the ritual standing and respect it had until very recently. It will, however, survive in some form, with far fewer Irish born clergy, for example, because many people will want rituals to mark birth and marriage and death, and not only the last item on the list.* With the sometime exception of Rome in its heyday, one of the problems with secular states in modern times is that they have never had any sense of theatre unless it served fascism and hyper, Communist driven nationalism, with soldiers in marching bands and armed soldiers marching like mechanical figures in full dress uniform in front of or behind, columns of tanks and lorry laden missiles of various kinds. The same armed display without, however, the very dated hammer and sickle, is now also seen again in Russia in whatever its new form of old fashioned top down rule might be called. Ironically, the Catholic Church in Ireland will also have to survive because of its immense wealth, which includes ownership of property where some eighty five to ninety per cent of schools under the control of the Church are built, including many aspects of access, which takes on inestimable importance in a culture which values education very highly [4].

*(Note: It will take generations until the bureaucratic links between the State and the Church in the Republic of Ireland are fully resolved, if only because of the Church ownership of both school lands and buildings and large tracts of land around these structures. The Church is now also selling land to supplement their falling income from the faithful. The cliché only in Ireland has also come into play where teachers teach the catechism to the younger pupils and classes in the Catholic religion and morality to the older students even when they themselves may only be Catholic in a minimal sense, if any. In another place I said that the majority will continue to believe in God and that we will all join those who have gone before us in Heaven for all eternity, which was proposed because it is in line with primary concepts and values in traditional Irish culture where being happy is a primary value. The biggest fall off in the numbers of Catholics will be among those who did not join in the march for education and who do not have or feel they have, a stakehold in the new Ireland. In some fifteen years, less than two generations, there will be a significant number of Irish teenagers who will not understand anything whatsoever about religion, some will think it strange and odd, and some will park it in the crazy zone).

The foreigner who lives cheek by jowl with us in the neighbouring island to the east, will shake his collective head and make *Irish jokes* again, but this time they will include the Catholic Church being the largest landowner in the country in terms of crude measurement and the richest in financial terms because much of this land is in the larger towns and cities. But this will only increase the numbers of those in Ireland who feel they might have some native talent for satire and we will be subjected to endless verbiage about the neighbour's particular system of divine rule. This next sentence is an explanatory *nota bene* for those who are not from these islands and who might not know that the monarch in England is *Supreme Governor of the Church of England*, which is the state Church and also the Mother Church, of the very large International Anglican Communion. But pots are never shy about calling kettles black even when they are smaller and sport the same colour, which is also a rather good summary in Irish demotic, of how symbolic violence works.

In Ireland today, blasphemy against Catholicism in verbal form, is now impossible. If I blaspheme in visual form, I might be criticized, but only if I breached the complex and sometimes fuzzy rules of what is demurely called good taste, in the more self-conscious and carefully articulated English variety of English of a certain class. And even then, this would be in the context of the sub-set of rules about bad language - itself a collector's phrase - or displaying visual crudity or sexual vulgarity in a public place. Giving examples of the last two, was always to be avoided in a semiotics lecture in the university in Ireland for obvious reasons. But what would recently have even been regarded in Ireland and many other Western cultures as vulgarity, has changed very rapidly, and this also seems to cross over as well to an acceptance - of the *does not really bother me* variety - of what would have been very recently regarded as taboo and religious blasphemy. There would be a very minor objection, for example, in the case of a poster in a bus shelter, but there would be little or no comment if the blasphemy was in an art gallery or a cinema or a theatre. Anyone who would object to blasphemy in literature would be lampooned; we did our best to learn the visual and verbal mix from the masters of the cartoon in the neighbouring island but our sometime obsession with *the words* section meant that the visual never got as much attention, unless, of course, it was words and how we put them together, on a page. Which also included as part of the game, not just unusual punctuation and distinguishing diacritical marks, but also the arrangement of letters and positioning of words in a phrase and doing whatever we liked with a sentence (others had done this and continue to do so, modestly, but that was a word we never seemed to like very much). As Joyce did when he *trailed his coat in Donnybook Fair* which was where the citizenry of Dublin's fair city began to do it seven hundred years before this in anticipation of his birth. Joyce would write a whole chapter with no punctuation which manages to be rude enough to embarrass you if you were listening to an actress reading it with your mother sitting next to you, but maybe not as much as might be expected in a swan song and last chapter that also happens to be one of the most beautiful, extended streams of sound in the long and wonderful history of English prose. I read parts of it out loud to myself as a lesson in the rhythm of language which has always been a glorious obsession wherever human beings were born.

Blasphemy against Islam is also largely unlikely in Ireland, if only because we would understand the emotional hurt it would cause to Muslims who now live and work in Ireland, but this could evaporate overnight if some Muslims resident in Ireland begin to *preach*, to preach about anything to do with belief and moral behaviour, and not just about things such as *the place of women in society*. Every cultural introduction for immigrants should say that we are in general a happy, welcoming people and we that we also know what preaching is, it has been going on in Ireland now for some thousand and a half years and before the Holy Prophet Muhammad, *Salla Allahu Aalayhi Wasallam*, was born. And, thirdly, that people telling us now particularly, what to do and how we should think, is marked as absolute taboo on top of the page of things to do and not to do for all new immigrants. The self-assigned preachers would quickly discover that the Irish are not all religiously illiterate and that if you want to talk about how we should behave, you will know before all of the words have managed to come out of your mouth that saying something does not mean that this goes unchallenged. If truth be told, we are not, in general, the greatest or most polite listeners of the world. We are also the world champions in what we call in linguistics *phatic communication*, and what my Scandinavian cousins would call talking about nothing much, if they are being honest with me; and that when we feel that someone is preaching to us, or worse, criticising or condemning us, that kind of of talk quickly becomes a two-way form of communication which means *You talk, I talk*, and if you talk hard talk, I will talk hard talk, and maybe even much harder talk. We have always talked as if we were afraid that we might forget how to do it, and this also necessarily meant that we talked about anything and everything - serious matters are very small in number, and I know very well as a teacher that they have quite a short natural life span each time they make an appearance - but in the world of religion we listened and generally did what we were told as best we could, even when sex was on our minds. But that changed in the great *overnight*.

The change did its best to mirror the cliché, such was the shock and anger at having not only our belief in the Church left in tatters, but also because those who went before us, which includes the generation before me, would have made *every* sacrifice for the faith - every is marked because here it means every in its absolute literal sense - and now many prople talk about religion the way they talk about most everything else. The younger generation do not care one way or another what you believe, unless you insist on talking about what you believe or telling them what to think and not think, and do and not do.* We will talk, because communication is and can only be, a two-way system, but also because *of all the people in the world* we are the poster country for the slogan *it's good to talk*. We never had to wait for any professor to tell us that talk is how human beings bridge the physical distance between them, we learned about communications from the best. From Swift and his disciple Maria Edgeworth, and more recently from Joyce, Beckett, Wilde, and Brian O'Nolan, who made communications and communications in all its very different forms, the centre of their writing, but also the writers of so-called short stories; if I were dying and had only time to read one short story, I would nod off arguing with myself and mumbling the somewhat profane litany of O'Connor, Trevor, Ó Faoláin, O'Flaherty, McGahern, MacMahon, Lavin, O Cadhain, Stephens, Binchy. Everyone now and not just in Ireland, had better know that the days of *one truth and we all say yes when we are told to say yes* are gone, forever. I was going to add and may God forgive you if you say there is anything hostile here to the teachings of Jesus Christ, but that will not bother the preachers either, no matter what their faith; and it will obviously not mean anything to those of *no faith*, as this new strange expression has it.

*(Note: It is extraordinary that we do not have multiple studies of how think and do have been combined in tandem in different ways, in different cultures and at various times).

There would, however, be a not so gentle reminder if there were any hint of blasphemy against mainstream Protestantism, because some would advise that it would be better if *these things* were not said because of the political sensitivities around Northern Ireland. Some of the guardians of the Dissenter denominations there, usually have their own distinctive *uniform* when they go on parade - bowler type hat, dark suit, shirt and tie - and they also swing tightly rolled up umbrellas like walking sticks. They will usually be accompanied also by a young and old marching fife and drum band and also a number of very heavy large Lambeg drums which are beaten with long curved canes and which can drown even the sharpest skirl of the massed pipes. Going on parade like this is a very Northern Ireland way of marking territory and sovereignty for particular groups within Unionism. Those who are members of the Established Protestant Church, however, do not usually march on the street like this, but this does not mean that they cannot use the example of such parades to say that they are only a pale reflection of what would happen if Northern Ireland were ever forced into unity with the confessional state in the south, the Republic of Ireland. Catholics on the broad nationalist spectrum generally shared the particular universal Irish Catholic assumption of being right which did not have to talk about being right, and did not use offensive language when talking about the religion of Protestant denominations. When Catholics had parades in the Republic of Ireland, they were solemn processions which carried the Sacred Eucharist through the streets while everyone sang solemn hymns and recited endless decades of the rosary. This was identity of the absolute kind which was also my young heritage and which is one of the reasons I chose religion and religious blasphemy as one of the case-studies in a series of essays on semiotics. In terms of system, identities based on purely materialist counters are banal and boring in comparison with the religious, which sounds pompous, but, in the semiotic world, it is also horribly accurate.

(Note: What is said above about blasphemy against Islam is no longer valid. Muslim immigrants - including an educated elite, from a wide variety of countries and cultures, including cultures where religion has a significant constitutional and legal influence - who have made Ireland their primary and permanent domicile with their families, have increased significantly. Some do not want to integrate in any significant way, and may take certain verses of the Qu'ran about the kuffar very literally, but when I lived and worked in a Muslim country which would be regarded as strictly or extremely fundamentalist, including by themselves, and not just most other Muslim countries, I knew some of my friends and students wanted me to convert, but I never felt I was always someone to be avoided and shunned at all costs, as the strange phrase says. I was, as was mentioned earlier, brought up in a religious culture which regarded other Christian denominations as being in error - it is marked in italics because this was the usual phrase - which might also have eschatological implications about the afterlife, and about who went to Heaven and who might go to Hell, but, as I have also mentioned elsewhere, we never actually believed that anyone in particular, went to Hell, with iconic exceptions, such as the old pox ridden enemy Henry VIII, as he was sometimes known in the King's English we made our own, and obviously figures such as Hitler and Stalin and Mao because they were mass killers. Maybe Mussolini was left off the popular list because Italian was associated with Catholic. In our very Irish adaptation of Catholic theology, if other Christians believed in what they believed, in good faith and did not persecute others because of what they believed - which could obviously include depriving them of being able to live as human beings and not killing them - then this did not mean they could never share in eternal life with us in Heaven with Almighty God; this includes those who are not Christian as well. There is no arrogance here, this is an anthropologist talking semiotics and interpreting his own culture. And they in this last sentence includes everyone, every group etc.

Terms like Sharia, Sunni, Shia, Salafist, Wahhabi, Jihad, Jihadi, Hezbollah, Hamas, the Nusra Front, the Muslim Brotherhood, and even ahl i-hadith, used to figure as part of media discourse in Europe until quite recently because of the wars in Iraq and then Syria, and also the massacres in America on nine eleven (9 11 2001) and in London on seven seven (7 7 2005), when many Irish-born and first generation Irish were also among the named victims and first line emergency personnel. But because the uprising in Syria has spawned civil wars within civil wars between the varieties of Jihadi and non-Jihadi, and within each of these as well, and because Russia and America are sometimes fighting varieties of proxy wars and have taken very violent and particularly vicious sides in the war in Syria, including war crimes against civilians which has ensured the never ending movement of peoples trying to escape, including coming to Europe, and also because of America's role with Muslim allies in Yemen, there can now be no easy demarcations in the fighting in parts of the Middle-East which began with the Iraqi invasion of Kuwait some twenty years ago. And because movement of refugees from Syria and numerous other Muslim countries into Europe though Turkey and Libya; but also because Muslims are now beginning to participate more and more in the national discussion in Ireland, for example, and else-where, and which itself often exhibits the dramatic denomina-tional diversity we have had for centuries in Northern Ireland, and which is still sometimes simmering and in grave danger of boiling over. The last two words can have all kinds of meanings.

There is now sometime talk among a minority in the wider community that certain Muslim groups have a public persona and also say very different things in private, which can hardly be a surprise in a culture which has created a world literature in two-talk, three-talk, and sometimes many-more-talk than that. Talk of many different varieties was also necessary for our neutrality during World War II and during the recent peace talks about Northern Ireland where whatever you say, say nothing became a theme in poetry and song and then a tired popular cliché. Great care is generally being taken on all sides, between the Irish and our numerous other immigrants, and especially those from the Muslim faith, not to give religious or cultural offence; and for the most part, comment which might be regarded as blasphemous, is being avoided, by all sides. But Ireland also serves as a warning to all those who may have illusions about inter-cultural, and especially, inter-faith relationships, progress can be painfully slow, sometimes a complete failure, and everything can even go backwards and get worse than ever. The erection of physical barriers between the two communities in Ireland has sometimes increased since the peace accord was signed some twenty years ago, and sometimes when one was dismantled some time ago, it was a prominent news item.

The new denomination of Islam mentioned above in another Note, however, has changed the agenda completely, for everyone, because now the rules have changed utterly, that terrible phrase that Yeats seemed to like so much he used it in a poem (and a phrase I have always found disturbing). The poor innocent little mouse who sits quietly here next to the computer is going to start squeaking if I make any more qualifications, but the group being talked about, is going to tag the phrase the new denomination as absolute blasphemy, because they are the original, authentic Islam of the Caliphate. There is now one rule, what the self-declared Islamic State says, is the rule, and more precisely, what it says now. It also decides when now is. Now is in Italics in this last sentence because IS, ISIS, is a dramatic, very public, and explicit reminder like no other today, that semiotics becomes a serious subject in every context when the explicit Whatever I say is the rule, is the rule, and the only one of any significant, logical consequence. If I were trailing my coat, I might call it a meta-rule which rules over every other rule, but even that is not accurate, because it is the only rule. The content of what is said may change and even absolutely, but that is of no importance, which you may also know very well from your own life and times. In another context, I might formally acknowledge the source which gave me a perfect example of the model being proposed to explain violence in these essays, where the apex of the model is I am, and one line below this reads, I am, you are not. I have bored myself saying from the very first drafts of these essays, in Parts I and II, and which had their origin in class notes for semiotics, that we all assign meaning in similar and often very similar and sometimes in the same ways, and we all use the same and similar rules, including the same contradictory rules, for assigning meaning, and the addendum is equally relevant, that this can hardly be a surprise, seeing that we are all human.

P.S. When it turns out that someone who was saved from death in his own country when he was a boy and taken to the West and given asylum and aid, commits a massacre a few years later, the West does not know what to say or do. Many of us in Ireland were in the same position when an Irish person committed similar grotesque crimes in England in the '70s in the name of Irish freedom. But Brendan Behan seems to have been the only teenager arrested in possession of bomb making equipment with serious intent, he was sixteen when he was arrested in Liverpool in 1939 - I am not sure he knew too much about all the trains that were coming down the tracks to destroy the world - and also probably the youngest ever arrested, charged and sentenced, on the word of an informant from within the ranks of the Irish Republican Army. I am more properly speaking a great fan of Brendan Behan's great classic of autobiography but not for the way he embarrassed the Irish born, Americans in the early 1960s who were struggling to get into and stay in, the lower middle classes. The second and third generations in my family in Boston and New York were not impressed by his literary fame and did not even bother to shake their heads at just some other drunk or other. They knew their American history on the street, every group has their spear side, and, anyway, they had the war in Vietnam and their sons' conscription to worry about; when I worked in New York to pay for my education in Dublin, word on the street even then was that certain other national and religious groups were not doing their patriotic duty which still now regularly becomes news again when it is said that certain named people used all kinds of reasons to avoid the military draft in the '6os, and I am not talking about conscientious objectors. I once wrote for a lecture in America in the '7os, the privileged know what to join and when to join, and what not to join, and that this is par excellence the mark of privilege. When challenged by someone with a touch of anger in his voice who asked what if you know but are not allowed, I said we are now in a political discussion where I - and I thanked God in public for the first time ever in my teaching life - have no expertise or pretensions. This, however, did not even get a faint smile which is hardly surprising. This was at a time in America when the ethnic atmosphere could still be quite fraught, so to speak. I had also decided very early on in my teaching career outside Ireland that I was not going to be forced into a corner because of someone labelling me, and I would say we Irish were not allowed basic freedoms for hundreds of years and at this time in my life - and I have said these last words for quite a long time now - I am not going to be bracketed with any group because you attribute this or that or whatever to me. I might even say it is not going to happen in a number of languages, which is really just to pass the time. Spanish is particularly good, lots of very long lazy vowels and a trilled r to finish, and French too because I can wave my arms around like an angry seagull does her wings).

But while someone may talk with impunity about Catholicism and religion in general, there would be a very audible uproar if what I said was regarded as blasphemy against Jewry. All of the stentorian classes, inside and outside the establishment, would rush to accuse me of antisemitism. It sometimes seems to be impossible to say anything which might be taken as criticism of Judaism, or even Israel - even if you are Jewish by birth or by adoption - without this being branded by some as antisemitism, and being interpreted as being against Jews as a whole, and without Nazism being introduced into the story somewhere or other down the line. This intellectual, semiotic equivalent of bare-knuckle fighting is very serious protection against blasphemy, but subtlety and complexity coupled with arrogance and symbolic violence often become a rich field for semiotics; in those areas of our lives which are material to us emotionally most of us can sometimes fight very dirty and use any every weapon to protect ourselves. And why indeed should religions, and religious denominations, and the officers of religion, not do what the rest of us do all the time to exploit the full gambit of ploys to protect the way they want to present their religion and religious identity, and especially Judaism which has faced endless expulsion and which was also the target of total annihilation. When those who attack religion use all the full potential of semiotics which they deny to those who are religious, the laugh I hear myself make is always very brief, totally insincere, and took years to perfect.

(Note: This was mostly written in the 1980s and '90s. The sometime manic pace of change which meant that a generation gap in terms of a multiple cultural shift, could be as little as five years from the middle of the 1980s, was noted because of inquiries about beliefs etc. I conducted informally, like a weather check, with undergraduates in Ireland, when I noticed that Limbo was well gone. Many, but not all by any means, had no idea what it could even mean, and cared less. Purgatory was on its last leg, and Hell was in a very serious wobble, so to speak, but not Heaven, obviously. We are Irish after all, and most people would not jettison Heaven for the privilege of being atheists and which you would have to talk endlessly about when people asked the why atheist question. This meant that sin, as it had been traditionally understood for multiples of generations had also been well on its way out and was now as good as gone, in comparison with what it was; and also that the traditional secret confession of penitent to priest in a dark box also became redundant and the concept of silent group confession which skirts all kinds of oxymoronic borders was introduced. There was a silent period when individuals could talk to God directly and acknowledge their sins and failings. Irish culture has very strict rules about what is said in any context - cultures always do but they differ considerably in the detail - and not just out loud group talk. But Joel was the Prophet we all had been waiting for - I always thought he had a touch of the divine as a writer - who allowed us to talk about our sins with God, in the merciful privacy of our own mind. Rend your heart, and not your garments, and turn to the Lord your God: for He is gracious and merciful, slow to anger, and of great kindness, and repenteth him of the evil. Even this translation in English gives a wonderful impression of the supernatural. Ireland was now in a mad rush to change everything to do with religion, attitudes, belief and patterns of behaviour which had been preserved in Ireland after the so-called culture wars had forever changed Catholicism elsewhere in parts of mainland Europe during the same time the Irish Church was allowed by London in the 1850s to begin to live again publicly in Ireland but without control of education. These religious disputes in middle Europe about control of education and Church appointments never had much traction in the London media, or in Italy where they were even called il Kulturkampf which as you can imagine, did not grasp the public's attention in Naples. I published Where did limbo go in 1986 without any traction either, Limbo was already very dead and well buried. It finally dawned on me that a tidal cultural change had been happening in Ireland while I was away - I left in the late '60s and came back in 1980 - and had probably had their first faint stirrings in the infamous '60s, but my curriculum vitae will not mention that sometimes my mind seems to do slow time.

But there are still three difficult topics which were and still are, totally beyond my ability. How can a culture change what seemed such core values and beliefs, so quickly and absolutely? Are there social and maybe other types of consequences as well, negative as well as positive, when a culture changes so rapidly and a generation gap can occur in such a very short period, which can also leave a strange niggling feeling of unreality of the did we actually believe that variety? And thirdly, what really does core values mean, a question that certainly does not need a vanilla dictionary or multiple choice type answer? I have spent a lot of time with the first question and might, at this stage, be a little prickly if given the clichéd answer which says nothing much more than they do because they do. The answer to the second question is already revealing itself and is not terribly difficult. Core values has sometimes been a research model which crossed over and was also appropriated in conservative America, and not only when it wants to pretend to avoid being explicitly religious, but we now need a new way of critical thinking about core values in Europe more than ever. The major movements of people who come from outside the continent and whose religion is different from the various and sometimes very different, religious cultures where they want to go, has made it relevant and rather urgent, because sometimes the religion is different which is said just above in this sentence, means that it may regard some of what we think and value very negatively, and even blasphemous. My very tentative working instinct now is that core values may not merit a lot of pages and if it also has a historical perspective, it might be better presented like many other ideas as a general topic for discussion; while also remembering all the time that if values are regarded as core values, this gives a very specific political semiotic perspective to the discussion. The European Union now also has a problem with core values, if only because it is becoming more and more embarrassing for those who want to believe in a new Europe to mention the steady emergence of fascism in different places in the Union, and not only in those countries which learned it from their Soviet masters from the '50s through to the end of the '70s).

I am not changing sides and I am not advocating that Judaism should use every twist in the book of semiotics to defend itself against blasphemy. Screams of antisemitism and Nazism would be a very dangerous strategy, for example, if I proposed that Judaism is fundamentally anti-woman in its scriptures, in parts of the Talmud, and in many of its hallowed, so-called orthodox and ultra-orthodox traditions. Symbolic violence feeds on untruth, to use a very old Catholic phrase - and which is always seen very clearly when blasphemy is also in play - and such extremism would probably foster, with time, a backlash and a rejection. Antisemitism still leads a vibrant existence just under the surface in so many European societies, and would seem to be only dormant, at best, in Western type cultures in general, like some virus which has the gift of everlasting life. Sometimes now when it comes on stage yet again out of nowhere, I hear myself saying when there is nothing to say, *please, not that again.* I should be more sober in an essay like this, but antisemitism has always frightened me from my very early adulthood. This is exacerbated now and in every sense, intellectually, semiotically and existentially, for its persistence and consistency, but also because it plays the nightmare of the 1930s and '40s again when much of the world could have been rendered uninhabitable. But it also plunges us all, as human beings, into the nightmare of this is who we are. Even some people calling for a reevaluation of the concept of antisemitism sometimes frighten me, just in case there are traces of old, viral agendas lurking in the soil in the undergrowth, which has also been a constant in the too many centuries-old history of anti-semitism. *Frightens the life out of me* is hardly the usual language in an essay like this, but the rough fields of unease and dismay are sometimes where a lot of semiotic gold is hidden. Fear which grips the mind like no other, can sometimes reveal meaning like no other, and in the world in general and not just in the world of religion, blasphemy has done more damage than anything else, figuratively and literally.

IF YOU NOW SAY I am wrong or accuse me in religious terms of being in grievous error, I must consider this, and if I am wrong, I must change it. This is the ideal perspective, and it may be too threatening to consider my own position, or it may take a long time to come to terms with such a *volte face*. I subscribe abso-lutely, to the cruel principle that in any intellectual endeavour, there can be no *a priori*, prescribed *terminus a quo* or *terminus ad quid*, in ancient shorthand. If you bring a bundle of ideas to the table which I must accept, and, if you also being another bundle listing the conclusions to be reached, then our discussion may not - I am trying my best again to be polite, *will not* is the reality - last very long. It is a waste of time for me to say that monotheistic religions especially, in the explicit theological sense, claim in principle that they want to follow truth. Or to say that it is hardly a matter of shame for human beings who sincerely profess allegiance to the God of Truth, even if they are official religious clerics, to say they are wrong, sometimes, and that this potentiality for error, has no time limit, past or future. That their particular writings or their religion, for example, sometimes define women as inferior, and not always only in practice, and which was something that reflected a particular culture at a particular time; and which may have been frozen in time because it was then taken as *an article of faith* by certain men who regard themselves as called by God - *called by God* was the phrase sometimes used when I was young, or more commonly *those who had a vocation* to be priests, for example - rather than sometimes a cultural happenstance which has nothing substantively to do with the religion itself. It is ironic that those who profess to be religious and who see blasphemy in and around every corner, are people who show a distinct lack of confidence in themselves, in their idea of religion, and in their own religion, but ultimately, and blasphemously, in their idea of a god created in their own image who is vulnerable to human opinion and behaviour. *Vulnerable to human opinion* also had *and gossip* attached, which it is, but that would also have caused offence, and not only to those from certain streets in parts of the global parish who (sometimes seem to) live their lives waiting to be offended. They insist and persist, blasphemously, in substituting themselves for God, *selves* that are distrustful of themselves, which is why they go around with termless bundles in the first place, including ones created at different junctures in their own or their own group's history, and which may have been assigned at some stage, early or late in their peculiar history, the seal of eternal truth. Note well the religions which have a consistent, historical pattern of different factions accusing others, especially those within their own religion, of heresy and blasphemy, including in the early days of the particular religion's history.* But talking history like this sometimes stokes accusations of blasphemy as well, and, predictably, the talk can become very extreme, and I am talking just about talk, and not other forms of behaviour.

*This factionalism within a religion sometimes becomes a

farce and a circus, as it does, for instance, now, when space is shared in turn in the Christian *Holy Places* in what is now Israel. But those involved do not see farce or even a mote anywhere, as we may also never do when something in our daily lives has intense emotional value.

In addition, there may also be strains of an obsessive fear that to admit any fault or failing, including the theoretical possibility of any shortcoming or blemish, is to risk cross-infection which could, in their eyes, expose their scriptures, and their whole belief system and religious practices, to criticism and ridicule, and worse. They are afraid, which is why they may be violent and dangerous. This is why they are also highly sensitive to blasphemy, sometimes verging on the pathological, and this is why, in an ultimate act of blasphemy, they project their own inadequacy on the god they have created. The violence they inflict may have no bounds, but it goes beyond all the lines of sanity, however this is assigned meaning, in popular terms or clinically, when, for example, unborn babies are regarded as legitimate targets. When it does not even merit the cliché *collateral damage*, which has been freely used in other war-type contexts for quite a long time, and is often Latin generated *talk* for what are often vulgar and sarcastic popular clichés of the *wrong place, wrong time* variety (to give one example which could be written in an essay such as this). When adherents of their own faith are killed in a bus which has been deliberately blown up somewhere in the *West*, it can be said, for instance, they should not have been there in the first place, which is a most extraordinary, chilling example of blasphemy. But no reason or excuse has to be given for those not of their faith who suffered a similar fate in the bus, including babies in arms who had no choice about being anywhere that day; they usually do not even bother saying it was done because these individuals were Christian, or even because they were there. This is all about them, be it an individual or group, big or small, and what he or she or they choose to be a symbol of identity, and nothing else: it is not religion, it just happens that this is the identity chosen in certain contexts, and it is absurd and absolutely blasphemous to say you kill babies in the womb because this is what God wants.* Your being, your existence, your life - and, worse, the life of your loved ones - does not rate in any sense, as if you never were, but it can also be classed as negative, whenever, and whatever the circumstances. I will get criticism for writing this sentence for all kinds of reasons, including for using phrases such as *your life does not rate*, which has its own relevance in an essay on blasphemy. Even in this kind of scenario we keep looking for *sense*, even when it may have none whatsoever, or ever could.

* I might have chosen to fight for Irish freedom in the second half of the 1910s, especially in the last two years of that decade when London kept insisting it had not learned anything in 1916 except always bring the gun boats up the river at the first sign of trouble. Of course I would have known that I might die, but I also hope I would have known as a good Catholic, that dying or killing others because this is what God wants is a heinous blasphemy. But even that pales in comparison with thinking and saying you know the mind of God.

I might also add as an attachment, I am Irish and was born before World War II, and witnessed blasphemy, religious and secular, and its violent consequences, and sometimes an anger and a violence which seemed to have no bounds, all in this little island which tectonics shoved out into the Atlantic to be all on its own. This could include religious leaders inciting their followers by denouncing other Christians and accusing their leaders of the most vile blasphemy, which has been and still is, a common ritual in many different cultures with different religions and religious denominations. I am not choosing examples from Ireland because of any personal emotional or religious or political agenda, but I could hardly ignore the parallels between such symbolic violence now and the historical context in Ireland, where religion was used in all kinds of ways as violence - as an excuse for and an instrument of violence - which I had already begun to write about as part of my own journey in trying to understand violence and as a case-study for lectures on symbolic violence. Sometimes it was a split screen experience when the language used multiple centuries ago mirrors the language used now. It was especially striking for me because I had returned to Ireland to find that the religious wars had begun again in the early '70 while I was out of the country, and not only symbolically, as a consequence of political agitation and terrorist violence from one particular sub-group claiming a nationalist and Catholic identity, but not from others of the same religious and political background.

The constant barrage of symbolic violence using religious language blasphemously, was from one side only and was coming primarily from fundamentalist Protestant groups and not generally from the official Established Protestant Church or *establishment* Protestantism, or from the Catholic side. The research I was doing was part of a case-study on symbolic violence going back to the 1200s and had nothing to do with the contemporary violence, but the centuries-old symbolic violence directed at people from my background - I had heard echoes of it in America when I worked in New York as a student in the early '60s and again in Chicago in the late '70s when I worked ther as a professor - was something I now heard all the time in the Ireland where I was living again. It also sometimes had implications for personal safety, if, for instance, I wanted to go to the very northern parts of the island and especially one of the iconic places in the world which is the long sweep of the almost open bay in North Antrim which has the Giant's Causeway at a kind of centre, and where I sit, do nothing, think nothing, and live in the landscape. I was going to say *where I just be*, but apart from the pretentious grammar, you might think I was a born-again something or other, or even an existentialist. Love of place which can be for a parcel of land and a house, or a townland or something much larger, has always been and in all kinds of ways, part of being Irish, but there is no chauvinism about it. Sometimes I even catch myself just staring even at a picture of the Great Blasket off the south western coast of Ireland, if I come across it somewhere.

IF BLASPHEMY IS to be understood, it also needs to be taken into account that there may also be an additional, insoluble problem with those advocates of a religion or an ideology who continually look for enemies after the manner of an obsessive disorder. No discussion which works on the principle of potential adjustment may be possible because it is this very attitude which is the overriding principle of their position; in the here and now and living in the here and now is usually a very particular fascination for such groups, and they may be incapable of being open to or honest about, the reality or implications of, their beliefs because of this; just as they will be incapable of being honest about the sometime major changes to their beliefs and practices in the past, in different eras, and this last part may be the most obstinate problem because now heritage also comes into play. They seem to be afraid that if they explicitly admit to any change, especially one that might be regarded by others as a fundamental change or a change in principle, including in the distant past, then the whole edifice would crumble, which means in practice, that sometimes virtually any change may become impossible, but only of course if it is regarded as significant change, even in a minor way, if I can sail close to contradiction again.* The problem arises when they turn their implicit fixation about protecting themselves and their man made institutions, customs and practices into an explicit, specious campaign of protecting their hapless god. Dysfunctional identity generates fear which generates anger and intolerance of every sort, and violence unlimited. The title of this particular series of essays, *Violence is easy, identity is the problem*, was a propitious choice, to use a phrase from an old book. But, looking back now, the essays also grew around the title which was in no great hurry to come out of its shell in the beginning.

*(Note: When this was written all those years ago, I was also going to include a kind of out loud sentence, We are humans, we are not God, we make mistakes, that is what we do every day, morning, noon and night, but I thought someone might wonder if I had lost it, as the popular expression now has it. This I had lost it completely phrase is genius in five words, it very cleverly leaves it to mean anything and everything, as required. What is regarded as significant change is a good way to get into and find your way around, a culture).

If your religion regards women as *unclean*, for instance, and you can weave and gyrate all you like with the concept of ritual cleanliness, then it does. You might even ask why not admit it? We have all been privileged *to be born and born of woman*, which in its own way echoes the beautiful simplicity of the Bible. But this could not be allowed to happen if fear (is such that it) forces us to adhere absolutely to the idea that there can be no explicit adjustment in principle, because we have to cling to the idea that every single aspect of what we think and believe is perfect - I am not talking about religion *per se*, I am talking about our ordinary lives - and no line in the script can be changed. Many believers could not afford to consider what I am saying, if I were to suggest, for example, that, theologically, God, the Almighty, is not to be equated absolutely with a religion as formulated in the here and now by mere mortals, and that to suggest otherwise is blasphemy, as is, *a fortiori*, the assumption, implicit or explicit, that we can know the mind of God, in any sense or any context.

We may want to strive spiritually to free ourselves from the ties which imprison us and even cripple us emotionally and intellectually, but this has nothing to do with the blasphemous assumption that we know or can know, the mind of God. A particular religion, as formulated by us, does not have to think that it always is the perfect formula, in every signal detail, for total and eternal acceptance, by everyone, at all times. The gospels had a very special warning about pride, and at Mass, we often heard the Bible story of angels who chose damnation because of empty, stupid pride. It may be the story of all stories, I used to keep asking myself when I was young how could anyone be so stupid (I did not know about allegorical then, luckily, that would have ruined the story).The admission of error in *humanum est errare* sounds so humble, but the Latin hides the embarrassing banality - but one which is, in practice, often masked by our fear - that we are sometimes wrong, that it is only human, and that it is inhuman to think otherwise, and sometimes even gravely sinful and much more harmful than many of *the sins of the flesh* which caused endless grief and guilt and occupied so much time in confession. The guardians of the monotheistic religions, however, do not always do humility, as the very informal, dynamic American expression has it, except in contexts which do not undermine their fundamental position of absolute, but very temporal, power. Which means that any admission of error may be impossible, in practice, except in very minor terms; but this is semiotic territory, and the phrase in the last sentence should read *are not regarded as undermining their fundamental position*. And to continue in the same semiotic vein. Most of us are often reluctant to say we were wrong, in the religious world there is also very often the awful fear that everything may collapse if there is the faintest hint of an admission of the slightest error - or even any discussion of what error could mean - or even the most marginal change, despite the fact that this has always been the reality. But saying this will be regarded as blasphemy too, by some. Fear can thwart reality in the context of belief, as it can in every other area of life, but *humanum est timere*, that it is only normal to be afraid, will never become popular in this peculiar world of a religion or any belief system or ideology - Communism in its practice is a notorious example - which is haunted by fear, and which only accepts *humanum est errare* when it applies to others, and every other *other*, that is not them [5].

RELIGION, however, has to be admired when it wants to manipulate a system in multiple ways. When, for example, some of those in a particular religion regard women as incapable of controlling their sexual instincts and then others say this is not a faithful interpretation of the religion. Differences of opinion has sometimes been the default in many different contexts of human behaviour, including in the foundations of religion, and not only Christianity and Islam. But I have a semiotic buzzer which bleeps quite loudly when embarrassed religious apologists start talking about an authentic exegesis of their sacred scriptures and traditions and then pull carefully culled examples out of some repository or other, to support their position, which may be regarded by others from the same faith as a liberal one or as heresy. This is again, the usual semiotic behaviour found in all of human behaviour, but if you do not accommodate yourself to their argument, or sometimes even to all of what they say is reality, they will be hurt and offended. After all the trouble they have gone to, you are just like all the others and you can now also be accused of being unsympathetic, or even hostile, to their depiction of their religion or denomination, and in addition, also to them. But a reminder always needs to be inserted, that they will be grievously offended if the word denomination is used to apply to their belief, which is why I have suggested elsewhere that ecumenism works best when little or nothing is said about certain aspects of what each side believes, and not only when it is two different religions, but also denominations - even the word seems to be stalking me - of the same religion. If you make a counter argument and dip promiscuously into historical practice, and also the scriptures and the interpretation of these sacred writings, as they do, in the original or translation or a modern language version, you may be accused of blind prejudice. The whole point of their story is for you to adopt their logic, and not just what they say. You are to keep rigidly to the script, as they write it, and however they write it, or however they change it. Talk about how key elements of the religion, in terms of belief and practice, have changed, may be a particular embarrassment, or worse, especially if the discussion moves on to relativism, which has been a particular bugbear for the strands of the monotheistic religions which have made a fetish of the principle of absolutism, and which can itself be just a semiotic creation like any other which has no basis in historical reality: this is also why some people made a crisis out of relativity in science when it was their own not understanding science which created their problem in the first place. In addition, you are to let them choose the quotations from scripture as well, and in the translation they choose. It may sound strange, and a little absurd, but I find it much easier intellectually, and emotionally, to cope with those in a religion who do not care what I think, and who proclaim their faith without any consideration for my views or feelings, unless there is cordite in the air.

(Note: I would love to get a present for my birthday next month of a time machine which would enable me to hear the reaction if I had published on relativism in the Ireland when I was growing up, or if I could have read what I write now, when I was eighteen. Relativism has often been a semiotic obsession in many of the strands of the monotheistic religions which made a fetish of the principle of absolutism, and which can itself be just a semiotic creation like any other that has no basis in historical reality. There has been a common fallacy abroad for centuries, that something is of lesser or no value, if it is relative, regarded, tagged as relative, in terms of meaning. As you might guess, I am a great admirer of semiotic games and blinds and bluffs, and being bilingual in two quite different languages as a teenager, gave me a very explicit awareness of and an admiration for, this aspect of semiotics which is just fun).

THE GENERAL SEMIOTIC problem is that I, whoever I am, may not be able to conform to the rules or enter into the spirit of your semiotic games, just as you will not play my game when I do not particularly like or when I reject, your story. This applies in many contexts all the time, and not only in the case of religion, denominations of religion, or different religions. I may, for instance, to give one example which can have serious emotional import, be expected to enter into the spirit of your *game* about what constitutes a relationship - much of literature would have a skeletal existence without the last four words - but you will not abide by my rules, which may not lead anywhere in particular, unless we are good actors and can pretend to each other and ourselves, and sometimes even to others as well, that there is no conflict. Or, unless we can adapt our expectations, at least implicitly, and work out a compromise set of rules, but with implicit as the primary guiding principle. In the situation where a group of religious defendants fail to have their reading accepted, the situation becomes much more charged than before and they may quickly draw the comforting conclusion that you are blinded by bias and that any attempt they make at reconciliation can only come to nothing.

On a different level, but for similar reasons, I smile at those, including certain Catholic theologians, who now sometimes expect the Pope and the Vatican to bend with whatever breeze is blowing in matters of faith and morals whenever these *experts* twist the handle of the wind machine. I may admire your semiotic arrogance, later, whoever you are and whatever field you work in, be it religion or some related field, but I sometimes get confused when you lay down the law that I accede to what you say, but you will not ever deign to listen to what I say, ever: if I included that *I accede to what I say* this might be taken as me trailing my coat, but it is not, it sometimes happens to all of us in certain contexts. For some reason I can remember very well when even pugnacious, obnoxious little boys knew that *you make the rule and I comply* was stupid and even dangerous - territory and boundaries were always key concepts in our young world - and not just in some implicit vague way. Let us agree to differ, or stay silent, or have nothing to do with each other. Forcing others to play by rules exclusive to you, be you a nation or a religious denomination, may be a recipe for grief or a prescription for violence, which we all know in our ordinary life; sometimes fundamentalists, secular and religious, do not and maybe even cannot live, in the world where the rest of us live. Those who cry blasphemy are saying they should dominate meaning, absolutely, and will demand freedom of expression as this is understood in my culture but this may be denied to me in their culture and also when they live in my territory and culture.* They may also proclaim that they can use symbolic violence of any kind and also sometimes physical violence in their own culture - and sometimes mine as well - whenever they like and against whoever they like, when they so decide. And *they*, the elite leaders, who may also be highly educated, will sometimes call on the masses, including those with little or no formal education, to join them vigorously in their religious mission to hurt and destroy others. Secular fascism also behaves in the same way. Blasphemy in the religious domain can also take on a mantle of *holy justice* - and which is itself also a blasphemy - to rationalize violence, symbolic or physical, where a context of symbolic violence by a mob can cross over into threatening intimidation, and where *the next life* can eternally come into play as well.

*(Note: This may now be an insoluble problem when the indigenous population in many countries in Europe are not capable of understanding that some immigrants - including second and third generation, especially if they have not availed of the education available to everyone - may regard their religion as a blasphemy and many aspects of their way of life and behaviour as despicable and grievously sinful, and hurtful to their god. Many of those under thirty five in Ireland come into this particular not capable of understanding category because they may also think any such thinking is not normal).

Here, as in other various essays, I want to look at aspects of our world from a number of different perspectives, in the hope that this contributes to understanding how semiotics works. Essays about meaning have had a bad press or been confined to a tiny minority despite the fact that meaning forms and informs, all of our lives, and every aspect of our lives down to the smallest and most trivial detail. Some students like *the trivia* about the endless variations and the sometime major cultural differences in clothes and in eating and drinking practices, including *table manners*, for example, but some seem to think this is *infra dignitatem* and that lectures should be about *higher things*, despite the fact that what is *not to be eaten* has caused all kinds of apartheid and infinite hurt and conflict, since time began, as the cliché always wisely says. If I lay claim, however, to furthering our understanding of semiotics, I am now in danger of proscription, because praising oneself in the slightest way can be an especially grave taboo in Irish culture, and the rules about when and how any such compliments can be expressed, may be themselves very complex. It is not, however, thinking about the value of one's writing which is taboo, it is, as in many other cultures, saying it, or worse, writing it, which carries the proscription.

We need a new Totem and Taboo to see how all the variations of meaning contained in these concepts can help in understanding the closely related concepts of taboo and blasphemy. But this time, one which concentrates not on the so-called *savages or wildmen, and the neurotics,* but on you and me, now, on us, in our very ordinary lives. But, especially, one that can help us understand, for instance, why saying something can often do more damage than the fist, or the stick, or the gun. In addition, it would be a bonus if the author could match the brilliance of Freud in literary talent, but also help us understand how we need to accept that we too, as a group or a nation, or as human beings in general, can also sometimes not only manifest the symptoms usually associated with the primeval and deviant in our ordinary humdrum lives and in our most sacred lives, but that the way we think and act in our familiar, routine existence can be far more intricate than the obviously special and exceptional aspects of our lives. It is what goes underneath the explicit public radar which is often the most sophisticated and obscure, and there are few aspects of our lives more strange, for instance, than when writing something can attract the label of taboo, including absolute taboo, and also the related accusation of blasphemy, which can carry interdiction without limit, including death. Sometimes, when trying to teach semiotics, especially when I am flailing around and in danger of sinking, I am tempted to proclaim that we are a walking, talking, sleeping symbol, and that there is nothing terribly important that is not semiotic.

I went to school in the same clichéd texts on the *savages* and *wildmen* as those who read the original manuscripts in classical Greek and Roman cultures millennia ago, and as the writers from middle Europe and England did many centuries ago, when they simply appropriated their terminology. The latter group applied them to my people after it had reduced us to material and often cultural penury and sometimes total material misery (in terms of shelter and basic hygiene, and what we ate and wore).* But it would add greatly to our understanding of who and what we are as human beings, independently of any peculiar historical or cultural background, if we could map, how a culture like that Ireland managed to keep alive a trace of what it means to be human. Freud would often adopt the same derogatory, two thousand year-old Classical language less than a century ago, which might seem all the more surprising from someone who comes from a people who have consistently suffered longer than any other major group in recorded history from such symbolic violence and whose long struggle just to survive and often thrive, needs the closest study to help us all appreciate more fully the depths of human resistance and what human beings can achieve despite being consistently subjected to the most appalling violence for multiple centuries. When I read the texts, in the original and translation, which were written as symbolic violence in the early, middle and late medieval periods against my people in my first major research on symbolic violence, the intellectual became personal and intensely political which can give a particular acuity to any analysis. Not that the research was taxing intellectually, this kind of symbolic violence is analogous with the classical *pie in the face* physical comedy of great English theatre and Hollywood movies (which I love in equal measure).

*(Note When I wrote basic hygiene all those years ago, I cried. I saw it in the late '40s when I went with my mother when she was ministering to the sick, as our religion called it).

The grounds, for instance, for using such descriptive negative language in the twelve hundreds to the fourteen fifties could only be spurious, because the Irish then, judged on the criteria of cultural excellence accepted by their accusers and the educated elite in general in Europe, were superior on a whole battery of measures, including intellectual, linguistic, educational and religious culture, for instance, than those who charged them with the most flagrant accusations of inferiority and depravity. This objective superiority would, of course, be demolished and beaten into inferiority and deeply felt, in the sometime manic colonial forge of symbolic violence; it also went on and on, and persisted in some of the same forms during the majority of my lifetime - *Note, this monograph was mostly written in the late '80s and '90s, apart from what is marked Note and in brackets* - and can still make an appearance like a psychotic cuckoo with no eggs to lay but which never ceases to dump the eggs out of the nests of other types of birds.* One of the strangest things about violence is that certain strands of symbolic violence against groups can manage to survive virally for centuries, and sometimes forever. Gender based symbolic violence is the finest example, and also the one which has been most influential in hindering human development and steering it into all kinds of destructive paths. Sometimes it now also seems to be getting worse in certain fields.

* I was quite small when I first saw three or four tiny little eggs scattered on the grass like this. It is still vivid and I hate the memory even now. But a good if ugly lesson, about how hard life can be for everyone and everything, including very small birds.

But this is only the secondary argument in portraying the ridiculousness of such language, the primary contention is that such language is symbolic violence, and nothing else. Its primary meaning is its use, similar to the name-calling of precocious nine and ten year-old boys in Cork who had the same linguistic talent the metaphor addicted Freud displayed in his historical travelogue about the *wildmen*, who would also begin to feature with photographs and drawings accompanying the text in the very popular and influential National Geographic when the great psychiatrist was still in his early professional years. The fixation which Jung and many others tracked in similar vein had a surge in popularity again in the early 1900s, centuries after it had first appeared as part of the language of symbolic violence against groups such as the Irish, and which itself was long before its use about colonised *people of colour* in Africa, for instance. When we were teenagers, those who came from rural, isolated places and not from the town like us, the sophisticated ones, would be accorded numerous *linguistic compliments* about their origins and their mental and linguistic abilities; but when I had to go away to school in the city, my classmates and I were now the *wildmen* and treated as such when we played hurling against day schools in the city. Our vituperative, sometime bilingual originality, woulf have been more than a match any day for the Greeks and the Romans and the plagiarizing Freuds. This was a game and the game was symbolic violence, and games can generate emotion and violence, like nothing else, in intensity. Neither did I have to wait *to become* an intellectual to know that game is a serious subject, and sometimes a very serious one. I was doing serious background research when I was a very young teenager and that is when I started out on the road to learn that violence is easy and identity is the key to understanding violence. It took quite a long time before I began to ask questions about what great thinkers have said about violence and which has often been accepted uncritically as intellectual insight and scholarly wisdom when it was sometimes stuff and nonsense as a Prime Minister famously said when he was accused of speaking dictatorially to his King nearly two hundred years ago in London. We sometimes seem to think that because violence has ruled and dictated history and secular and religious cultures of every kind, that violence itself must be complex and, worst of all, that the reasons for violence must be complex. My little formula I am, You are not, is banal, and has to be, if it is to go toe to toe with violence.

I TOOK a small trip around my own life story to show how semiotics works and how we all manipulate and exploit in similar ways, the worlds of meaning, including the worlds of identity and violence. I am nobody very much, to adopt an honest expression I grew up with, and my efforts at managing my own life have sometimes been deplorable, and might even be amusing, if it were on the stage, but talking about some of the stories in my own life might lead to thinking about the bits and pieces that go into making up all our lives. I think it is not a bad way to get an initial understanding of how the world works, to use our own life sometimes to try and understand the worlds we have created. This is no grand proposal for self-analysis or cloying confessionalism or the misery genre which is now also becoming very fashionable in Ireland, it is a way to probe and find out and understand maybe a little better how we assign meaning in areas of identity and violence, for example, which often prefer to stay in the shade and which sometimes hide away under impenetrable wraps in pitch dark places. When I first came across the phrase *black holes* when I was reading a long time ago outside my own particular curriculum in the first year in the university, I understood little or nothing about general relativity etc., but the phrase spoke to me and has stood me in good stead ever since, especially when I ever I begin to feel foolish because I understand little or nothing about something or other. You can only go part of the way in understanding how we assign meaning by looking at how we arrange the world from the outside, you have to go inside in the shadows sometimes, if you are to see even a pale reflection of the whole picture, and you cannot get inside anyone else except yourself; there is the extra advantage that this is also somehow your meaning, when you see it in this way from the inside. This act of *seeing ourselves as we are*, is an essential ingredient in any essay which uses violence as a case-study to illustrate what is meant by semiotics. I know my colleagues in the natural sciences will send me back to the cave again for saying this - I have been rusticated so often I know my way out well by now - but this may sometimes, often, be the only option available. We have lived too long in the unconscious with those who give us explanations for violence, when, for example, even on any simple scientific criterion, it never said anything very much about blasphemy which is continuously destroying lives and is now again, for example, threatening to destroy various parts of the Muslim world, including places which were thriving centres of culture a thousand years earlier.*

*(Note: When I later read some of what I have written in the past, I sometimes wish I were wrong. But it did not take a

genius to write threatening to destroy various parts etc. in this last sentence. What I missed completely, however, was that two superpowers would again go to war in locations outside their own countries. One of them is on a campaign to settle old scores and get revenge for humiliations in the recent past, the other seems to appear everywhere and anywhere and is never going to lose an opportunity to humiliate this old enemy again. I am never surprised at little boy violence but the scale of the destruction of innocent civilians caught in the middle between these two proud dogs of war who never seem to tire of wreaking mayhem and destruction, is another reason to be very humble about what levels of violence will be used when male pride is on the battle field yet again. One fine day as Madame Butterfly says in her song, one of these dogs will go nuclear if it feels it is being humiliated again, and the other side is going to win the game. Parts of the world will never again have a fine day and other parts will never have any kind of day. Pessimism is not driving anything here, and never drives me or anything I write. There is a very old tradition in this our world, if you make tools to fight, they will be used, and we are now at the stage where ordnance is able to wreak total destruction, as happened in the old days, when every wall in a village was razed to the ground and everyone living in it was slaughtered).

EVEN THOUGH WE create everything in the worlds of meaning, for some inexplicable reason, we sometimes want or have to, pretend that we are the playthings and victims of these worlds. I decide what things mean, I decide what you mean. I decide when I am hurt. I decide when you are not hurt. I decide when you do not have the right to be or say you are, hurt. Semiotics puts the focus back on us where it belongs because it is we who decide what things mean, it is we who implicitly decide every-thing, including what hurts us symbolically. Sometimes, people are never more hurt than when they want to be hurt, which is why blasphemy was chosen as an example to explain semiotics. They decide what hurts, and I should hardly be surprised when they bite my hand if I pat them on the head and tell them that there is no need for them to be hurt; that if they were more sophisticated and progressive and a liberal like me, which now also reads as parodic as it sounded when I tapped out the letters one by one, they would understand the right of every human being to think and to express his or her own views. *Mutatis mutandis*, we all play the popular *I am right* game, what I have called elsewhere the *One-Truth* position, when it is a strong theory, as may happen in the case of religion or a particular political ideology about race or colour, for example, which carries intense emotional attachment; it is a weak theory in contexts of meaning which may not be as sensitively charged in any consistent way. As individuals or as members of a particular culture or group of related cultures, we may not go around calling those who disagree with us blasphemers, we may not sentence those who disagree with us to death, but we are all involved in the very serious game of deciding what things mean, and what meanings we do not like when proposed by others. And when these meanings assume important emotional import, then the game can become serious, and very serious, and even a matter of life and death, and not only figuratively, for all of us. There are many ways to die, and death by dramatic violence is only one of them, and still the exception.

But back around the corner again to classic blasphemy. Is there any answer to or defense against, such blasphemy? This is cruel, but the best advice is not to blaspheme if you live in a society where you will be killed or punished in some way, for blasphemy, or if those who take violent umbrage with what you say, have long tentacles which will find you wherever you are. I would not have been able to publish essays such as this in the Ireland where I grew up. The Church would not have issued for a nobody like me anything as grandiose as an edict sentencing me to torture or death - in certain periods, in my religion, they sometimes even had the rather perverse habit of combining both together - they have not exercised this type of prescript for some time in Catholicism. But sometimes a type of fascism coopted a particular brand of religious fundamentalism in our Irish Catholic Church and made it part of its social and cultural sets of rules which we all happily accepted because we had adopted holus bolus, their initial principle that they were *in locus dei* and were consequently regarded as and treated as, God on earth. Instead of a prescript of physical violence, the bishops and priests under their orders, would have denounced me off the altar at Sunday Mass which everybody attended by choice and obligation, and the print media would have carried the story as told by the Church, unless it was decided that even this itself would shock and cause scandal to the faithful, which is what we were strangely called in a wonderful example of regarding the ideal as already in permanent existence.* Some of those who liked to have a more active role, would have engaged in old style trolling in the local talk circuit - I once said in a class about cultural patterns that we Irish fashioned what might be called the classic language of trolling - some would have had a swipe at me, or put a few stones in my mother's window, or maybe worse. I, and, in the very unlikely circumstance, if there was anyone of my family or friends and acquaintances who had not already denounced me or shunned me, would have been subject to public censure and abuse. And I would have lost my job in the university or school or shop or sweeping the streets, wherever I worked, and I have happily done all four in some way (the latter two enabled me to have an education).

* And another example, as if we needed another one, of why semiotics could only come from such a Catholicism. Even magic realism pales in comparison.

In practice, I would have been forced to leave Ireland to be safe, and not just to write as I do now and to earn a living as an academic or teacher of any kind. I hope I would not have been surprised at the reaction, whatever it was, and I hope I would have been too good a Catholic, which I was, and would not have bothered delivering a heroic philippic from some symbolic burning deck on the banks of my own lovely Lee about freedom of expression. I say hope, because I find it disheartening to imagine that I could have been so pathetically ignorant that I would have had such a rotten grasp of how my own culture worked. I am not much for the grand theory, I am sure you have seen by now that I am more the mole who happily scurries around in the margins of the fields of culture where weeds sometimes creep in from the ditches. In today's Ireland, a religious blasphemer against Catholicism would only merit a mention if he were adopted by one of the mosquito groups put on this old earth to fight old battles for freedom of speech when it is much too late, and very safe. Employment in certain areas could still be a major problem, because the Catholic Church often owns and manages the schools, but there are little signs here and there that it is beginning to lose that battle too.

Some years ago I wrote an essay on a model of meaning which tried to explain how we process meaning. It was not a model in theoretical semantics or psychological or neurological linguistics which sometimes have the habit of leaving me outside with my face pressed against the window looking in and feeling foolish, it was a model which was useful for showing how we assign meaning in practice. When I was small, I loved being out and about on the street, even if it were only ten or twenty yards each side of the front door on our side of the street when I was two and three, and I am still most at ease semiotically on the street, as it were, where we all live and have to live our ordinary, sometimes cruel, sometimes magical, sometimes boring, lives, but I am lucky, I am still the boy from my home town who sees everything and loves everything. That we are all God's creatures was a very early lesson which has, analogously, stood me in very good stead in semiotics, when I began to track the notion that we all assign meaning in the same and similar ways, which is the secular equivalent of the miraculous religious belief - we are all created by God - we happily shared when I was growing up. The model shows how we process meaning in different ways, in different contexts, to suit ourselves, and in classes, I gave lots of examples, including the use of language by certain religions to categorize people who do not share their beliefs. Lists of words which were used commonly in Ireland, for example, in the second half of the nineteenth century and which hiss and crackle with anger and fury were sometimes not much different from the *name calling* we enjoyed when I was nine or ten and when we were already at doctorate level in the creative demotic which we used generously when we wanted to call others a wide range of derogatory names (you could also show how brilliant you were at the same time by coining new metaphors, *donkey ears* which you might know are a ridiculous shape, would serve as an example of our sometime brilliance). The words on the vernacular list - which included pagan, heretic, infidel, schismatic, apostate, idolater, atheist, adulterate, pervert - were thrown around like confetti and must have dramatically increased what might have been predicted as the normal word count in other similar societies for people in our socio-economic situation; in a draft for publication I also mentioned that the various orders of religious in Ireland, Franciscans, Jesuits etc. must have been engaged in a contest about who could come up with the most defamatory and slanderous items on the list, but I thought that this might not get past an editor. I also set up schemata to show how they were graded and how some of them worked in practice. The few more benign benefits of colonialism never managed to have any effect on our cultural tendency to *fight dirty*, even in intellectual and literary fields, and this includes our own Jesuits in Ireland who were for a while around the time of independence, the undisputed champions in the very special Irish category of scurrilous writing in their tirades of impeachment against whatever was *not Catholic*. Which could sometimes mean everything English, even though the great little man himself, Gerald Manley Hopkins S.J., had had to grace our little island for a while because of his vow of obedience. When he was a professor in the humble university where I too would happily go to school, however, the poor misfortunate man sadly wrote *each day dies with sleep* and *I wake and feel the fell of dark, not day*. In the article, I proposed that ultimately, religious ecumenism now may only be an agreement to say nothing, and that this is possible because certain aspects of religious dogma and belief are already fading away and that they will wither away like *dead letters sent* if they lose much or all of their *One-Truth* status and are barely or ever mentioned. Which I knew - and the knowing of it did not unduly tax my intelligence - would sound like a terrible blasphemy to those scribes, including the secular ones who had not cast off *the old ways* and who guard their superiority zealously.

I sent this article to a periodical in Dublin run by an elite society of male religious who became, as was sometimes said in more recent times, the Pope's *storm troopers*, to counter the Protestant Reformation. But even they too had had to learn the hard way about the vow of obedience when - *to encourage the others,* as only the Vatican can do when it is on form, and warn them what their fate could be if they too were ever to step off the track of absolute subservience - the Pope banished those *who serve as soldiers of God* into humble exile in the wilds of Germany and this was some two hundred and forty years after they were founded. This publication was known for being a serious publication, intellectually, and sometimes a daring one, but daring in that Ireland in the early '8os still had a quite restricted meaning - this was before the Irish Church ignited at the same time as Tom Wolfe's *Bonfire of the Vanities* appeared in Dublin - and was always exercised in ways that would avoid *a belt of the crozier* as those who religiously waited in the morning in South Anne Street for their favourite hostelry to open, would have said then. I knew the article would be rejected and I did it for the *craic,* as we often say when we use the vernacular in English, to tickle my naughty boy gene, but I think a little bit of me wanted, as a bit of *blackguardism,* to pretend I too was a member of that glorious tribe of genteel and seditious Irish writers - many of them became my mentors because of their brilliance, not because they had that pecular gene - who were often not published in their own country, or sometimes in their own lifetime, in the not so old, not so good days. The editor wrote a worthy epistle of rejection which went into the bin with a smile and the usual gentle expletive reserved for such rejection. I was not that naïve. I duly sent the piece off to England where it appeared and died, as usual, in a university publication.

The model has been useful for students doing research essays and theses on a variety of different topics, from advertising to sexual assault. The reverend editor, however, was right to reject the article. Those engaged in the sometime very political and often brave battle for religious ecumenism, do not need someone saying *ecumenism can ultimately be an agreement to say nothing about the truth-value of certain religious proposi-*

tions, and which itself has important implications for any study of blasphemy. But looking at it again, the part marked in italics is not the dumbest thing ever written in semiotics, if I could indulge in the old, very Irish, sacred tradition of false modesty. Maybe it was insensitive to point this out because of the religious overtones in the violence in Northern Ireland in the early 1980s, but that is another discussion. I would have been stupid if I had expected Studies to publish such an article. They do publish faintly unorthodox views, but only that type of heterodoxy which conforms with the usual rules for accepted divergence with regard to content and expression, and which are often worthy of study in their own right, if you are looking for a lively, quite difficult topic for an advanced seminar in semiotics. The long winding road between the what is regarded as orthodox and what is deemed unorthodox, is also obviously a splendidly rich place for the study of blasphemy and for a close examination of the rules about how meaning is assigned in various contexts. It can also be a dangerous road to be on as well, in every society, including, sometimes, those which fly a very explicit, liberal flag of honour and convenience.

My students, for instance, usually gaze at me disinterestedly when I say that we communicate with each other because we live in a rule governed world and that it is because we share meaning and the same rules for assigning meaning that we understand each other. Nor will interest be quickened a great deal if I then go on to say that this is inevitable, that we have to live in a world which is, by and large, a semiotic dictatorship. But when I say this means that the rules for so-called radical behaviour are every bit as rigid and predictable and usually more inflexible and exacting, than the rules for general behaviour, there may be an increase in interest, especially if I give examples relevant to aspects of their peculiar side cultures. The self-designated non-conformers, who somehow always seem to have the hermaphroditic ability to self-procreate in every country where I have ever worked, may grin with less than gracious resignation which I understand. It is not good news for older teenagers in the last hurrah of their rebellion to be told that all your efforts at being an exclusive individual, and a deviant one at that, are a chimera. It would have been worse and just plain immoral to have also added that some manage to stretch their imaginative foray into radical fields well into their thirties, and even beyond that. When I say that it is inevitable that the rules for being radical are very constrictive, if only because of their tiny number, the majority drifts back happily to their normal state of detachment. Saying that the reason Soviet style Communism and Hitlerism went rogue and over the edge completely, so to speak, was because they lost control of what their radicalism was supposed to be; but saying that they kept adding and adding the inevitable *everything and anything* way beyond what any ordinary absurdity can cope with, was a step too far, and some who were doing their very best to exhibit a certain predictably Irish critical sophistication about religion, might have thought my inner Irish Catholic was churning out all this negative talk about Communism.* But despite the sudden loss of interest and the students beating a quick retreat to the company of *Hypnos* and *Somnus* that I learned about when I too was a happy teenager. I always, however, continue with the story, it is, after all, as some academic stories go, not as tedious as some such stories. That it could hardly be any other way, when the numbers of rules for being normal are infinite and largely implicit, at least in many important areas of life. And that sometimes the rules are so generous you are allowed a fair amount of leeway, while the rules for being different and radical, especially in ideas, are minuscule in number, and may be starkly rigid and unforgiving, and also very explicit. At their age, understandably, and rightly, most students are not very interested in why, only in what, and then only if it is dramatic. We also often forget that why questions are sometimes what questions in other clothes, and this is not confined to the young.

*(Note: It was of course my inner Catholic which gave me the wherewithal to understand such Communism on the ground as it were. I have said elsewhere that in comparison with Irish Catholicism, this Communism, as a system of political, social and cultural rule, was beyond simple and crude, and way beyond what any first year student in a university in Dublin might imagine are the borders of stupidity. But I am always afraid that people will think I am on the type of anti-Communist rant I often heard in America in the late '70s when I worked there, and that I do not know, and in great detail and depth, the horrors this Communism caused, all day, every day, and about the millions of lives that were wasted and lost, in all kinds of ways. I still have a very old Irish Catholic type of puritanism which regards wasting what we traditionally called God given talent, as very wrong, so you can imagine how I regard disposing of people as if they were garbage. When the Irish are not very bright made its regular every five years appearance in various media in different parts of the English speaking world in the last fifty years and more, I used to say that is why we work so hard to make up for what God never gave us. In Cork we had special classes in how to put the boot, figuratively, of course, in without people noticing it).

BUT IS THERE anything else you can you do if you are accused of blasphemy. You might tell your accuser to go away, or some graphic variant, depending on your linguistic talent and your attitude to flamboyant language or salacious taboo. That only works, however, when the religion is wary of being called insulting names or of making a laughing stock of itself, and, as mentioned earlier, where large numbers in a society will come to your defense. But there is another little local problem here, as would be said in Ireland in such circumstances, if a significant force would put their heads up over the parapet to defend you, then the blasphemy would not really have *worked* in the first place. Blasphemy is only blasphemy when there is majority support among the population for accusing you in the first place, even if it is only a lukewarm endorsement which would not advocate anything other than a verbal chastisement or the kind of admonition reserved for someone engaged in any kind of not very serious impropriety in that particular society. And there is also a secondary, very practical rule of thumb about blasphemy, that if there is a quiet, polite discussion, this means it was not really blasphemy, and not higher than one or two maximum, on a blasphemy scale of one to ten. But if you are accused of blasphemy against your own religion and you are living in a theocracy or quasi-theocracy, the help of intellectuals or *human rights activists* from outside does not count; it is of no use, and may be of negative benefit, if it fans the feeling of uniqueness among the believers, and increases the paranoia among those in the society who accused you in the first place. If your accuser has a big stick, run, hide, emigrate, have plastic surgery, or ask a rich, generous foreign government to give you asylum and protection which only works, however, on very rare occasions.

And if you are a genuine believer, ask God to protect you, and, if your belief extends to a higher power who sometimes intervenes in the world, ask Him to smite your assailants down, or at least, to remove them from their positions of power in your land and

if you have access to that wonderful explosive Semtex which, rather romantically and ominously, is said never to corrupt or die, and you find a goodly number of the godly fanatics who want to kill you as a blasphemer gathered together in one place, turn the room into a booming crematorium and you will be doing the world, now and in the future, a favour; if they regard dying violently for their religion as an act of martyrdom which guarantees them a place in paradise, you will be doing them a favour too.

This is what might be called *doing a Swift*, albeit very gauchely, but he sometimes did the gauche to match what he regarded as the intellectual level of his opponents. It may shock because it is explicit, and the fact that it is written and not just spoken in an informal context which is not broadcast, increases the taboo quotient. But it is not meant for shock effect, it is a common garden variety example of the talk which sometimes swirls around in the worlds of blasphemy. Swimming, and sometimes up to my chin, in violence for so long means I am not easily and can hardly afford to be, shocked.

This indented paragraph in italics, breaches all the rules for intellectual writing and all the laws, and then some, of decorum and good thinking, in an attempt, feeble as it is, to show that the world of blasphemy is *sui generis*. And while it has always been a very violent world and sometimes an extremely violent one, there are signs now that the potential for widespread, international calamity is more ominous than ever. Because the traditional media outlets are now featuring synopses on the Internet and also because of the increasing use of the Internet for very individual communications in the whole world, the synapses of communications have become a potential monster in every sense, for individuals and groups of every kind. A blasphemy here is reported there, one small, modest mob here becomes thousands there, a spark here causes an explosion there, and worse, much worse, when religious identity or an amalgam of religious and national identity is seen to be threatened. Then there are regimes which feature a fusion of the political and the theocratic, which can call on the religious as the *raison d'être* - there is also the very dangerous theocratic versus theocratic which may even nominally *share* a religion, which is, of course nothing new in itself, except that now weapons of mass destruction may also be in the frame - and then the *post hoc* justification as well, for whatever they decide is the politic. Some of the explosions seem to be getting much louder as well. Just observing Northern Ireland from a very short distance away, when I came back to Ireland in 1980, was an education no one needs to have, if only because I was now hearing *talk* in the public world I had personally never heard before and which I would never have thought possible anymore, on the island of Ireland: people who did not know I existed were sometimes apoplectic when they talked about me. This was hate talk of the very explicit vilest kind, and the physical violence itself had no bounds either, of any kind. Sometimes the *any kind* was of a kind that I cannot write, for personal psychological reasons, not because it might be censored. I gave up wondering about censorship very early on in talking and writing about violence, not for any brave, worthy reasons - anyway, I was not present when the hero gene was being handed out - but because I very quickly realised that if one eye is keeping stock of the censor, be it your neighbours' forewarning or your own some-time very noisome self-censor, you cannot even begin to think about violence, not to mention talk or write about it. I never even bothered to ask my legal colleagues who know about such things whether an accusation of incitement to violence or harm, or some such, might be brought against me or stand up in court. There was always as well, however, the little boy wanting to take meaning and symbolic violence out for a walk in public, and being publicly accused in Ireland of *saying things you should not say* would guarantee endless publicity far and wide and not just at home, for what I write for humble lecture notes.

(Note: The third paragraph above in italics which began with If you are accused of blasphemy against your own religion now reads like a newspaper which is barely legible. It was written, as was the subsequent paragraph in italics in the last century, albeit in the final years of the millennium. Since then, talk about Islam went global, and sometimes with violence unlimited in its wake. Some commercial American websites where everyone can post their musings are now also being exposed as web carriers of hate. So my chances of my book getting any copy have vanished unless legal aid is also available in Ireland for someone who wants to take a book to court in Ireland).

An accusation of blasphemy which carries the death penalty, be it official, unofficial or everything in-between, is a crime against humanity, but do not waste your time taking this proposition to the United Nations. A significant number of member countries will abstain, and I do not want to list the quite large number who will vote against bringing it to the table or who will not even allow it to be raised in any form which gives it explicit existence, including having any discussion about bringing or not bringing it, to the table. And I might also suggest that if some member or other insists on tabling a motion or whatever it is they do in the UN Assembly, this will usually be a clear signal that one member wants to embarrass some member or other for another reason completely. If your prosecutor and hangman will not communicate with you when you are accused of blasphemy, other than to harm you, your only option left is to communicate in the manner they have chosen. I am not trying to be smart when I say this. Your action will lead to further violence, but - and I will argue again and again that violence is a form of communication and that every young child knows this - if it is the only communication being used, it is the only *language* that will be understood, which is itself teetering on the brink of a tautology.* Violence communicates. It is that brutally simple and obvious, and we learn it at a very young age. Your culture may tell you in all kinds of ways that violence is bad and say lots of other very different things, in practice. Sometimes we speak in trilogies and tetralogies to convince ourselves or to pretend to ourselves, that what we say about violence is true; many different cultures have even incorporated words of wisdom such as the awful spare the rod and spoil the child, into the culture. I am saying and this is not any grand proposal, that sometimes violence is the only answer to violence, a proposal which may banish me to the nether regions of the untouchables, which itself can be a very large group even when it is only figurative, but not necessarily any less vicious for not being literal. We usually accept this sometime moral principle in the *West*, and not only in large-scale warfare, to put a stop, for example, to ethnic cleansing and genocidal massacre, but sometimes, as we all well know, we do not like certain things being said both explicitly and out loud, because then there is no escape or denial. We all become members of the deniers' club at a very young age when we begin the long and sometimes difficult process of learning when to keep certain things locked in a world which is not allowed any form of exposure, and sometimes even to ourselves, to avoid having to deal with the consequences of being open and direct. Irish uses the expression *an modh díreach,* *the direct mode,* and itself a clever metaphorical transfer from Irish syntax, for the latter.

*(Note: I should also have mentioned that when this was first written I was not talking about violence in any particular type of context. It borders on the perverse but it is no less valid because of this, but whatever is said about or even sometimes whatever is proposed as an explanation for, violence, has a habit of becoming relevant because of the never ending torrent of examples which never ceases. The only reason this deluge

seems to happen more often in America is because America always dominates the world's media almost in every sense, and it also seems to have what would be called in many other Western societies a fetish about violence which also has all kinds of discussions spinning around endlessly, including about the right of the people to keep and bear arms in the Constitution).

You cannot, however, want to understand things if all you are doing is pretending to be sincere and honest, while you continue to wring your hands and mutter platitudes; violence, predictably, has always had a special attraction for platitudes, and some of them, act as hides for the most outrageous examples of blasphemous violence. I have decided that this (pretence) is what the Bible means when it talks in certain English translations about whited sepulchres, one of the unfathomable phrases I loved as a child, and which was also the perfect gobbledegook to insult other twelve year-olds. Boys of this age in the ubiquitous everywhere are experts in the semiotics of symbolic violence, and they also know very well, that saying nothing, doing nothing, when someone or some *gang* is calling you *names* - which was a very vicious form of symbolic violence when we were that age - can mean that the violence may then escalate very dramatically, if silence is taken as an implicit signal that those in the other gang can say anything they like, whenever they like. This is a reading of reality, not advice about what to do, coping and dealing with violence are other worlds, and those who help others deal with this even in any minimal way, are saints (which was the ultimate compliment in my youth). But semiotics will also say that those worlds are very strange, complex worlds because identity is in play, be it in the context of young males or religion, when *identity is the problem*; and which sometimes cannot be changed or cannot be seen to be changed, at least, and the best that can be done is to work with the *violence is easy* first part of the generic title of each of this suite of essays on violence.

In our everyday life it may often be easy to accept that it is often better not to say certain things, even when some group is shouting nothing very complimentary at us. But there is a danger surely, if what we say to others, and ourselves, is always restricted and censored, that we, as individuals or a society, will subconsciously lose control of the parameters of intellectual life and of any semblance of an ethical culture. We will happily condemn people, after an event, for not speaking up, and we would not accept (anymore) systematic, artificial, and voluntary prescription, either in terms of concept or methodology, in the natural sciences. Yet, we accept such a demarcation almost without question, in some of the other sciences and in intellectual life, and in life in general, with the sometime exception of creative writing, and this only in certain cultures, certain types of literature, and in certain periods, which is not a happy trilogy. I often witnessed journalists, academics, intellectuals and trade unionists from the *West* who explicitly *supported* the Communist countries of Eastern Europe coming to Romania and choosing silence as their considered response to the regime in Bucharest while also sometimes receiving carnal rewards and favours too abusive and flagrant to be mentioned in an essay such as this. There are even still a few Stalinist exceptions in France who suffer from a chronic form of withdrawal symptoms and they have been joined by a younger cadre who are gallantly stalking *the march of history and historical materialism*, or some such, and who say that such Communism was not true Communism (in the manner of some of the talk in the early decades of Christianity which still finds a strong voice for authenticity two thousand years later). I am sometimes tempted to revert to my happy young self and ask out loud if Jesus ever gets tired of us squabbling about *true this* and *true that* every week and every year, but semiotics will, of course, always sourly remind me if I ever step outside what are sometimes very rigid semiotic lines, that we all follow similar principles in our own lives and that sleep is the only chance we get to indulge our fantasies about being different and special. But we all know unfortunately, that sometimes even sleep can intervene and spoil the fantasy. The other morning I woke very suddenly and had to get out of bed and walk around to shake off the image that I was a double and we were both attached in some way, which was not a very pleasant feeling for some reason. Before the analysts seat me on the couch, I willingly confess that sometimes one of me is more than anyone should have to suffer.

(Note: Some of the above about the reality of Communism is ugly, but I will furnish multiple free red pens to make marks on every page I write and an endless supply of doughnuts to keep up your energy, if you think the exploitation of young people was not accurate).

I WAS ALWAYS fascinated by how people talked and what they talked about, which sometimes seemed completely absurd, but it is ironic I suppose that it was in Eastern Europe where I began, and very slowly at first, to become completely committed to semiotics and not because of my very Irish and very Catholic young life: doing semiotics later, also meant that I realsised my very intense Catholic upbringing might as well have been in the service of semiotics, if only because, in comparison, Communism as an ideology in practice - forget Marx and Engels, what they said never had any relevance in Communist countries other than students had to study the acceptable parts of their writing - was utterly banal. Communist Romania was also the antidote to the absolutism of my childhood culture, because no matter how different people and groups try to put us in hermetically sealed containers, semiotics can sometimes bore holes to let in the air others do not want us to breathe. It all began when I was trying to make any sense of what was happening around me when I worked in what was a Communist country - officially, of course, and itself a very important word in the real, everyday world of that Romania, it was still only in the Socialist phase, but Communism and Communist always seemed to want to be the dominant, ruling words - for some five years in the early 1970s. Some of those who worked in the University and the Academy were international experts in linguistics and semantics, but they usually seemed to live professionally in a world which had nothing to do with real language and the worlds of meaning all around us in the university and on the street. Language scholars, as had been the historical practice, were dealing with selective and sometimes artificial samples of language and meaning even when studying Chomsky's Generative Grammar which was all the rage with young scholars in linguistics - and I think that is when I began to move to semiotics, psychologically as well. My colleagues, and many of them were theoretical linguists either of the new linguistics or of the older, philological tradition, seemed to have entered a cloistered world which was a reaction and escape - and both at the same time - that served as a cocoon against the raw reality of public meaning in this sometimes very cruel Socialist state which was originally established in what would turn to be the swan song of Stalin's era. This peculiar type of system was called Socialism by its (tiny number of elite) proponents who believed it was umbilically related to Communism, because it was eschatologically regarded by its proponents, as being *on the road to Communism.**

*(Note: Elsewhere I have said that nobody in Romania apart from the Communist old believers - they had rather a lot in

common with those who resisted the imposition of the peculiar state church in Russia in the 1650s - believed any of this and they often suffered penury and much worse, because they were completely out of step with the system put in place by Moscow and which was also then put into practice by the Romanians appointed by what was in that period, the Soviet Union. Out of step in this last sentence is a rather good metaphor for anyone in that type of Communist system who could not walk the very straight, narrow line, for whatever reason. What were current rules and doctrine could change which could itself cause confusion and anomie, and not just for older people, and this could be in the context of minutiae or the very substantive, when someone or other in an authoritative position, to give just one common example, was no longer in favour or had been quietly or very noisily disappeared).

It might have been the secular version of *the yellow brick road in search of the magical Wizard* if it were not so cruel and violent and depressingly dire, which also managed to make boring a new form of cruelty and the ultimate nightmare for those who were extraordinary and sometimes extraordinarily talented and brilliant. The battering language took continuously from the regime was constant and particularly oppressive for those whose *métier* was language; it was, in particular, a form of merciless secular blasphemy for academics and intellectuals over the middle age of forty who had come of age before such Communism was put in place by an extremely violent Stalinist Soviet Union. But a consequence of living the intellectual life of a hermit crab also meant they seemed to be bereft of normal, empirical instincts, as if they were imbued with the same terrible deductive instincts of the regime (and what seemed another cruelly ironic consequence of living in such a system). There is no moral condemnation here, I would have behaved in exactly the same way, or worse, if I too had been a citizen of such a Socialist state whose foundation was based on an apodosis type belief in a future which will be the full manifestation of Communism. This belief in *bread tomorrow* which was sometimes not just figurative, illustrates the dearth of imagination and sophistication compared with the richness found in the kind of religion - and its eschatology and exquisite gentleness and beauty - I sometimes experienced living in my own community, with my own people.*

*(Note: I also saw the awful and sometimes official, systematic cruelty in my own society, as you will read elsewhere. I sometimes witnessed more than my friends did the appalling poverty and misery when my mother would minister to those who had nothing and could not and could not afford to, take care of themselves even minimally when they were ill. The standards of hygiene were sometimes appalling in parts of that Ireland which also made everything worse, but some people did not know anything about basic hygiene. This is not a personal criticism of anyone, this is what happens when poverty and not taking care of the self becomes endemic. I never ever wavered from the absoluteness of my Christian belief that we are all equal which also includes knowing that, in certain circumstances, we are all capable of indulging in any and every type of violence. Doing research in and writing about, violence has been the worldly bulwark for these last thirteen words).

I THINK I share DNA with parrots, which regularly embarrassed my poor mother when I would imitate the walk of people walking in front of us on the way down to the shops; if their peculiar way of talking were particularly distinctive, imitating that as well would win me very glaring stares from my saintly Mother who had suffered too much in life (which I discovered later, after she was dead). Sharing a talent with parrots means I learn languages quite easily and I had learned Romanian - a very common variety, as some learned colleagues constantly told me when they finally heard me speaking Romanian, but not of course actor friends who used to ask me to perform the spicy argot of the unsophisticated *mahala* for them - on the street, queuing for food in the few shops that existed and might some-times be open, but especially when I travelled to work in the buses and trams. One day when I said in the university staffroom - I spoke only English in the faculty, nobody in the university in the first year or two knew I had learned Romanian - that I loved, for example, the way, independently of gender, age, or biological relationship, the term *Mama* was used in every single possible context as a term of address, there was a frantic rush to jump off the cliff and contradict me, which was very unusual in a society where very measured, formal behaviour was the norm among the highly educated, unless they were in an informal trust group. I was *the English professor*, and my colleagues had classed me as the stereotype unilingual *Englishman*. Ireland did not really exist then for most people, and was, at best, an appendage like Scotland and Wales, which was surprising at first (to me), given how intense patriotism and chauvinism was in that Romania, for example, *vis-a-vis* Hungary and Moldova which had been united with the *Kingdom of Romania*, if you please, in 1918 and then later russi-fied - which even sounds *an awful class of a* verb - when it became part of the Soviet Communist Empire. When I came back to Ireland for the summer in the mid '70s before I went to work in America, I also got a very timely lesson in semiotics: when I said that in large parts of Europe, Ireland is still umbili-cally tied to London, this could mean nothing. Can mean nothing is a very important, mean concept in semiotics and one of the most important cluster of ideas for any modest understanding of prejudice, racism, classism, and all kinds of symbolic violence.

(Note: I must be loved in a special way by any and every god in the universe to be given such presents. I just heard this very morning the most powerful man in the greatest country in the world list Ireland with Wales and Scotland as satellites of London. It is some twenty five plus years since the above was written, and now coming on fifty since I experienced Ireland did not really exist in Eastern Europe. I once said to a former Professor of mine from a university in England who commented one day that we Irish are always talking about ourselves that we do this in case we forget that we are a free country again. In a couple of years, we will celebrate one hundred years of independence but counting years like this sometimes sits badly for me, it is a bit like thanking someone for giving back money they stole from you. We should have always been free and never shackled and humiliated (which also proves, to me especially, that I can sometimes write short sentences). No one has a right to indulge in gross symbolic violence and humiliate and deprive others of their humanity and their future. For hundreds and hundreds of years a lot of their future was denied to my people and even sometimes for no gain whatsoever for most of this time to the coloniser. Even when there was what might be regarded as the very first decent gesture from the establishment in the 1830s and we were able to go to school, this too had a self-serving twist and was put in place so that we could better serve our masters if we knew English and were literate and numerate).

But Romania was also a paradise for learning semiotics for lots of other reasons. I had heard, for example, *Mama* being used by older men and women to their very young grandchildren of both sexes - I once said to close friends that children in that Romania seemed to be especially treasured and pampered to compensate for the misery they would know intimately soon enough and no one rushed to say I was wrong - but my university colleagues maintained, in principle, that I had not really understood. This type of gross, exaggerated chauvinism about their perfect language which could not have any such seeming illogicality - or much worse, a whiff of the dreaded peasantry - sometimes almost seemed to be an attempt to paper over the embarrassment of living in a humiliating, cruel system which had been imposed with overwhelming force by a foreign power that had defeated Hitler in one of the key battles in the war which had just ended and wanted to carve out a new empire *on the backs of others*, be they other nationalities or other social groupings within Russia, as their reward. The denial of reality was not just beyond irony, this was also an exercise in denial, and it was impossible that I a foreigner, might understand anything,* and not just the system in Romania but also *the street*. But, of course, that is *easy for me to say* - in practice, everything there was easy for me - I was safe and could leave whenever I wanted which meant that acknowledging reality came without any cost.

(Note: It was almost a type of perversity that foreigners - the very term was constantly used - could not understand anything about Communism in Romania. It was a kind of crazy compensation for the ridiculous triteness of reality).

When I told them about my observations they dismissed them to the point of rudeness, but one or two strained to be more polite and say, if I had heard such a thing, it might have been from *very lower class, uneducated people*, a five word string much in use then in Communist Romania, and not only in the university. They were theoretical linguists and experts in literature, who would have known, and sometimes professionally, that Romanian like other Romance languages such as French and Italian, works with two very different, sometimes extreme registers, high and low, but this must have somehow meant also, that the *low* somehow did not and could not, have any real existence, a way of thinking and assigning meaning which is not that unusual in certain other worlds.* In the early years of colonialism in Ireland which might also include intense symbolic violence, Irish - and we are now entering the portals of a type of blasphemous denial of reality which sometimes has no limits, and also, of course, endless potential for violence - was not deemed to be a language (in any real sense). Only those who are properly human in every sense, including in terms of cerebral, intellectual development, could have created and then also use a language as such. The latter part meant that we could, for example, learn a certain, very limited range of English words, but could never learn syntax - putting various kinds of words together and changing their form and appearance as necessary - because such a language rule system was beyond our ability in terms of evolutionary progress, at best. Pronunciation, in any proper sense, was also beyond us, and this was used in particular, as a signal that we were not able to pronounce and speak language as it should be; underlying all of this implicitly, was also the assumption that English was *the perfect language*, the form of words and concept have a very long, often dubious, sometimes racist history, and the assumption often gave way to an assertion and absolute certainty.

* Semiotics is always happy when any group, be it a nation, religion, or social group, are so generous in giving examples where what is real is used and abused and sometimes tossed around like a rag doll. We would have used the sarcastic *they will get their reward in Heaven* as a way of thanking them.

Mama used in such contexts did not exist, it could not. The proper and educated use of language was the single lifeline for educated people when the rest of their life was endless oppression and constant humiliation from Communist Party members who would have, in the eyes of my colleagues in the university and other such sub-groups in society, little or no intellectual or social sophistication. They, in their own mind, knew everything about how language is used and any evidence to the contrary could not be entertained, the *modus operandi*, exactly and hauntingly, of political regimes such as the one where they had to live their daily lives. Romania was in social and political terms, regarded as on the extreme end of the regressive table of Communist countries, including by their neighbours imprisoned in the same Soviet area of interest, and when the dark descended in the 1980s, even the early '70s when I lived and worked there, would be regarded as the good times. I was dumbfounded and shocked because such absoluteness in principle not only undermines the empirical basis of all scientific inquiry, it shows how classism and hauteur can ensure that sometimes we do not and cannot, see reality which *stares us in the face.** That meaning can create competing realities and parallel worlds of meaning is a very good lesson in semiotics, but it is also frightening because it is ultimately inhuman: when reality is deemed not to exist, is a common theme in various fields of violence. I hate not being able to say this in language that does not sound ridiculously pompous and condescending, but this often happens when we are in places where violence exists and where things are magically made not to exist. Elsewhere, I refer to this as the antonym of creation, a power not given by man to God, the Almighty. But it is not magic, it is what you and I do, and sometimes not infrequently. But it was also very personal for someone like me who has always been besotted with how we play with language.

*(Note: I had wanted to say when this was first written in the '90s, that Communist Romania was a sclerotic, class-ridden society, but I had become totally worn out by friends saying but I thought it was a Communist country if I ever tried to tell them what life in Romania was like).

Romanian is full of affect terms and affect adaptations such as the term *Mama*, above, and also in its widespread use of suffix diminutives to indicate affect, and here were highly educated people living in a state of suspension from an extraordinary part of their own culture. I later wrote about this briefly, in 1985, in *Babel*, an international journal on translation, as a modest gesture to a language which embeds affect like this into the very structure of the language itself - including using double diminutive suffixes to indicate affect - and which can be particularly striking in those Romance languages which work with very distinct high and low registers which is foreign to spoken English and particularly foreign to the colloquial English we speak in Ireland. This incident was only one of many of the same genre, and I think it was then that my absolute conversion to semiotics began. I needed to be able to deal with the principle that all our constructions and reconstructions of reality and meaning must be taken into account and that these too must be subject to empirical investigation, in whatever way they can, which, I know, also sounds clumsy and affected even to me, but I do not know how else to say it.

But my most joyful discovery in such a Socialist state was my old Catholic friend blasphemy - I was now at home in familiar Catholic territory which wrote the first and last book and every book in between, on blasphemy - which could be a very serious problem in the satellite Socialist countries in the eastern Communist part of Europe. They could sometimes be even more serious than some of the religious varieties in most other societies in Europe in that era, except those with a very fundamentalist denomination which could also affect very practical areas of life that are often seen by those outside such communions as having no direct relevance to religion. The same problem did not seem to arise after a certain initial period in countries which had adopted *National Socialism* in the 1930s, or in countries like Ireland which had adopted a socio-religious driven fascism after independence, when important aspects of the ideology seemed to take on the trappings of *a one true faith* for the vast majority of the people. But it was sometimes a terrible, desperate problem in countries such as Romania which did not, and could not, adapt in this total way, even remotely, partly because of the genesis of the *Socialist* ideology in Romania; it was an import and had no possibility of being grafted in any way to anything in Romanian history or culture, but this also meant that it was easy to wander into blasphemy as it were, by accident, which could be very dangerous. The ideology also chopped and changed which added another unhappy opportunity for saying the wrong thing. Sometimes the only thing you could be absolutely sure about in certain contexts was the unitary, assumed principle which stated that things meant what the Party leader and his minions said they meant, at a particular time. This could refer to anything and everything, and not just to what would usually be regarded as the political and economic aspects of an ideology; you had to know this, of course, and know it very well. It was a great place to learn how meaning can descend unexpectedly from on high, but *the common people,* and ninety plus plus per cent, were classed as *dirt common,* paid a terrible price for Romania being a semiotic laboratory for an unelected fascist oligarchy which wanted the country to live in a demonic world that had been created out of nothing with visiting Soviet Communist cadres of different kinds, including the Russian army, military police and the ubiquitous secret service, and those in the ordinary Romanian police who had not been ousted in some form or killed. The Romanian Communist cadre would have hardly been able to administer a medium size town badly on their own, if the Stalinist regime in Russia who had brutally occupied their country did not also stay in large numbers in the country. The privileged few directed others to manage according to the Communist book, but sometimes the others were not sure what they were trying to do because the directives of the privileged few might make *no sense* which has also proved to be a very useful two words in trying to explain many other areas of semiotics.

(Note: I have suggested elsewhere that a couple of countries, in particular, from the Soviet Imperial, Communist empire in Eastern Europe, seemed to have been so particularly degraded that they were not able to begin building their society in order to fit in, in some proximate way at least, with the EU, even after they were given initial membership. There are now signs, however, that a number of other countries which had been trapped in the Soviet enclosure are regressing again to a state incompatible with the minimal political standards expected in a democratic EU, and if incompatible reaches the impossible, the EU will collapse. The 1919 poem warned us that turning and turning in the widening gyre... Things fall apart; the centre cannot hold.* Those who never knew the reality of the degradation and the semiotic chaos and sometime insanity of Romanian Communism now want the democracy my little country enjoys; they do not want any fascism, of any type, but the problem now has been exacerbated because some former countries which were also part of the Soviet bloc are themselves trying to move again towards top down systems of various fascist kinds where, to give just one example, the judiciary serves the government. The six words are in italics because they are one of the classic corner stones of every fascist state, where the first move in every kind of embryonic fascism is to control or completely, replace the judiciary. Even the Supreme Court in America regularly becomes a unique spectacle when well dressed, highly educated people behave like hooligans, one of the fine sounding words gifted by Ireland to the world of English, and also adopted by Russia and a slew of other countries.

*These last seven words and others, from The Second Coming have always featured in various ways in other writers, but Yeats has now again taken on the mantle of universal wisdom when people want to talk about the chaos our nearest neighbour has engendered for itself and also the European Union, including the unrest mentioned in the first sentence above, in this Note, and also the legal, social, political and constitutional bedlam in America since the election of a new President in 2016).

It was impossible to explain to friends in the West that nobody in Romania believed or could believe, in Romanian Communism. I had been brought up in a belief system and knew very well what believe means in such a context; the system imposed on that country by outsiders was not acceptable in any sense, in practice. They were told, for instance, they now lived in a land of plenty when the reality was that there might be some, limited types of food today but maybe nothing much of anything tomorrow. *Food today, none tomorrow* needs the voice of Chaplin in a horror film; when I was very young I loved his tomfoolery but later I also began to see his hard satire which was also in its own way, terribly frightening. But one has to remember as well that blasphemy was always the joker in another way also, because nobody was ever sure what might be regarded as blasphemy. From some fifty five years before this, during the first years under Lenin many members of the Party itself in Russia were jailed, tortured and killed because they were accused of blasphemy, which meant whatever those in power at a particular time said it was, and which is another reason why examples from Communism are being included here in an essay on blasphemy. What might be regarded as blasphemy might also sometimes be called *no sense* as mentioned just above, and there was an abundance of that and also the absurd, and I am not using the term in its safe, bourgeois, intellectual or theatrical sense, but in the sense of just dumb, stupid, ridiculous. And sometimes a type of cruelty dreamed up by someone who was trying to be the new Dante and create the new Tenth Circle of Hell. The Communist leaders in Romania would not know how many books were in the *Divine Comedy*, but I would not put any money on the very talented Stalin not having read some of Dante in his seminary days in Georgian, and in Lenin and Trotsky not knowing him in some language.

Someone might quibble with the use of the term believe, but I am not using the word with any sarcastic baggage - semiotically, I am a genetic, hard wired Irish Catholic of the old prick me and I will bleed type, and would never pass on any such opportunity - but there is no alternative word in English, or any other language I know or am acquainted with. It is a word that also has an importance without limit in all our lives and many aspects of our lives outside the religious. What could create a worrying problem for the people living within such a system with no escape, was the constant fear of not knowing when you might blaspheme, unknowingly, because you were not always exactly sure what rules were operating at a given time, or even what possible meaning such rules could have in the first place - which even I was sometimes asked about, in the hope that fresh eyes might bring a new perspective - or what meaning certain terms had at any particular time, or any time. I am not sure anybody did, which has always meant in Communist systems that anyone and everyone can be indicted for *unorthodoxy*, which famously happened also to certain *Supreme Leaders* in various Communist countries and is still happening regularly today in places like North Korea, and not only when they had already passed to whatever paradise Communist leaders go. Or because you might blurt something out unknowingly, if your responses were not already honed to give the right answer instinctively, or because you had just made a gormless mistake using the wrong words because of fear and panic. A Communist culture could reduce adults to little children caught in a classroom with a volatile teacher with a foul temper, and it was awful to witness their humiliation when it happened to friends in Bucharest. Ideologies with structures which also induce an acute fear of sanctions, infantalises adults in all kinds of ways. Mrs Malaprop and the Reverend Spooner would have been dispatched to the Romanian reconstruction of a notorious Russian *gulag* in the Danube Delta in double quick time, and in the first day or two.

MISTAKES - AND BLASPHEMY is sometimes the ultimate mistake because the penalty can be severe and sometimes terminal - are not allowed in artificial systems except when allowance is cleverly made to cope with the deviancy, or in absolutist authoritarian systems which assume a dogmatic system of rightness, which have absolute control of the apparatus of state power, and which arbitrarily use this facility any way they like. It is a frighteningly simple principle but the capacity to generate and tolerate mistakes and contradictions which indicates whether a system is human or fascist. The most extraordinary aspect of my experience with Catholicism was that the absolute belief that we were just human and not perfect could also predicate a certain Christ like gentleness and understanding, and a certain tolerance as well. This did not always apply, however, in Irish Catholicism in matters public, when scandal came into play, but especially the sexual. The fundamentalist, puritanical Vatican created many centuries before this, was often the primary judge of blasphemy in history, but they also had never read all the pages in the story of Jesus Christ who was all-forgiving except when, you might remember, hypocrisy, corruption and the sins of officials came into play. Correlatively, any social and political system driven by an imposed, artificial system of meaning can only cope inadequately, with all of human reality and meaning - Communist talk of the Romanian type, was designed to exclude the many awkward *bits* of reality, if I may use my favourite new *techno word* in its old sense - nor indeed with a miniscule part of it. It goes without saying that systems of meaning formally and informally communicated from on high - which could also include self-important, very lowly bureaucrats in that Romania - were so silly, that to compare them with artificial systems, as this is technically understood, is itself ridiculous. It is just that some people in artificial intelligence have sometimes become like a cutout of those leaders in Romania when it comes to merrily issuing decrees about real meaning, in a say anything you like fashion.

(Note: Some might conclude that I am saying in the last paragraph above, that it was harder for the well-educated in such a Communist country, and it was, in the sense that we usually have an expectation - often a very sad, naïve, not very intelligent wistful hope which can sometimes take a terrible psychological toll - that things should make sense, which is itself a somewhat strange four word expression. Things is vague, does it actually refer to anything or everything? Is should make sense a cry for help type of expression from a semiotician who is having a crisis about meaning, which we all should have from time to time unless we have taken up permanent residence in a make believe world to hide away from the sometime harsh reality of meaning and semiotics. Everyone sometimes has the feeling that things should make sense, including small children; you might think we were born with it, and itself a string of words which is one of my sacred taboos, if only because of the violence it has caused throughout history. We may also have an expectation that prominence and promotion in every sense, are our birthright. This was exacerbated, for example, when Party stooges at every level in Romania were put in charge of prestige institutions which was regarded as personally hurtful by many people, and not just those with a university education. The jokes about the various leaders' lack of education in polite society in the palaces of Rome, Paris and London, were legion and sometimes funny, and always pathetic and awfully sad, of course

Their boorishness was particularly hurtful in a society which had learned about class and style from France; the French patrimony also meant that I would sometimes pretend not to know French because older people preferred to speak French to a foreigner rather than Romanian.* My friends who told the jokes - some were brilliant actors and theatre directors - were enacting their little gesture of rebellion and revenge, but they, of all people, knew Faustus was laughing off-stage at them. They were also the ones who had to play the part of the fool in real life when they performed paeans of praise in public for the Heroic Leader and the Glorious Future which was Communist Romania. This was the equivalence of the dance a jig and sing for your supper in our culture if you wanted to stay in your job, and your apartment. If you were a student, attendance at public demonstrations in your designated group - designated was a very well used word - was compulsory if you wanted to continue in university and also not put your family at risk, in terms of work, living arrangements, education, if there were other siblings, and etc., etc. Not attending was a sin, a crime, a blasphemy all in one, which was a constant in all Communist systems and also a reminder of the reign of Caligula when attendance in the Senate when the horse was also in the chamber, was similarly encouraged. Life could always be precarious, and the fear of losing whatever advantages you might gain or have accrued one way or another - use your imagination to flush out the details of one way or another which were sometimes awful, and done because of infinite love for one's family - could sentence you to a much more precarious world, and not only materially, especially when what was regarded as private had gone to an extreme more exigent than in most other Communist countries which had been similarly annexed into the Soviet bloc, including even Mother Russia itself. And to add a personal, very unhappy postscript, I would have been no different. I learned in the religion of Christ which my own people in the town where I was born had made their own in a very peculiar, very human way, that I am, at best, no better than anyone else, and that if truth be told, there are always multiples of those who are so much better than I am or could ever be.

 * In the article I later wrote for a journal of translation about high and low register of terms of address, I mentioned when I also gave examples from Romanian, that language experts in Romania would sometimes tell me I could not have heard what I had heard. This last string of nine words is a frightening example of what can happen in a culture which is so completely obsessed with class and status indicators that it continuously gives new life every day to William Penn's very pithy is for the Pot to call the kettle Black. Communism never really had a chance in Romania because of the absolute ties of language and class in the culture and society, which I know is a beyond bold statement. It would have taken a good fifty years and three or four generations for those bonds to begin to fade away, and this only if the society were to be totally sealed off from the rest of the world which could not have happened anyway, when the Internet made its entrance not much more than a decade after I had left. But there was always something else in play as well. Communism in practice and as it was ordained in Romania and in the other Imperialist, Soviet satellites was objectively designed to alienate. Qua system this is what it did and could

only do. It was stupidity incarnate. It was repugnant to everyone over six when it was introduced and destroyed completely the lives of those over sixty completely).

Systems, be they religious or secular, which do not want to cope with all of the reality which exists usually engage in a process which defines reality *ab initio*, as if the world was a *tabula rasa* and you could write whatever you want on the blank page. The Communist system imposed in Romania after World War II said this is how it is now, not just how it must be, as if reality already was as they said it should be, which gives a little hint of the absurdity which continuously rattled around in how this *Socialism which leads to Communism* was supposed to be put into practice, not to mention what this Communism itself was supposed to be.* I have always assumed that there was able to be a famous school of semantics in the outreaches of Russian Communism in Azerbaijan because it was far from the centre of Soviet control in Moscow but also because it was theoretical. It avoided the empirical fields - what words and phrases and sentences mean when we use them in our lives - which are often packed with embarrassing booby traps which jump up like a jack in the box and laugh in your face when you act as if you were a semiotic *gauleiter* and all the worlds of meaning are your fiefdom. Semiotics makes a monkey out of any system which works on the primary political principle of imposing meaning, especially when it makes a *tableau vivant* of living breathing people of all ages forced to pose without a break, in whatever scene leaders ordained. The masses posing, and also sometimes waving little flags and shouting slogans in unison, was the primary feature of rallies, including lining the streets when spontaneity, popularity and enthusiasm had to go on display.

*The *supposed to be* which is used twice in this sentence, is the key. The system never necessarily knew what it was supposed to be doing which is why it was and could only be, a mess. And God only knows what the Communism part - which was the second and last phase - was supposed to be. I am being very Irish here in my use of English, I used *And God only knows* as a signal of complete desperation about what this second phase could mean. One time I read everything I could find in the various languages I knew about Stalin to try and get away from the *tableau mort* he had become. He was an educated, intelligent, literate young man who began to write poetry early on in life and see the world very differently from the one he had experienced in his religious schooling, and all very 1880 to 1920 Ireland. His father was a drunk and had beaten both him and his mother who had left home and taken her son with her, all very Ireland as well, except for the part about leaving your husband and taking your children with you. She had managed to get him into a school which was reserved for sons of the clergy (which could not be Catholic Ireland). Lenin died five years after the October Revolution which had its own bit of paddywhackery *a l'anglaise* about it because it was not in October. The beginning of the end of Trotsky began in 1925 and Stalin was not yet fifty when he began his nearly thirty year absolute rule. Opposition from within and from without was staggering and he became what he had to become, if he were ever to create this new world of Communist rule. That Communism became what it became in Russia was inevitable in every semiotic sense, it became what it became to survive: this meant doing what was necessary for survival which had nothing to do with any philosophical, social or political theory of any kind. This was semiotic absolutism on a state level in a ten, fifteen year evolutionary phase and trying to fit Marx or Engels or anyone or anything else into the picture is silly; which often seems to happen in semiotics when fixed ideas, and not just theoretical ones, try and force their way into the picture. When he died in 1953 at the age of seventy five, he had had twenty long years where his personal survival was still dependent on his political survival; power in the Soviet Union was sometimes just an exercise in survival, as it has always been in every Communist country since then, and most fascist states as well. When the first elected leader of a free Ireland was murdered he was thirty two and the leader of the group which staged the most short lived armed rebellion against a sovereign state in history was a republican whose first allegiance was to his religious faith, and you do not need to be a racist tinged wag of any kind to say this is a very Irish take on republicanism: someone who knows nothing about Ireland except they we are great jokers might think everything from *When the first...* just above, is also one of our famous jokes. None of what is said in this asterisked part of the text has anything to do with prejudice of any kind, it would not be clever to do semiotics without being conscious of my own too many to count, battery of meanings, including prejudices.

What amuses me in a particularly Irish way, is how Fascisms of every variety, be they the Italian or German type, or one of the many Communist brands, Stalinist, Maoist etc., are always addicted to grandiosity and ostentation on a grand style, not, of course, that it could ever be said that the older Egyptian and Roman models were ever lacking in pomp and circumstance either. The Catholic Church has great Churches as do Protestants of the High Church variety - but the latter get little credit, they modelled them on the ones they stole from the Catholics in the countries where religious ascription generally followed the political leadership - but the leaders of the Catholic Church in particular, dress a little too ornately for our age now, and not just their age and portly silhouette. I have always kept a close watch on children, they can be very clever semiotic mentors, and, in this context, they also remind us that dressing up and *putting on a good show* starts very early in life.* But all of these groups which glory in pomp and ceremony have another thing in common, they do not like to be laughed at. Children hate that too with a special vengeance. It was Communism's ultimate nightmare to be treated like a fool and if people could see they were wearing nothing underneath, they would be exposed with nothing left to cover up the naked nothingness underneath their imported *Made in Italy* pure silk suits, extra fine shirts and silk ties of various colours. Which is why political satire is always regarded by many such leaders as the ultimate blasphemy and which must always carry grave consequences; it is no wonder that this last word can itself function as an ominous threat. *The Emperor's New Clothes* might well have been written for the Second Romanian Emperor in that first half of the 1970s.

(Note: The Communist variety constructed their own impossible, sometime farcical problems with regard to male dress when they might sometimes work, for example, with the principle of whatever you do, you cannot wear a collar and tie. In Eastern Europe in the '70s, blue jeans - bluj in Romanian - could be almost the symbol of I am not a Communist. Some Communist countries now wear the collar and tie - and suit as well, including the silk variety - as a signal of modernity, even when suit, shirt and tie, had never been part of their own tradition. Male dress in general, provides endless material for seminars in semiotics on a wet Friday afternoon in Dublin, and the American version, smart casual, has become so complex it could fill endless wet hours every day of the week, particularly if you can show clips from older American films as well as example of No Change).

IF YOU KNOW your own religion and culture, you can usually

predict when the allegation of blasphemy will come your way and bring the wrath of the vengeful soldiers in arms of some man-created god on your head. Unless, of course, you have an unholy desire for notoriety, or you have been afflicted with an irresistible urge to dice with death, or you are a fool of the holy or one of the other many varieties. You should be able as well, if only for the good of your health, to estimate your chances of withstanding the attack, verbal or physical. You can only tell people, for example, with impunity, that their scriptures may need a proper translation or to be adjusted or rewritten, in whole or in part, to account for varying cultural ways of writing and also attitudes over time, if you live in a culture where the majority will declare you should not be punished for this, or for almost anything else you say. Or if you live in a culture such as Ireland today at the turn of the new millennium where many of my students now do not care, or know, what it means when it was said that *the scriptures are divinely inspired*; they do not necessarily have any points of reference which would enable them to relate to, or understand, the phrase marked in italics just above, or the belief which has endless complex implications, including those which extend to a *next life* [6]. When people do not share, even partially, a common set of points of reference, there can be little shared understanding - look how girls and boys even at a very young age may have already learned very different and sometimes contrary, points of reference - which means, for example, in Ireland, if someone claimed Jesus had a sister, this would not bother too many anymore, one way or another, in Ireland, including those who would mark the box *practicing Catholic* in any census or poll, a phrase which could mean they go to Church once or twice a year, maybe, and never pray in private (which now also give particular newspapers and *chat shows* who like to vent their sarcasm on the citizenry endless copy). Some also say it enhances religion and makes

Jesus more real, more like us, to know He had a sisters and brothers. This, of course, would not now be regarded as blasphemous because we recently lost many of our shared reference points which would have regarded something like this as blasphemy, but those who believe absolutely and who now practice their religion as they have always done, now also seem to be adopting the adage made popular in Northern Ireland, *whatever you do say nothing* if only to avoid being pilloried in some form in public.

(Note: The last two lines of the last sentence in the body of the text is now in need of serious editing because of trolling of every kind. Everyone is now a target and the Irish are again breaking world records for writing, but this time also for slander and scurrility written by the ubiquitous anonymous. Hate talk was often a most extreme form of blasphemy, slander and symbolic violence of every kind, but now it has become a monster which can be read by billions which can give everyone the impression that what they write is being read and that they are now published authors, which all of us scribblers know can be a very toxic drug. I personally find it particularly depressing that believers in Ireland can now be pilloried and mocked because of their Catholic beliefs. I must be getting old, but I thought we were better than that, and maybe we are and it is just because these trolls also make good copy for the traditional type of journalism which would never look the clichéd gift horse in the mouth).

I am very conscious, on the very same principles, that many people do not share my points of reference when I talk about violence and will absolutely not want to adopt them. If only because this would compromise, and sometimes fatally, the acceptance of very different ideas and values, but also because it might involve moving many of their ideas and values from the ideational to the real, and from the implicit to the explicit, which can be bothersome and sometimes tiresome or worse, or even impossible. There is not an iota of condescension on my part when I say this, it is simply that it is extremely difficult or sometimes even impossible, to make such a cognitive move to figure out, not to mention identify with something in some way, if this means key factors in the overall picture of our life have to be changed even somewhat, not to mention substantively or radically. Religious cultures are usually predictable if you exercise minimal intelligence, but I am not taking here about cults which can spring up out of nowhere and disappear just as fast. But in some political regimes it could be sometimes impossible to predict with any surety what might be regarded as blasphemy. In the Socialist countries in the eastern and southeastern sections of Europe which were created by invasion with colonial, fascist intent after World War II, the Russians *made up* this new world as they went along as the popular phrase has it - which always happens in colonial crusades of every type, other than in the feral, violent phase which sometimes happens at the beginning if there is resistance to the fascist intent, but this highly successful form of colonial crusade was always substantively different from anything that had ever happened before, anywhere - which sometimes meant changing the rules or the interpretation of the rules, on a continuous basis (which the great Pavlov will tell you can induce breakdown of different types very quickly). And which also meant that when this colonial empire imploded in some thirty something years, it might as well have never been; it is not that nobody mourns its passing but there is no memory of any kind of the majority of the people whose lives were completely destroyed. Some of the Russians who managed the system in the various satellites are now back home again as leaders of a Russia which is still an absolute dictatorship but which no longer makes buying hammers and sickles compulsory.

LIVING for some five years in Romania frog marched me into semiotics which is some form of revenge I suppose on Soviet Communism, the ideology that first destroyed more people physically, spiritually, morally and psychologically in a short amount of time than any other country ever in the known history of the world except for those countries in various parts of Asia which would adopt the same system from Moscow more than thirty years after Russia had started the cycle in 1917. Russia is still plying its violent trade in a more orthodox, fascist, ultra-capitalist form and is sometimes even more unpredictable and dangerous, to the sometime chagrin of countries like China and North Korea which are now more like the oligarchs of the old traditional varieties, but now with state of the art military cultures and equipment. Dangerous took on a very distinct echo of Armageddon when states which exhibit unpredictable semi-otic behaviour began to harbour nuclear intentions or went nuclear, which makes it time to say that these essays on violence are themselves a constant reminder that semiotics names it in *the here and now* and does not care what anyone thinks, be it Lord or peasant, or whatever the contemporary equivalent might be. Walter Benjamin's pithy *Jetzteit* was a clever attach-ment to help us understand how meaning is assigned when he pared away the apparent changes of meaning in his very caustic *homogenous empty time* of the semiotic overlords which is detached from history.* Semiotics has no necessary interest in the past as such, even as a guide to meaning now, which can be a serious source of annoyance to many historians, but while the patterns of meaning always remain the same, the peculiar expression can be very different which some can assume also involves a radical change in the meaning itself. Nor does semi-otics show any particular favour for those who want to impose fictional meaning, be they ideologists, religionist or cultists, secular or religious, except when semiotics uses and exploits them, and often quite shamelessly, as peculiar case studies.

* Some might say this is not an orthodox reading on Benjamin's work, but semiotics treats ideas such as orthodox in the same way it does everything else, including, for example *homogenous* table manners.

SEMIOTICS IS the ultimate form of reductionism, when everyone and everything is a potential case study, no more, no less, including how we assign meaning to the divine, which is extremely varied, and which obviously does not concern God in the least. It can hardly be a surprise that it can be very unwelcome, and unacceptable, and many more such terms with *un-* and its many relatives with a similar negative prefix, to all of us, without exception. It is also one of those infelicitous universals on the personal level, except for those who want to exploit it, including Freud and Jung who began to mine its deep and dark underground again in the manner of the Greek dramatists and myth makers; and also those in our various worlds who created their stories orally in the early stages before literacy, and who left us traces of various kinds, and not only in reported form.* The great creators have the special gift which helps them to see in the dark, and I am not referring to just those who use words; it also includes all those in our many worlds who have changed the expressions of meaning, substantively, in history and in the street and in all the ever growing forms of new media, including sometimes by happenstance.

*(Note: The summer of 2018 was particularly dry and hot in Ireland, drones showed us the outlines of multiple ancient constructions in the Boyne Valley - which is also the home of

the burial site at Newgrange, which is thousands of years old and was constructed to catch the light of the Winter solstice for three to four days in its inner chamber - which we never knew about. The first time I was inside the chamber waiting for the new light of the solstice, I caught myself not breathing and then almost hyper-ventinating, I was so happy to be from such people).

THE FIRST FIVE decades of the last century in the so-called second millennium are one of the great historical case studies in meaning change, as was the popular adoption and exploitation of phrases such as *millennium* etc. as a way of counting time. Changing the rules of assigning meaning and not just the meaning of time, arbitrarily and quickly, has always carried great risk on the personal and group level, including the risk of relative or total destruction to the self and also to others. We are a group and live and can live in a group because we share meaning, or, at least, because we assume we share meaning, or, at least, again, because we assume we share certain levels of meaning, in key areas, which includes very strict, very complex rules about what latitude we may have with regard to certain rules; this, of course, is always threatened or destroyed when meaning is imposed from the top or from outside, especially in a very short space of time, unless the majority of the population in question can accept it readily and promptly. As the title of the two parts of these essays says, the violence part is easy and predicable, identity is the one which may get complicated beyond what we can cope with, especially in certain explicit contexts of sudden, top-down impositions. This is why the nuclear example is mentioned above, as one of the new ways of delivering violence on a gigantic scale, and which was hastily developed and brought to its first conclusion because of the ever creeping threat of Hitlerism and its own nuclear ambitions and substantive progress. There are now increasing numbers of ways of delivering violence virtually and on a grand scale, including through the Internet and the very recent developments in technology. It would not be a mark of genius to say that this will see multiple *ends* in various parts of the world - this is who we are, this is how we think, this is how we behave - and not only from those claiming a very special relationship and mode of communication with their god, but also from those who give themselves absolute status. End of the world language has been a historical constant in many cultures as has origins, but beginnings and ends and quarrels about them have caused and are still causing endless controversy, and violence, and not only when contention also carries accusations of gross blasphemy.

Those thirty some years in the first half of the twentieth century which took the world to the portals of an apocalypse are a grim reminder about what happens when major shifts in public, international meaning are wanted by some but not by others, but the lesson might as well have never existed. In the years following those few ominous decades, sharing meaning in parts of Europe was also then made impossible within many of the so-called Socialist countries of the on the way to Communism variety, if only because many of the attitudes spawned by this creed meant that any and every measure could be said to be necessary to achieve an ultimate goal which was purely ideational and a classic example, if one were still needed after all this time of the artificial imposition of *no sense* in the public and international domain. This dogma which had already been in an evolutionary phase in greater Russia for more than twenty years before the beginning of World War II carries clear traces of the mystical fantasy of reconstructing time found frequently in many very different cultures, secular and religious, across all eras, and which was given an eschatological type twist of the Biblical kind by Karl Marx and his like-minded colleague Engels who spanned much of the nineteenth century. The nineteenth was also the century which spawned a very peculiar *middle Europe* intellectual culture which has often exhibited self-hatred and intellectual embarrassment towards traditional ideational religion, and especially Jewry, but this, of course, did not save them from transferring the apogee of life to a future time.* We are all for obvious reasons, predictably tracked in one form of another to be future orientated, but this has also in many different cultures involved creating stories about the future which may be and sometimes can only be, no different from the kind of day dreaming we all indulge in, at different times in our lives; examples can often even bring a large class of students to attention. You can, however, play all the tunes you like and all the variations on a tune with the great fiddlers of Dooney, but a model which exclusively projects reward into future time is a reward in the future, no more, no less, no matter what tunes fiddlers in other places might play. Stalin's and then Hitler's adapted models of what the future must be, brought total disaster in many places to add to the millions and millions of deaths and lives destroyed in the fighting in World War II and its very long aftermath. Children are the great exponents of semiotic inquiry and find many of the adult worlds of meaning strange and sometimes senseless and contradictory, and, as they well might, they some-times resent their experience bitterly. They are the ones who very particularly conscious of meaning because they eat, breathe, sleep every shade of meaning, and are always involved in the process of learning what meanings are in play, including the contradictions, but they must also learn how to assign these various meanings, and when, which can cause endless confu-sion, trouble, and sometimes, thankfully, great humour, and not only when contradiction has the baton and is conducting a mad orchestra.

*(Note: Deep self-hatred in a context of a group is also mentioned in other essays. It can often be a peculiar form of extremely virulent symbolic violence, and also, sometimes, one of utter, destructive sadness. It is has never been confined to any ethnic or religious group, but its consequences, however, have sometimes been more visible and dramatic in Europe which often had good ecclesiastical communication systems and which also shared Latin as the common language of literacy; but despite sharing a religion and language, and long before the 1400s, the hatred was also projected onto others who were living in the same national territory or who were living cheek by jowl in other sovereign countries. Hatred, including self-hatred, which is driven by ideational variants of absolutism be they religious or secular or what is sometimes a toxic combination of both, is also often exported as is, or in an adapted form, as happened, for instance, within Europe itself - including in my own small island when religious factions which had a faith driven hatred of Catholicism were brought into northern sections of the country as colonists - but also to many parts of the rest of the world as well, including America. Such toxic hatred can also flare up unexpectedly and fade away just as quickly, as if it had never been, which can also cause great disquiet for decades later, in many places in Africa and Asia, for example, and also in many places in Eastern Europe as well).

The sometime Marxist twist that this was *the working man on the street's take on* reality and not philosophy, is given the lie when it can hardly be claimed that, in semiotic terms, this is different in kind from the model of my childhood Heaven. It may come with philosophical trimmings couched in very particular language which is often due to a language style which is topically expected in a peculiar culture and has no necessary relationship with quality of content, however this is measured. This is not a criticism in any sense of economics which, like the rest of us, has to and should, deal with social and political reality. To mention Marx's own overt personal take on the value of philosophy - and never in my life would I have expected that Karl Marx would spark my naughty little boy gene like this - that *philosophy and the study of the actual world have the same relationship to one another as masturbation and sexual love*, might seem not to have any place in an essay on semiotics. But intellectualism, everywhere, and not just in the *mittel* European traditions, has sometimes been vitiated by an absence of a critical awareness of the idea of model itself, which runs through everything, and especially our ordinary language; and also the sometime fallacy that the value of ideas has any correlation with the type of language used, including its impenetrability. This is one of the major problems with semiotics, because it is *common - dirt common* was a particularly vituperate popular phrase when I used to overhear someone's reputations being shredded when I was twelve and began to hear things like that being sometimes said by certain people who lived nearby and who came to visit my mother nearly every day about people in the town that I knew - and it can hardly be anything else when it is and must be, about us, which also means it is sometimes vulgar as well, because we sometimes are.* Name calling is one of the ways we put meaning-tags on everything and anything, and every culture has a love hate relationship with rudeness, and also sometimes, levels of rudeness which cross over into *vulgarity*, as Freud cleverly *exposed* in one area of our lives, when he openly talked about the sexual organs and which duly caused a cultural shock when translated into English equivalents, which is one of the reasons we formally and informally banned so many books in Ireland. We were so good at doing this, many of the offending books might as well have never existed.

*My mother schooled me in absolute equality which was for her a primary article of her deep personal faith, which also meant that she was uncompromising in her belief in equality. She did not have to be told in a sermon at Mass, not to take the name of the Lord in vain, her belief never had to use phrases such as *before God*, they were superfluous. God was present, the adverb *always* was superfluous. She never prefaced or finished any sentence with *I swear* (if she had used that particular five letter word in any context, I would still remember it). We lived in His world. It also meant that she would never excuse bad or sinful behaviour which could obviously prove difficult for a young teenager in the house; she would even stand there and say nothing when someone's life was being shredded by someone who stopped her in the street for a chat and a rant, because walking away would be offensive (if I were with her I would turn my face to the street to hide my stifled laughter). The sometime uncompromising belief in equality sometimes made life awkward and difficult in the various places where I worked, as can easily happen when conviction of any kind is very intense.

THE CONFUSION about what meanings were operative in practice in Communist Romania, but especially those currently deemed blasphemous by the power in place, could sometimes be more obvious to an outsider than to those who had to live the meanings morning, noon and night. The endless sanctions for getting *it* wrong, even about what might ordinarily be regarded in my world as trivial, not important or not very important etc., could make everyone at some time confused and nervous, and fearful. Young children often have to suffer this humiliation in the first years of school and in society, but it was particularly hurtful to university professors whose identity was closely bound up with having been - and still being seen in a parallel way of social thinking - a member of a highly educated, intellectual elite, which had very high standing in a Romanian culture which had regarded itself as part of the French tradition where intellectual is prestige, and not a snide remark as it can be in our highly English influenced Irish culture. I remember making the following list one day about someone who was the key lead in the faculty as they say it in America, for *political doctrine. She does not believe a word she is saying, the students do not believe a word she is saying, she knows they do not believe a word she is saying, they know that she knows*, and on and on in an anal cycle. But nobody could step out of the circle. I remember a young colleague smiling, a little nervously but happily as well, that I understood her reality when I mentioned this. Communism, and I do not mean the intellectual exercise which was Communism in most countries in Western Europe and which often had and still have, many features of a cult, bullied me into semiotics. This same Communism was responsible for producing such wonderful absurd and comic writing in certain Czech and Russians writers, as often happens when the top-down rules imposed in a concentrated, aggressive way in a nation state make little or *no sense*.* This had also happened in Ireland in the early years of the eighteenth century when Swift said to the English in A Modest Proposal, if you want to destroy the Irish, which you are already doing quite successfully, do it with some benefit to yourself. Fatten the children for market and sell them as prime veal for the English table; in the poor days in the 1960s and '70s, Ireland sent truck loads of live young calves to the fine tables of the elegant cities in Northern Italy.

*(Note: Many of these writers are no longer read at the end of the second decade of the new millennium as the Joyces and Becketts are for example, because what is talked about has no cultural resonance now for the vast majority of those under forty in these countries in Eastern Europe, or anywhere else. Many were great writers but they were caught in a trap because writing such satire did not always exercise and exploit their obvious literary talents to the full. Nobody ever wants to remember such misery if you are lucky to emerge and not have been destroyed).

In the first half of twentieth century Ireland, Joyce and Beckett would also use the pen and pencil when many of the rules of religion, morality and behaviour which were imposed and accepted without question in Irish society before and especially after independence, could be seen as life destroying or just plain stupid by certain writers who often share the stage with children as the best semioticians, and sometimes as the best communicators as well, if only because the young ones use live English, and even the odd innocent, off colour word as well and which may be a special, unexpected delight coming from their innocent mouths. These two Irish gentlemen are like Swift, their godfather, among the greatest experts on blasphemy in world history. They were very easy, almost nonchalant, about their place in the intellectual and literary canon, but they also had very ambitious international aspirations, which included holding up to ridicule many aspects of the way we think in secular and religious Western cultures, in that order. They are now applauded for their genius and talent for exposing the arcane secrets of life and are then often duly ignored in practice, as the cultural commentators they are. I once added they are ignored as if they had written a treatise on the comparative semantic changes in the Greek of Lower Egypt in the first half of the second century of our era which has an important bearing in the study of the conceptual, linguistic models which would later influence European thinking, but I think now that was an immodest step too far.

When I went first to the University of Bucharest, I was particularly interested in the logical aspects of linguistics and semantics but I was forced out into all the wider worlds of meaning by that Communism, to try and understand how meaning was assigned, not only in the context of language, but in every other aspects of life as well. Since I was quite young and foolish and inquisitive, I have always wanted to know about what I see and hear around me - it was also sometimes a game - and it was only later, after university in Dublin, that I began to try and put what I was seeing into some kind of conceptual frame, to see if the various parts fit together, or if there are aspects which stand more alone, as it were. It took me quite a while to realise that it was also important to focus on the process of assigning meaning and not just on meaning itself, if one were not to miss some of the multiplicity of meanings we work with and use, in the same and different contexts; my sometime crazy love of language as the ultimate game from when I was quite young, also meant that I was also beginning to see how meaning was sometimes assigned, and also manipulated. The Communism imposed by Russia in various countries in the late '40s was a semiotic *hurdy gurdy* and, as I would quickly realise in Romania, a place where semiotic dangers lurked in every corner, including corners which had never existed before: and which is why Romania in the early '70 is used here to serve as a secular example of blasphemy. The meanings assigned to anything and everything could depend on whoever was conducting the orchestra on a particular day which meant that people were not always sure what was always the party line on a whole variety of issues, which included, of course, the language and writing being studied in the universities. I got to know quite brilliant traditional intellectuals and great poets and artists and world class theatre directors and actors, but its Communism could and often did, confuse and degrade everything. We all know from when we are quite young that confusion can sometimes be particularly taxing because we may be very unsure about the multiple meanings given to anything and everything, including language; people would sometimes laugh at you for saying *the wrong thing*, which was also very confusing and not just humiliating when I had no idea why they were laughing at me, but they could also get angry. This kind of Communism infantilised the population and never regarded, let alone treat, the people as adults or as having any right whatsoever to think for themselves or as having independent rights of any kind. This was do what we tell you to do, say what we tell you to say. And the two terrible words *or else* framed every *do* and every *say*, and never had to be made explicit as sometimes is the case when absolute meaning is in play in many other different contexts, including the seeming ordinary and banal. Sanctions were multiple and sometimes not knowing if there would be sanctions or what they might be, could also make the situation more harrowing. Children can deal very badly with such confusion, but we can all deal very badly with not knowing what to say or do in particular situations, but especially those of us who have a certain standing as experts in expression and communication.

Some years before I went to Romania I was spiritually a socialist, and still am, and in some ways more strongly than ever. I also knew Russian Communism was an aberration, any regime which kills millions of its own can be nothing else; the version I met in Romania had the added colonial aspect which was something I had understood for a very long time because of own country's experience. I had also been a *total Irish Catholic* for the first twenty something years of my life, but you can really only properly lose your innocence once - it has now become a very boring repetitive story in Ireland that the official Church was not just cheating and dealing off the bottom of the deck (of cards), but had also been double and triple dealing in hypocrisy, which is everybody's way of behaving sometime or other, but when the opposite had been trumpeted morning, noon and night, it was both repulsive and shocking to be told what had been the real story all along. Of course we knew that was not the whole story and that there must be more, but the stories already on the table were unthinkable and gravely sinful which meant the country was completely blindsided and did not have the capacity for righteous self-deception which certain Western intellectuals and writers have always had, for example, *vis-à-vis* Communism in all its cruel reality. The only thing that ever surprised me in Communism was its endless, crass, cruel stupidity, and not just in comparison with how Catholicism had successfully inserted itself in Ireland in the 1920s as an integral part of Irishness: which itself became what certain churchmen in leadership positions would say it was. When I got my first smell of the reality of Communism *in situ*, in the first week, the stench was everywhere, and the fear, especially in the University when people sometimes looked through me as if I were not there. Very soon after the change of regime in 1989, I was invited back to Bucharest to lecture in my former Faculty and I talked about symbolic violence which I had begun a decade before this, including in literature, especially in Swift and the twinned Joyce and Beckett, and a number of female professors came up to me later in the corridor in tears, apologising for never having said hello to me in five years, despite us all having shared a not very large common room for some time, and often cheek by jowl between classes.

This was the first time in my life I had ever been so humbled by honesty in this way, but I was also embarrassed because I was the one causing embarrassment to people because they had not say hello to me years ago. No writer would have the courage to write *I am sorry for never saying hello to you when we were in the same room for five years*, but maybe in its own way it says better than anything else how awful and degrading that kind of Communism was. I could not name even one of the many great absurdist writers who would put something similar in a play, and this not a criticism of them, it is just that this apology cannot have any real existence because it deals with a past that now makes *no sense* of any kind whatsoever. I had originally come to Bucharest by train from Vienna, and the senior Hungarian police officer who came on board at the border with Austria in his high, highly polished cavalry jackboots might have been auditioning for a part in a silent camp production by Brecht and Weill in a make-believe 1934, but here he was in all the splendour of a bad dream if you had the *wrong* passport or a problem with your visa. I also learned very quickly that the Irish myths about Irishness being an international currency did not operate in Eastern Europe. Ireland then, because of an accident of random morphology, could morph morganatically with Holland and Iceland and with every other place deemed of little or no importance, which shared *-land* as a suffix. We had no credit in Communist Eastern Europe for beginning the riot against colonialism in the Easter Rising in 1916, or for anything else (this ideology had no confidence in itself and would be afraid of any such comparison in case it might belittle its historical absolutism). Our so-called absurd writing was also in English and was especially totemic in some of the so-called Communist countries which had been annexed by Russia. Beckett had been smuggled into Romania and was canonised while he was still alive, but he wrote in French and only sometimes in English; actor friends were the only ones who had no problems with Irish identity, and I think this was because they could see that our writing could sometimes be nuanced and different, and of course, they loved being able to play absurdity when also had to live it every day as well. But, in general, if we existed at all, we were an appendage of London and did not exist in any singular sense, and even then this was only among the elite. It is easy to forget that this was also before travel became accessible to everyone in many different parts of Western Europe and when very few people knew anything in detail about other countries or the exact positions places occupied relatively to each other in the map. For many people now in Ireland and Britain, Scandinavia and Eastern Europe are still the *over there* countries.

(Note: The last few sentences now need serious amendment, but ignorance about where certain countries etc. are, can still be quite prevalent even in the European Union).

A political system of governance defines itself by its institutions and personnel in very important ways, and when the *Security Police* in Communist countries - the phrase *securitate* always seemed to be said in a special voice by friends - regard themselves as living in a sealed space independently of the world of public meaning, then there is something rotten in such a state. This is a very simple rule of thumb, but we need symptomatic indicators for the health of a state and society, and the attitude of those who work in the various areas of control of the citizenry in a country is never a bad place to start. In semiotic terms, the state tells us in multiple ways, what meanings they assign to us, and the Hungarian border police told me I was *trash* and did not have to be afforded minimal respect; police in most countries in the world live two lives and their public persona can sometimes easily indulge in quite random symbolic violence. The Catholic Church and the Irish state in tandem, also sometimes did the same when they told the children of Ireland, born and unborn, that they too were *trash,* as outlined elsewhere, in other essays. *Children of Ireland,* in its Irish or English form - even despite the exquisite five-syllable cadence in

English - was never part of our public language. *Women of Ireland* became a meme in the 1980s when the first woman President of Ireland *called it out* in a firm voice, but we are still waiting for someone to call out the *Children of Ireland*.

I remember one autumn in the early seventies when I was in Romania, the President triumphantly announced that the corn harvest was in and had broken all records. In the world where corn actually grows, there was still corn waiting to be brought in from the fields and the workers in one of the particularly large collective farms who had tried to bring in the remainder of the harvest were told to put it back. The *Great Leader* - titles in certain cultures and not only in secular contexts, can tell you very quickly that you are now in a very strange Caligula like land - had declared that the corn had all been harvested, and by their action, these collective *peasants* were contradicting the President himself. Local Party bosses were more sensible, they just told the hapless workers they were putting everyone in danger; by their action, the collective was contradicting the President himself, which was blasphemy of the absolute order. Contradiction of the *Lord and Master* could have very sombre consequences for the workers themselves and their families, including those yet to be born. Secular blasphemies of different kinds have always been known to have very toxic tentacles as we saw in the case of Cicero's assassination. His only crime, as English can say with a fine sarcastic twist, was to write the *Philippics* which called for the restoration of the Republic after the manner of Demosthenes, and the penalty for any such blasphemy was death. This Roman example was not your usual run of the mill heinous crime, any such proposal deemed to contradict reality was unadorned blasphemy of the highest order. There is irony of some mad perverse kind hovering in the wings that I was given intense training in Greek and Latin because of their role in Catholicism, when you realise there could also be no better preparation for the study of symbolic violence - we will not mention sexual perversity in an essay - and violence of every kind, including the cruel and grotesque.

(Note: It is only reading what I wrote more than twenty some years later that I realise that one of the added benefits of being introduced to Greece and Rome as a young teenager was that I implicitly accepted their histories as no different from modern history which I was also studying at the time - twenty-year old history was history in my way of seeing the world then, and two extra noughts did not change what history is - but that it was also introducing me surreptitiously to ideas, and ideas of the type which had stood the test of time. Studying very recent Irish history was sensibly excluded at the time because of contempo-rary party political resonance - my home town was riddled with party pris politics which had its origins in the fight for freedom and the civil war which had been in preparation from before independence and, by chance, all my best friends' fathers had also been on the side which rejected the new Ireland after inde-pendence - so my introduction to revolution as such, and also very bloody revolutionary violence, was the somewhat aristo-cratic *French variety in 1789* and its dramatic *guillotine*, which was a foreign one from a safe past. I put the two phrases in this last sentence in italics because they were part of the iconic language of the time which had a special existence of their own; they were not memes or anything else necessarily linked to remembrance).

In storybook terms, *The Emperor*, as Dali would call this particular Romanian leader satirically - and, *en passant*, Dali's sculptured moustaches would not have survived long in that Romania which regarded the most modest variation in male hair style as an absolute taboo which also resulted in me seeing my hair grow steadily and relentlessly in '60s style in the '70s - had decreed in a radical variation of *Cogito ergo sum*, that the harvest was all in. This kind of Communist thinking, however, did not have much time either for the more feeble *I think, therefore it is*, this was a new epistemology and ontology. *I say, therefore it is*, the harvest is in, and it is a record harvest. If the corn was all harvested and recorded, how can you say the impossible, that there is corn still lying in the fields waiting to rot. Meaning, and in this case the grand, overriding semiotic, imposed by the *Imperial Leader* and the system as a whole, determined what reality was, could be, and should be. This is the trilogy of fascism which defines what is, and any contrary notion even of the faintest, concocted variety, could take you into blasphemy and taboo, two very severe ideas which can harbour the gravest purpose and penalty, when united in tandem. I should say that I went to school in fascism when I was a teenager and did not begin using the term in the '60s which passed us by in Ireland, apart from the music which we listened to with religious intensity on Radio Luxembourg.

Any such ideational system which has the arrogance to declare the absolute semiotic lordship of *what is, what can be, and what should be,* is serious about exploiting semiotics to the full, and this was Romania's peculiar system's fourth decade in operation; it was also this particular leader's first decade in power and in the early 1970s he was already relaxing into his destiny and was very determined to mark his place in Romanian history. The wags among my theatrical friends would say his knowledge of history would not need one whole side of a very small page; they all, as you might expect, had a penchant for colourful language (which also introduced me to the very articulate world of obscene taboo in colourful and creative Romanian, but its gravity was somewhat lost on me because taboo in a foreign language learned after adolescence often loses much of its shock effect). With this kind of political ideology, a special power had been introduced into the world and one not always envisaged in the related scriptures of the three monotheistic religions and whose practice could never be accused of being shy about assigning meaning to the magician's anything and everything and whatever they wanted. Because such Communism was intensely preoccupied as an ideology with material minutiae - which is hardly surprising when Communism had its intellectual roots and its peculiar Germanic type lexis in so-called dialectical materialism - sometimes it seemed as if there was hardly anything outside its potential scope. It struck me after the first few months in that Romania in the early seventies - and it was ridiculously striking in a very particular way - that while the Catholicism of my upbringing could value poverty in the midst of plenty, and often in a very spiritual, human, and sometimes even in a very practical way, Communism took the mad hatter, absurd route. It valued plenty in the midst of a total abject poverty, and forced people to humiliate and degrade themselves in moral, spiritual ways, and also sometimes in physical ways that were beyond every vestige of human decency and dignity.* It was people I knew well and admired, many of them infinitely talented, in all kinds of ways, people I respected unconditionally, and who were often *better human beings* than me, in every sense. The wonderful thing about a very spiritual Catholic upbringing which sometimes ran parallel with the official triumphalism and pomp and ceremony in Ireland, was that it was easy to acknowledge that these friends and acquaintances could be much *better people* than I was [7].

*(Note: It is too depressing for me even all these years later when most of my friends are dead, to say anything more about these last thirteen words. When a very good friend said to me when Communism collapsed in the end of '89 that he had told everything the Security police had asked him about me, I told him that I had told them myself when a very senior member of the Security had asked to talk to me when I was in Romania).

What did these blasphemous stupid peasants expect the *Great Illusionist* to do, confess on television he had made a mistake, that the harvest was not finished, yet, or to make a complete ass of himself and say on television the harvest was even bigger than he had already said. This is a translation from memory of one of the declamatory rants an actor friend who was also the only actor I knew who had come from a very humble background. I remember arguing later, and sometimes rather heatedly, with a renowned American academic whose work I greatly admired in a number of quite different areas, that, fundamentally, *we all do the same thing all the time*, but that sometimes we do it with regard to different things, so that your absurd may be my reality, and vice versa, *ad infinitum*. I am more convinced of this than ever and would now suggest that all cultures and sub-cultures use the same semiotic tropes and follow the same primary semiotic patterns and principles, be this in personal relationships, or religion, or fashion. But the expression, verbal or non-verbal, may, of course, seem very different, especially in what might be sometimes regarded as totally different cultures, on the surface. Christ too, as you might expect, knew His semiotics extremely well, and was very partial in his moral teaching to the metaphor of surface and what is hiding underneath the surface.

In similar vein, Aristotle's *substance and accident* model is also very useful in semiotics, and not only when meaning is camouflaged. This American scholar mentioned above, belonged on the radical side of the ideological road, as I still do now and in a much more anarchist fashion because of semiotics, but, in principle, he did not like echo or mirror-models - they can make us all uncomfortable, and much worse, when even thinking about looking below the surface may be impossible, in practice - and, in particular, he did not like the *we all do the same things semiotically* part. Sometimes I do not like it very much either, but he had not had the *good and bad fortune* to have had like I did, such an intimate experience as an enthusiastic very young insider of a political, religious absolutist system which was Irish Catholicism then in the 1950s, and which was also capable of the most terrible cruelty and violence, and not just the symbolic kind.* My education and training in Ireland also meant that I sometimes worked implicitly with quite different models to look at society. My American colleague also did not have the insider, outsider experience of an absolute political system (as I had had in Romania for five years) which exercised total control and whose cruelty and violence could also sometimes be completely different in kind, from anything in my Irish Catholic experience. Chicago was pre-kindergarten, in comparison

*(Note: There are now stories coming out of the barbaric cruelty visited on those in Ireland who violated the rules and which includes babies who were also deemed objectively sinful and repugnant and not entitled to any minimal decency. There are also stories coming out now of how ordinary people broke all the rules in the name of Christian decency and conducted services themselves in their own way in Kerry, for example, for those who had died but who were not deemed fit for Christian burial. I am not the least surprised it was in Kerry, but I am sure they were not alone in their brave, Christ like decency. I could never imagine doing any such thing in the dead of night when I was growing up. Humiliating myself by saying this now is a special kind of awful, but I am too old to pretend otherwise. I seem to lose some of my ability to pretend with age, as if there is no point any longer pretending what I could never have been).

Nor did he seem to be able to cross over cognitively and allow himself to understand that the often gratuitous, endless cruelty of such Communism made *no sense* of any possible kind and could not, when nonsense and violence of the most awful and degrading kind was often the common currency in all such Communist nations or satellites: this *no sense*, of course, played a very important role in everyone's life. He seemed to think their *no sense* was a few grades below our everyday *no sense* and was uncomfortable with me saying it was different in kind, and not just relatively. He was still on the first sentence of the first paragraph of the first page of the book which deals with theory, and was blinded by external and superficial differences. He had not turned all the *pages* and had not come to the ones which *talk hard talk* about the semiotic reality of a society where everything is potentially precarious for everyone except a tiny number of people who live in the region of the apex of power, but who also never know when *the end is nigh* for themselves. Which itself also introduced *precarious* into their Communist world too and also paranoia about their own future, and not just their long term future, but which - I am sure - many thought could not happen to them, if only because they would make sure it never could (which is a wonderful example of what human optimism can be despite all the evidence to the contrary, but which has also been the driving force of a lot of behaviour in many types of lives, in lots of very different contexts). I do not find it very flattering either that I was a religious fascist of the Irish variety for some years, albeit of the kind which also believed absolutely and genuinely in goodness and equality, and hell and damnation as well for good measure and balance, but then I had not yet turned to the page where other realities begin to speak. But maybe the no sense of that Communism was not difficult for me to understand because I had been weaned, without any trauma of any kind, in ideas that were fantastic and eschatological, and which had no bar either too high or too low. And because I was explicitly conscious of what blasphemy means and can mean, in the context of religion from my earlier life, I now recognized it again in its secular manifestation, which was on any scale, crude and inanely simple when it often just meant *it is what I say it is.*

But I am now much more critical of this colleagues's attitude. He was wrong, and if we even dream, in our happy daydreams, that any society is not capable of being Nazi Germany and Soviet Russia, given certain circumstances, and that, similarly, every society is not capable of producing multiple *Stalins* and *Hitlers*, then we need help to (be able to) think like humans; but again, no accusations of cynicism etc. accepted, because it has no place cognitively or emotionally, in my life and way of thinking, and never had. To know when dreams like that are just happy nonsense and sometimes dangerous nonsense is part of intellectual development and maturity in any society. If some of our anthropologists, for example, had been more attentive to their own cultures and more open and objectively honest about them, and been more aware of how meaning is assigned *at home*, as it were, they would have discovered that the principles of the unity of mankind are all listed on the first page. That ultimately, we are one because we assign meaning in distinctively and significantly similar ways, when we are not doing this in exactly the same ways, despite the often apparent differences in expression, in all of the ways we use to communicate. If we sometimes, at least, do not see, and are not explicitly conscious of the roots of meaning in our own society, we are blinkered; and if we have to go on an intellectually racist safari to what is grotesquely called an exotic culture, be it in the past or the present, to be able to see how meaning is assigned socially and culturally, including politically, we run the risk of making a complete ass of ourselves, and anyone and everything will make a complete fool of us as well. This is taboo land, and I must have read over this last sentence ten, twenty times, but as the lawyers used to say *stet*, it is going to stand. I am not changing anything, not because I am being stubborn or trailing my coat Irish style, which I can sometimes do with some aplomb. But is there anything more depressing at the end of twentieth century - the century when we seriously diced for the first time in history with variants of Armageddon - than educated people being surprised at what we do again and again, and when this is not enough, we do it again in a serial, vicious cycle.

These last sentences are from a member of a tribe that was hunted for centuries. The first reported safari some eight hundred years ago in the lands now known in English as Ireland, was by tribes which could hardly have been considered superior on any contemporary criteria, if I could use the very English *could hardly* touch of sarcasm; but their descendants would later go on safari to places that were unknown in the twelve hundreds when conquest and domination far from home became a peculiar type of group compulsive behaviour (which can sometimes be very bad news for other groups). At the time, those regarded and treated as the natives in my homeland even dismissed the invading colonials as boors - in poetry too, which, at the time, was a waste of sarcasm if anything ever was, and not just because it was written in Irish - and a variety of pejorative equivalents which are embedded in the deep structures of Irish culture, if I might be permitted to indulge just a little in silly racism.* In a variety of publications which have a particular semiotic interest, I have suggested that it is a pity that it has not been properly recognized that anthropology type writing has a history that goes back centuries before anthropology became an established driving force some two centuries ago in that genera-tion of *denkkollektiv*. Ludwik Fleck's used this striking phrase *thought collective* to refer to ways of thinking, thought patterns, thinking styles, Carol Dweck could use the clever metaphor *mindsets*, and I am borrowing from both scholars to refer to peculiar studies carried out in the nineteenth and twentieth centuries by people from the colonizing tribes who often followed on behind commercial thievery and exploitation and occupation. And enslavement of various brutal kinds, and also absolute destruction, including the mass slaughter of peoples in particular areas. Those engaged then in what might now usually be called cultural research, would often not be able to be conversant in any real sense with the people where they were doing research because they did not have absolute, first language competence in the languages and dialectal variations of those they observed and *studied*. Such competence is the initial *sine qua non* and those who wrote about Ireland some seven centuries previously - and also, for example, some of the American anthropologists who wrote about Ireland just half a century ago - did not have any such competence. There is no faux polite *did not seem to have*, and those who wrote more recently did not seem to know that the English used where they were doing research in the West of Ireland, for example, might be very different from their own English. I would also have been very wary, if I were using Irish or English, because I would know very well that we like to play games with outsiders, and that I would might also be regarded as an outsider outside my own parish, as it were. I will quietly pass over the sometime trend in American anthropology to become the *handmaiden* of the government in the context of World War II and in the post-war period, including in the Communist regions of Europe, where I sometimes met them with academic and familial cover in various places in Romania.

*(Note: My identity as Irish has always been deeply rooted in my own people, in the people in the town where I grew up, in the county, and later in the country as a whole. It has always from very early on included poetry and song - including singing the very distinctive, old style in Irish where certain categories of fricative consonant are distinctively lengthened, for example -

and writing of every kind, in Irish and English, in a completely natural way. The scholarly interest in the writing came some time later which I now think was also an advantage).

The claim I am making for the semiotic basis of universality is a simple, basic hypothesis and satisfies, for example, the critical criterion of making the smallest number of assumptions, and this is just one. The history of the Western world is littered with such hollow appeals, but how else could it be, how could it be any different, how could we not assign meaning in general and sometimes very specific, universal ways, unless, again ominously, you work with a very active assumption that we are *missing* something and are somehow not fully human, and that we do not all share a common *humaness* which is the foundation of ways of thinking which spawn phenomena such as racism and sexism and *childism*, and worse, much worse; you might assume I know there are important strands of difference, which is also happening now with diverse patterns and threads of evolution, and also rates of change. But that last part is only the general argument, the argument from the particular, a multiple set of particulars, is the empirical argument. And I feel very safe making the empirical argument, that in many areas of life, we, from the very different cultures of the world, often substantively assign meaning in the same and similar ways, despite the seemingly different external expressions of our individual and peculiar cultures, including what one group makes explicit and another implicit.* We are often dazzled and easily trapped by external expression, by appearances, especially when the representation is not just exotic - the poor word is now creaking under the infinite meanings it has to carry - but which is something we are not used to and which may be counter to peculiar cultural expectations which we adopt very early in life and in an infinite number of fields. Blasphemy, for example, is a cultural universal, in religious and secular contexts, and it exists in all our lives and is not confined to religion. It belonged, for example, in a very intense, particular way to Ireland from the 1920s to the end of the 1970s, to Iran between 1977 and 1997, to pick twenty years at random, and to the Soviet Union in the time of Stalin and China in the time of Mao.

*Of course account has to be taken when, over time, a peculiar religion, for example, or a wide-ranging ideology, may successfully change particular patterns of observable behaviour. When it is said above about assigning meaning in the same and similar ways, this accommodates an extremely wide variation in expression, which is often extremely limited because language itself sometimes is in many different contexts, and also because we erect barriers, implicitly and explicitly. One of the sometime effects of aging is that some people *forget* some of the endless rules of what cannot be said in public which cause excruciating embarrassment to loved ones in public contexts and sometimes painful hurt to the person saying something which carries a taboo of various kinds; the taboo can sometimes be so absolute it has no place in consciousness, so that hearing a loved use a certain expression may also cause terrible hurt when intimate details about the family are made explicit and which may also be unknown to the children and friends.

When anthropology decided to study other cultures as part of its professional training, it committed multiple forms of violence and also sometimes made a fool of itself as well - our English adopted the special term *gom* for a fool who keeps insisting on being outstandingly stupid - which affected both theory and practice. The risk of racism was increased exponentially when it concentrated on what seemed, superficially, strange and bizarre external expressions of culture which did not usually conform to the customs and practices of outsiders. The *National Geographic*, for example, which targeted the educated elite is a classic example of extremely clever marketing but it was also perfectly exploitive at a time when such lustrous *porn* was not readily available or even remotely respectable. It began to publish some hundred years ago brilliantly written, anthropology type essays which were sometimes illustrated by photographs in glorious colour of bare-breasted Black African women and also sometimes pubescent young Black girls. This type of representation was regarded at the same time in France at the exclusive *high artistic end* of pornography when the pictures were of white women, and at the extreme end of deviancy when it featured young girls. Today, publishing such pictures of eleven and twelve year-old girls of any ethnic type would be regarded as paedophilic pornography and can attract a criminal charge of indecency in some countries, but not always anymore in practice, in the so-called West.

In the last two decades, some in the mainstream print media still coyly play with partial pictures of younger women's breasts almost as *side-shows* and *haute couture* often does the same, if only to flaunt its artistic, *au courant*, voguish credentials. Some of the mainstream, both high and low, often plays teasingly with this, but does not feature *full* nakedness, yet, but when pubescent girls and boys are used in advertising and merchandising, including gigantic billboards, there may be posed sexualization and manipulation of images in the process of the development of photographs, and also the use of quasi-diaphanous and gossamer type material, and also sometimes *double entendre* in the text. Full nakedness can now even be touted as a signal of liberation and artistic freedom but nobody has ever bothered to tell me how a woman's public nakedness is an archetypal symbol of human liberation. I said once in a lecture that it might be noted that explicit male nakedness was more popular in classical statuary etc., but I think the semiotic comparison got lost somewhere *in the translation* and the very quiet polite titter which never reached laughter pitch. The diaphanous type portrayal which is particularly popular now, plays complex games with expression, pornography and *secular blasphemy*, and would not have been regarded as pornography of any note, especially in the portrayal of male sacred figures in certain Christian cultures in our own era, while the general tendency at the same time, was to attach more and *cover* in the portrayal of female figures so that sometimes there was only a partial representation of the face.

(Note: Those who exploited nakedness for commercial reasons have now finally won the day. Some people are now saying nothing in public, because they are afraid they would be laughed at in many circles in Europe as atavistic and a throwback to the dark days of sometime or other; their knowledge of history and dates is often a little challenged. The famous multicultural America, however, can still be depended upon to give popular examples of every view, which sometimes attract epithets such as atavistic and much, much worse, in Europe, but which themselves may also be very useful as examples when talking about semiotics in countries which give the lie to equating nationality with cultural homogeneity of even the remotest kind, in the context of attitudes to values, for example, except in circumstances when there is a perception of threat or even criticism, from outside).

But the risk of discrimination in anthropology on the basis of *colour* mentioned above, should hardly be a surprise when anthropology itself has often been open to question. Semiotic interest was always a common feature in the earliest manuscripts and in cave type drawings and very early statuary as well; look, for example, at the lineage of just body adornment alone in every culture in the world and the portrayal of such adornment which should hardly be a surprise when the body is ultimately, and at the beginning and at the end, all we have to show. But the intellectual driving force of some of the early studies and writings in anthropology in the closing third of the nineteenth century has often been objectively suspect; if I were to give a relevant example from today, male students are often surprised and shocked that underlying all kind of patterns of thinking and behaviour are ideas and values which objectively define women as inferior, in principle. I am not saying that the ideational driving force of early anthropology was on the level of explicit intention, One of the most difficult factors in the assessment of and writing about, violence, and obviously blasphemy as well, is the introduction of the idea of implicit intention, if only because it puts the discussion on another, very different and sometimes acrimonious and also very difficult, often impossible, level, in terms of access. But this is nothing new. Descriptions of cultural habits which were intended to give a factual impression, and which used whatever contemporary means were available, including illustrations of the sometime very dramatic and lurid variety, were used in my own island from the early periods of colonization, from the thirteenth century onwards. But what happened in the closing decades on the nineteenth century could sometimes be very different. This was the period in Europe when there was rapid growth in the science of genetics, including, importantly, its widespread popularisation for educated readers, which would also play an important role in the various forms of *genocidal type blasphemies* in the first forty to fifty years of the twentieth century. I mark those three words towards the end of this last sentence, because I felt myself gripping my thumb between my index and middle finger which is a habit I have had since I began writing about violence when an aspect of violence of the kind inflicted and to be inflicted on, Jews *weighs heavily*. I do not know how to describe what sometimes happens to me physically other than that two word cliché.

(Note: Magazine type publications since the late nineteenth

century, have also used photographs of African male adults, often tattooed, in codpiece variations, and sometimes boys fully naked. The mainstream media, including giant billboards, has now also come full circle - which itself gives a lesson in progress - and can also feature faux codpieced, heavily tattooed, intensely photo shopped, adult white males, and pubescent virginal young males, of every ethnicity, but especially, in the case of white subjects, those who are pale, white and blond, but there are no codpieces, no tattoos, only sheer without being fully transparent briefs. Advertising is a cross between a cuckoo and a magpie, it steals from everywhere and exploits semiotics and how we assign meaning like no other, including cuckolding, but it brilliantly plays with the rules as well - which is why I always exploit advertisements in class - and In some instances, it may also be for good or evil as the old cliché used to say, and be an instrument for driving significant change of meaning as well, which can be an attractive seminar in semiotics, including when the meanings touted, reek of symbolic violence, and not just against the usual suspects, children and women, but grown men as well.

Public relations and advertising is the clichéd Wild West but with far fewer manners. It will sometimes even ransack the Holy Bible and turn the message on its head for its own semiotic ends. Woe unto them that call evil good, and good evil; that put darkness for light, and light for darkness; that put bitter for sweet, and sweet for bitter never bothers them. Nothing does. Artists and writers have always done this of course, and not only for filthy lucre's sake either, an expression which is not common currency anymore, and a terrible linguistic loss. I loved Filthy lucre and whited sepulchre and all their cousins when I was growing up. I loved the sound of them but they also provided prototype patterns for using language creatively to insult my friends. I learned very early in life that meaning is sometimes its use when language is used, for example, as generic offense and derision. My home town was a Harvard, Oxford and Sorbonne in small, and I learned aspects of semiotics which I can hardly express now, as you can see in this last sentence).

If we, all of us, often find it difficult and sometimes impossible to see or to be honest about, not to mention understand, the underlying meanings in our own cultures, what hope do we have when it is shrouded in *curious and weird* external behaviour. But the rot often lies in the Greek roots of our intellectual culture when theories of meaning were devised and which were often divisive and elitist in the deepest and widest possible sense of the two terms, and also deductive and dictatorial, to boot. In Ireland, outsiders, and not just the English and the Americans, used to say that we tell strangers who ask for directions out in the countryside where I come from, *If I were you, I wouldn't start from here.* We have taken a lot of wrong roads by following the directions for studying meaning on old Greek maps sketched on papyrus, and by indiscriminately adopting without intellectual and ethical due care, terms from Latin such as *natura* - which would give us natural and unnatural etc. - and *norma* - which would give us norm, normal, sub- and abnormal etc. - and *sanus, insanus* - which would give us healthy-sane, and pathological-insane etc. - to list just a few from what sometimes seems an unlimited basket of terms. It is an awful thing to think that a word can wreak endless violence and that some of these words have been doing their worst for millennia. My people have also used complex poetic forms to do this *awful thing* for centuries also, and it is interesting to note that while the Irish exploited poetic art to express violence, many other cultures used visual art. But maybe even this will give more boring energy to the racist minded who used to say the Irish are visually challenged.

I WAS lucky to have had two quite different ideological experiences when I was growing up which might have been peculiar in some ways to Ireland. I was well trained in the principles of religious rule in my Catholic education and we also believed in a sometime parallel way that we would all live forever with God in Heaven. All is the word to note here because it never caused any friction which is itself a wonderful example of how clever a culture can be. In our real belief system, as mentioned elsewhere, we ordinary people would not go to Hell, which was reserved for the kind of ogres mentioned just below, but, of course, you might like to make your own list, even if it is only a game and you do not believe in an afterlife as such. Studying Greek and Latin intensely for five years in school also opened up two other, very different worlds, with the latter sometimes seeming to veer on a very random, bizarre curve, including the quite mad, as this has usually been understood in all eras and most cultures. Learning the two classical languages became a memory game - I have a slightly freakish memory which I never equated with intelligence, which was very sensible and saved me endless potential nonsense about myself - and being locked up, as it were, in boarding school meant I had little else to do during the long hours of compulsory study except to study and read Greek and Latin which I liked from the outset as a kind of game. I still use the two languages in quite a natural way, whenever I need them for research or fun.* Such a variety of exposure to completely different systems would later turn out to have been very useful especially when compared with the ultra-crude tactics of the regimes in Russia, Germany, China etc. in the twentieth century, whose leaders - Stalin, Hitler, Mao, Kim il-sung, Pol Pot, is the short list - were more a throwback to crude warlords and despots such as Alexander the Great, Genghis

Khan and Suleiman, than the very clever ideological overlords we had in Ireland. We have a special term - *cute* - in Cork English for someone who cleverly manipulates others in their own very selfish interests (it is always followed by a five letter noun which could not appear in an essay such as this). I might be tempted to scorn the boorishness of the former group above, with their sadism masquerading as a moral ideology, if they had not also murdered countless millions of *their own people*, which is a sacred expression in Irish culture. It was a blunt, philistine semiotic which worked under the cover of a discordant morality you would not find in any sort of a half decent story told hesitantly and marked by frequent gasps for more oxygen by a ten year-old reading her first attempt at a grotesque horror story out loud.

*(Note: Knowing any Latin or Greek now is often taken as a peculiar mark of intelligence and not just learning, but no one should disabuse anyone of this notion if by reason of strength they be fourscore years as the sacred song says. I should also mention that just because I did not mention above in this last paragraph, what was done in Africa by European overlords such as the Leopolds and their foreign lackeys, this does not mean that I do not know and sometimes in too much awful detail, what was done in Africa in the nineteenth century, to mention just one period and one continent (and incidentally, also in China). And I just caught myself catching my thumb again between my two fingers because one of the many bonfires bequeathed by colonialism in Africa has flared up again for the umpteenth time, and some people are still writing, if not as brazenly as before, that such people are not suitable for self-rule (itself a fairly bizarre phrase). Some of those talking like this are now even Irish, which beggars belief if you know anything about what was done to our people. Bur also, and almost equally important, how they were regarded in various parts of England

and Scotland and in America where the Irish had flocked in their hundreds of thousands in the hundred years after the famines in the mid-nineteenth century and which has scarred us like nothing else has ever done, through to the end of the second decade of the third millennium where we are now. There is now a group of lest we forget, famine sculptures near one of the bridges on the banks of the Liffey and I hate the sight of them with a deep, visceral hatred. I do not need a sculpture to remember that many who died in the famine sacrificed themselves, so that their children could live).

And, in a similar way, having immersed myself for years in research on the multifarious identities assigned and imposed in an extensive variety of ways including legal charge, for seven and eight centuries on my own people, I have hunter's instinct for spotting ideas and models implicitly or explicitly designed to be vicious or tyrannical or elitist, or all three acting sadistically and brutally in tandem, as they can sometimes do. It is an important part of the thesis being proposed in all of these related essays on the semiotics of violence, that social meaning is and can only be a dictatorship, which can sometimes be humane or reasonably so, or just ruthless and cruel, or with significant levels of *no sense*, which human beings can find particularly difficult when it is imposed by force. But this is very different from the deductive systems mentioned earlier when a small number of educated, middle and upper middle class males posing as intellectuals in the areas of politics and economics, transposed and modified an eschatological notion from the Christian religion to this our everyday life in a particular place. In this secular protocol, a single leader emerges, a Messiah type figure of some kind - *un soverain pere, cui ge voldroit m'ame rendre* - who enters immediately from stage left or right, as this pair are used as ideological, political metaphor. A codicil always attached to this appropriation says that the role, and only role, of the eternal and ubiquitous everyone, is to give their collective soul to this sovereign, and who, in keeping faithfully to the script, must be a male figure. You might know that Christianity always issued grave warnings about selling your soul to the devil, but in this exchange, Heaven is now on this earth, in the future, an unspecified future. That this followed on from the collapse of a similarly sovereign ideology which was already in place and which was itself the source of its own inevitable social, political, and economic disintegration, was also part of the background story.

The ideas and language sometimes reflect the story of the monotheistic religions, but especially Catholicism, which is bizarre enough, given the explicit, intensely savage antipathy and blanket discrimination shown to religion, any religion, by regimes advocating different varieties of such Communism, but also the brutal savagery inflicted on millions of religious believers, and millions of others as well for no religious reason (because they might be self-sufficient farmers, for instance, or because those those doing the killing for the state had become brutalised and killing of this kind had become a habit). In other circumstances, the racist eurocentricity of the ideology and its origins would have ensured a never-ending barrage of accusations of imperialist lackeys and many other such lines from a multilingual hymnbook which featured cultural differences only in how insults were framed for those regarded as the collective enemy, and which could be everyone *not them*. This last phrase is one of those simple sounding phrases which tracks the general model *I am, You are not*, which is used in all these essays to focus on symbolic violence.*

*I have long tried to think how the Communism instituted by Lenin in Russia, and then Stalin - especially when the latter moved quickly to clear the stables after Lenin's death and dispatched Trotsky in the mid- to late '20s - and then also taken up later in many other very different cultures, is integrally bound with certain Christian notions developed in Europe and also even by intellectuals who might not have been or who might have trenchantly not been, Christian, and who might *not have a very rich and extensive reading of Christianity and its theology in various eras and traditions.* I am trying to move around delicately to avoid accusations of racism and religionism etc. which may also tactically change the focus of what is being said, and which would have no basis of any kind in reality or anything bordering on reality. Zhou Enlai might now tolerate a brief hearing about the mystical, transcendental, Christian roots of Marxism, but it is probably still much too early for Mao Zedong and probably Lenin too, but maybe not for Stalin if he were ever to visit his younger life again. There are all kinds of very dangerous traps hovering around the borders of any such discussion which involves European intellectual influence and dominance, as often happens in the realm of the ethnic and racial, and also of religion and blasphemy. But at the end of an essay on blasphemy, it is probably a little late to be worried about religious, ideological and political correctness, and all the other traps which may be lurking in the tall grasses.

THE ESSAY BEGAN QUITE some time ago when *I went out to the hazel wood, Because a fire was in my head,* but at this end stage, it might be no harm to think about the damage many of the accepted aspects of our Western culture are also doing to our lives compared with a religion which is now sometimes expected to take all the blame and which is also losing much of its public influence in many places in Europe, including Ireland. Many of the myths, for example, about romance and relation-ships have dramatically increased in force because of the radical changes in social and cultural structures and the increasing presence of the myths themselves in the ever expanding use of the Internet and their constant exploitation for commercial interests.* The myths about romance and relationships, for example, are now also causing all types of problems in all kinds of ways and in very different areas across a very wide age spectrum, which has never happened before in any extensive way. As we come into the third decade of the third millennium, females aged ten and fifty, for example, and every year in-between may be using the same media which is possibly the most radical aspect of this new world, and which may act as a contrary force to what is now also a major movement towards justice for women, including sexual equality. Many of these myths which sometimes go back into the fabled mists of history, have remained intact despite the critical attention they have long received in literature and theatre, and more recently in film and television and also sometimes in popular music which has recently even begun to give women a new and different voice as well. *Even* is said towards the end of this last sentence because it is a new phenomenon; in the past when women were given singing roles, *the book*, as is said in musical theatre, was purely male. We wrote the music, we wrote the lyrics and put what was thought to be women words into the mouths of real women, be they words of love or words of hurt done to women by their not very honourable lovers. The old myths of romance and relationships are still the untouchables in all the hustle and bustle of change in many areas of social communication as if they were still the new faith. They may be scorned sometimes in public - including in popular music - but they still leave a void *in the book* that can be filled by nothing else, which is as good an example as any of the power of everyday, often implicit, social meaning. It is an old dictatorship, but it has unlimited potential because it has always ensconced itself in every new form of communication that comes along, be it stories of all kinds, oral and written, or music, folk, popular and classical, and film, and now on the Internet as well where participation has fewer barriers and is potentially open to everyone.

*(Note: Some years ago after working very hard to understand any and every idea and to keep asking the magical child friendly question why, I decided, in the absence of another option, to be open with myself about what I do not and will never be able to, understand. Included in the latter was quantum talk but also much of the money talk which was beginning to dominate the media and public discourse of every kind more and more in the years just before and after the new millennium. As the new year began to lose its newness, I began to wonder if some of this money talk which had taken on a whole new life of its own was some kind of millennial cloud and that - maybe - nobody really understands the ever increasing volume of the verbiage and jargon in any real, absolute way. Even I could see that some of those wearing the label of experts were patently talking nonsense and had no idea what they were taking about. As a teacher you are paid to know also what nonsense is, but in the context of linguistics and semiotics, to ask does anybody understand is a very strange ask. I was always used to lots of people in quantum talk being modest about what they understood and did not understand, but when there was never the slightest hint of hesitation, I was becoming more and more suspicious about the cavalier money talk. Even a summary walk in linguistics and semiotics leaves you with humility as your only option, which I never said to first year students, in case they asked for their money back. Or, worse, if they began to question my knowledge of the two subjects. In fact, I now consider myself a bit of an expert in what we do not understand about natural language and meaning - I learned the hard way, every time I hit a brick wall - and about the arrogance of

thinking we will ever understand them in any complete way. Now I find it exciting to think that we too complicated for us to understand, that we are too complex and will never fully understand about human language and meaning. But people tell stories and sometimes stories take on a life of their own as happened in the early years of the new millennium. Why did we ever think that money would be any different, when history is full to the brim the way I liked a glass of milk when I was small, with stories which tell us that you can pay very dearly for thinking you understand money. But thinking you can understand things when maybe you never will, is the vanity and fun, in equal measure, of being human).

International communication is now generally in English and it would be very clever or very silly to predict what effects this will have in the world. Not only because English will change much faster and in all kinds of ways because of this ever increasing universal use, but also because a particular form of English will probably take the form of an ever changing dialectal variation. This will happen particularly when instant communication will feature what used to be referred to as sound bites, whose analogous form has now also made an appearance in writing, including in places of work when face to face communication may still have quite strict rules about polite discourse compared with writing. Especially when these are very brief messages written very quickly with no review, and not only when English is a second or third language.

BUT IF I ever come back, I will be able to continue writing about blasphemy where I left off; nothing much will have changed, it hardly ever does in the world of blasphemy. Blasphemy in every era has always used a restricted field of ideas and expression, but I always thought that I should not say this too often in class, in case someone might think that blasphemy was also too simple a subject for serious inquiry, or that I was somehow restricted. My sometime contrary culture is not a great help here either when it advises me that if everyone thought they were able to understand, my reputation as an intellectual would have a very short life, but you would also be advised to be very careful about using that word also. If people in Cork thought you were talking about yourself, it would not enhance your reputation in any positive way, so to speak; we have a lot of ways of talking about people who like to praise themselves in public and very few appear in writing. But we made a virtue of this as well. The ultimate skill in communications is how to praise yourself without anyone thinking this is what you are doing.

POSTCRIPT

I took out the following paragraph some time ago from *Endnote I,* in case too much background detail for *satanic verses* would take away from the semiotic thrust of the essay as a whole. But I am putting it back here in the main body of the text as a *Postscript,* because it gives a very peculiar example of blasphemy. But also in the hope that it may be of some help in trying to understand the religious anger which was fuelled as a result of the tripartite political interference, military invasion, and regime change, in parts of the Middle East and North Africa. First, in what were called Operations Desert Shield and Desert Storm, in a seven month period in 1990 and early '91, and then later, in the Iraq War from 2002 to 2011 (the latter is a formal convenience). The two *Operations* and the long *War* were initiated by an America which marshalled an alliance of white, European countries which would also have been generally regarded as Christian; such an alliance would have an obvious parallel with the *First Crusade* against Islam, which was initiated rather hauntingly, a millennium ago by Urban II, a Catholic Pope. There are a number of groups listed in the last sentence and this itself creates an impossible problem. I may also be listed, for example, as part of that *combatant congregation*, and, wherever we are, I and *all those deemed to belong to me*, if I can change a popular expression in our English a little, might be chosen as the target for any and every violence. I first wrote random violence but that is a lazy cliché, this is targeted violence. I am random, which is nobody's identity of choice in any such context. Everywhere is the battlefield when the person or group using such violence says it is, and everyone in that space is the enemy when the person etc. says they are. Which also means that if a Muslim child of three is killed, she is killed in the space which is defined as enemy space. Language cannot cope - this is not just *copes badly* - with human behaviour of this kind, but the problem is much worse than this. Trying to talk or write about it may itself lead us astray because in trying to capture such reality in language may itself create a different picture of reality than the one that happened or is happening or is intended.

This and the other paragraphs below, are being put back again here in a Postscript, because public discourse is now again off the leash in the West after a very short period of quiet, and has gone back to the brutal age of Swift and his detractors. An American President has suddenly appeared out of a world which nobody seems to have known existed and has torn up the pages of the book of polite discourse which Western Europe began to write during the final decades of the second millennium. What is also causing special difficulty now in this new age of international communications is that it seemed to have arrived overnight and is being driven by the leader of the free world who is also the leader of the greatest country on earth - this, ominously, of course, had always been the phrase du jour for every American for decades, including, for example, every talk show host from every shade of politics - and who has adopted public channels of particularly brief, instant communications written by himself, and often many times a day, and which are also sometimes inconsistent even when written almost in the same time frame. If I may step out of this peculiar essay for a minute, the only surprising thing is that a maverick President had not been seen for quite a long time in America. It happened now because the Republican Party made a whole series of errors in choosing their candidate and when an outlier slipped in, he used one of the new modes of very brief, instant communication to bypass the usual, very predictable media. America soon discovered there were tens of millions of Americans they did not know about and who had never identified with mainstream politics other than America is the greatest country in the world.

Satanic Verses, the title adopted by Salman Rushdie for his 1988 book had already had a certain history a very long time before this. There was text supposedly spoken by the Prophet Mohammed as part of the Koran and taken out later, because it was said to be the work of Satan who had tricked him into thinking that the prophecy was inspired by God. Those familiar with Christian texts will know the various stories of Satan's machinations, including the triple attempt to tempt Jesus Christ, the Son of God, when He spent forty days fasting in the desert after His baptism by John. The iconic story also says that He, the Son of God, the Second Person of the Holy Trinity, was also born of woman like you and me. It was said that these particular verses were excluded from the Holy Koran because the Holy Prophet was protected from error by *Ismah - infallibility, immunity* from sin - by God Himself. The story from *qissat al-gharaniq, The Story of the Cranes,* was included by the scholar and colonial officer Sir William Muir in his four-volume 1861 Life of Mahomet, and the English phrase *satanic verses,* seems to have originated then as well. A contemporary review of Muir's Life used a generic Latin phrase, *odium theologicum, theological disgust*, about such religious controversies - a phrase which also seems to have had a certain traction a couple of centuries before this, when *hard talk* was common talk in public debate if the religious and the political were in play, and especially when the two streams met - but a variety of such phrases goes back to the most extraordinarily bitter disputes about heresy and blasphemy in the first centuries of Christianity, and also in a variety of analogous forms in many different cultures and religions in different parts of the world, including from long before our era.

In an extended essay in 1990, for instance, I wrote in some detail about how Dean Swift talked of the toxic anger and loathing generated by such religious and theological disputes, and also by a similar type of analogous, often lethal stories which talk of certain peoples as being less than human. In another essay a few years later, I also wrote about how Maria Edgeworth regarded what she was writing in An Essay on Irish Bulls in 1802 as completing and complementing Swift's writing about such lethal, pernicious stories about who is human and what being human ultimately means. There was often an implicit overlap of the secular and the religious in such stories, and sometimes any such distinction would itself have been regarded in many quite different quarters, as blasphemy. Her writing was hardly ever figurative but it could always match that of her mentor for vicious sarcasm - the daughter of an ordained clergyman, however, would avoid his outrageous taboo and profanity - when she wrote about the symbolic violence which was targeted against the Irish. Edgeworth's Essay has the distinction of being the first scholarly work in book form, on symbolic violence and followed what would be regarded now as the usual scholarly practices: and of particular relevance in this essay, it featured a parallel, analogous reference to an earlier French book about the harm done to Islam and those of the

Muslim faith, by the type of symbolic violence used against the Catholic Irish, which was the primary focus of her research and analysis.

If I were to ask now if the *West* would have been different if Edgeworth's masterpiece on symbolic violence had become part of common knowledge in the world, that would be an annoying little boy born on a waterway which goes south to Spain and Africa and west to America trying to get *a word in* at a time when some of *the big people* in America are now shouting very loudly again, and sometimes in ways never seen or heard before. The island which lies to the East between ourselves and the mainland of Europe, is also tearing itself apart in every which way which has never happened before on this scale in England since the 1640s, and which has also happened in history to countries which once dominated whatever *much of the known world* meant at the time. It has been a consistent aspect of history that great powers sometimes suffer from quite severe catoptrophobia. They like the pictures they draw of themselves, but they also sometimes exhibit a severe allergy to mirrors, unless they drape a picture of themselves over the mirror. But we are now also in many different ways, in a new world. From the last decade of the second millennium in our era, *the big people* from the *West,* allowed *the dogs of war* onto the streets in the Near and Middle East and many places in North Africa, and now there is chaos in many places.

In the different religious worlds of Islam various factions of their *big people* are also fighting with each other again, and some of them have recruited some of *the big people* from the *West* in their internecine conflicts, including those who are *haram* and sometimes called some variant of the historical *Gog and Magog* or *foreign devils* in the very recent present, which gives some idea of how chaotic this chaos now is. Add *the big people* in the *West* who have aligned themselves with some of these religious factions within Islam and there is a new world disorder and a *big bad world*, as an old fairy tale used to call it when the poor hapless wolf sometimes had to represent the big bad world all alone. A special form of potential chaos, however, is now looming, because many of *the big people* in the West do not (know how to) talk religious talk and can now never learn because much of the competence might come not from formal teaching in the school or the family. It is said too often by the boring teacher in this essay on blasphemy, that if you do not come from a deeply cherished religious culture, you will have to make a superhuman effort to understand emotionally - and then probably fail as well, unless you have a very special rare gift - what religious ascription means to someone who is a religious believer, or you will have to try and find an analogy with ideas and values which are a real part of your own very personal, emotional life. Otherwise you will understand nothing much of any real import about blasphemy other than the ideational, which very often has no emotional resonance, and is no different from most social and historical commentary. Even in the original paragraph above in italics, I was reluctant to talk about *Ismah*, because concepts such as *divine inspiration,* are not accessible now to the vast majority in the West. Those who practice absolute literality with regard to the Bible are saying *It means what I say it means*, but my saying this will also be taken as an insult. There is nothing factional in this last sentence, this is hard, very ordinary semiotics, all of us practice absolute literality in various forms and contexts.

I have used the unusual, awkward, childlike phrase *the big people* above in the absence of any other, to talk of peculiar groups of people who regard themselves as special in certain contexts, and which may sometimes have widespread popular approval, and sometimes none. English has a motley collection of phrases such as the elite, the elect etc. but I have decided to stay with *the big people*, if only to include the international coterie of *big money* which has existed for millennia but now often operates secretly, independently of national ties, and which may be confined to one generation, be it an individual or group, and is not accountable in any usual sense, including internationally (although the Corkman in me also wants to jump in and say there was never much of the *accountable* on view whenever the big people went *on the warpath* and engaged in *smash and grab*). The phrase can apply to religious cultures as well, where belief extends *beyond ordinary life*, and where *the big people* also have a significant eschatological dimension in some contexts, as Popes and Bishops had in Ireland from the 1850s into the early 1980s; there may also often be absolutely hostility and a history of extreme violence between *the big people* within a particular religion and between peculiar denominations of this religion, including the ultimate claim of having divine authority on earth.

[1] THIS INDIAN WRITER OF MUSLIM ORIGIN WAS LIVING IN England, writes in English and famously became the subject of a *fatwa*: nobody at the time that this was to be the beginning of various Islamic groups regarding Europe and what was deemed to be the *West* as part of their sphere of interest and concern. The chief religious authority in Iran issued a public ruling which deemed the writer guilty of blasphemy and solemnly declared that it would be a moral and religious act if any Muslim were to kill him. There was also a large monetary reward, equivalent to multiple lifetime incomes in most countries in the world but this would probably not have been given to those who are not Muslims. The particular Ayatollah who made the ruling was also the Supreme Leader in Iran and wanted to assert his dominance in the Shia world - Shia constitutes some fifteen per cent and Sunni more than eighty percent, of Muslims - but this also afforded him the opportunity to mark his authority in the Muslim world as a whole. This meant, for instance, that the Sunni world and the eleven century old renowned Al-Azhar Centre of Islamic theology in Cairo, was now seen to be following the very public Shia lead which could

itself cause disquiet in many Sunni jurisdictions. This particular *fatwa* now seems to be somewhat in abeyance in these two major persuasions for all kinds of reasons, but as sometimes happens in religions and even other types of secular belief systems as well - state Communism insists on being a prominent example - not making certain decisions explicit means that certain aspects of change do not have to be explained. Islamic clerics in Iran and elsewhere, however, may reiterate the continued existence of the *fatwa* for devout religious reasons or to position themselves politically within Iran or in Islamic theocracy in general.

P.S. You might know - and now it is all the more relevant to know because of the related implosions in the wider Muslim world and in many parts of the wider European and Western worlds - it was Muslim masters of scholarship at the end of the first millennium of our era who mediated the primary concepts and patterns of Greek thinking which became our ways of thinking. The polymath and scholar, Abū Alī al-Ḥusayn ibn Abd Allāh ibn Sīnā who is known outside the Arabic world by his Latinate name Avicenna from the region of Bukhara in what was then Persia, and who died, Peace be with him, in Hamadan, Iran, was one of the most important. *There is no real knowledge, and no knowledge worthy of the name, unless the causes are known*, and this and countless other essays and studies have been guided by this same principle. Avicenna was the first Muslim writer I had ever read, and it was a happy chance that his writing matches his absolute genius, even in translation. For most people in the *West*, including politicians and even the majority of highly educated intellectuals, religious talk was *a foreign country far away* so the religious edict and the bitter factionalism within Islam was generally not understood, and *primitive* and all the other old poisoned darts came back into prominence again. I was the last generation in Ireland who knew a lot about this kind of language, however, because it was used about us all the time by certain *parties* in England and their *cousins* in America which, unfortunately for the Irish, could sometime include sections of the prestige and mainstream media, and certain strands of popular culture as well.

(Note: The first paragraph of this Note which was written more than twenty years ago, is now part of history. All of the usual authorities in Islam have been blindsided by the emergence of the Islamic State which advocated and established itself as The Caliphate which declared itself the Supreme Authority and which regularly issues a fatwa, including recently, the killing of the new born deemed to have certain defects. The Shia world mentioned in the first paragraph of this Note above, has been particularly caught unaware by IS, which is a Wahhabi variant of Sunni Islam usually associated with Saudi Arabia, but the Sunni worlds which are accused of compromise and even betrayal, have also been impacted by this new group which sometimes uses language marked as sacred and iconic and of historical provenance. In the case of IS, whatever language they use is regarded as having exclusive, emblematic self-reference. Accusations of ideational betrayal and heresy have always been regularly found in religions other than the monotheistic ones as well and our secular worlds are all liberally tagged with signature markers too, even in worlds not generally deemed as having any special status, not to mention any standing of the absolute kind. In the different countries where I have worked and which also included very different political and religious cultures - and not just those which have absolute rules about what is not to be said - I have often failed abysmally to explain in any adequate sense, that some absolutes of the secular variety may also often assume the same level of supreme status as some religions or denominations of religion. The

failure is mine, but if I could now write as I would have sometimes talked when I was eighteen, Excuse me, please, but absolutes are called absolute because they are absolute, if I thought
they were trying to bamboozle me with words. Regarded as
might have been more properly inserted in brackets between are
and absolute, but including it would have ruined the pretentious
bite. My West Cork accent with its sometime crazy mix of high-
rise and flat patterns of intonation, would have also facilitated a
particularly dramatic emphasis).

Some will condemn Islam for having a system which
decrees that a sanction imposed by a mere human may not be
able to be lifted because it is said to be a divine sanction. Those
who suggest that men - it is always men - assuming the power of
God in this way to punish and kill people in this life is itself
blasphemous, should know that it is a semiotic strategy shared
by the two monotheistic religions which followed on from
Judaism, and especially Christianity, but also sometimes by
other religions and also what are referred to as cults. Some cults,
and not only in America, sometimes occupy a space which is
beyond criminal within the nation state where they operate, and
this sometimes in countries where the rule of law may also be
regarded as paramount. But, in general, it is naïve to express
surprise that there are people who are deemed or who deem
themselves, to be God's agents, to be the instruments through
which God acts on earth, to be in the place of God on this earth,
to be God, in practice. This was also, in one form or another,
documented in various, very early types of extant writings.
Some who also declare officially that someone, or some statement, or some action etc., to be a blasphemy or some such
cognate term - and this too has a very long history in many very
different languages and cultures - will usually also decree that
the punitive decree and sentence etc., once invoked can never

be retracted because it comes from god, their god, and is there-fore eternal. They may well also say that they have no right to repeal or abolish the sanction, whenever they say they cannot, but at other times they will insist they have this power, because they know the mind of god; the immutable stands, until it is changed, which is sailing very close to being a rather good candi-date to be considered as an example of a classic tautology, but not all my responsibility, this time.* It is the predictable result of certain groups operating a top down assignment of meaning which ordinary language may not easily be able to cope with, or cope with in any way, when language is made a hostage in this way. Language itself is also sometimes structured semantically, to do this as well, including in the most mundane contexts.

*This implicitly blames their god, but they can now reply that their god can do whatever he chooses, including changing his mind radically. But, predictably, accusations are avoided because they could not, in principle, have any validity.

Those who act like this serve as a convenient archetype of semiotic terrorists. They alone can decide, and often do so with absolute aplomb, when and how to assign this meaning or that meaning, including life or death, as the casual cliché menac-ingly puts it. I come from a culture where the term terrorist has itself been used and abused endlessly and constantly since the early 1970s - I was in a quandary about saying this in case someone thought it was *an Irish joke* - and the term is being used here for common or garden semiotic reasons, and not for effect. Any such group, religious or secular, is a semiotic phenomenon and construction, and is often explicitly conscious of this, and must be: it defines itself primarily by its insistence on the right to assign meaning in a whole variety of contexts determined by itself, and, sometimes, these contexts may be of an absolute fundamental kind. This can include saying any number of very diverse things such as a particular state's rule - be it a confessional state or a secular, fascist type dictatorship, or a nation state which regards itself as democratic etc., but which may regard itself as having the right of intervention in other states for all kinds of reasons and not just the various financial varieties - is not confined to its own borders. Or, in the context of a group, that meaning can be assigned differently to those who are members of the group, or, at least, to those who are the leadership of the group, than to those who are not members or leaders. Or that the group has the right to punish and kill etc., that is, when the *terrorist* group, for instance, is not also co-terminus with the state. But the claim to authority changes absolutely, in kind and not just in degree, when a group claims, in practice, that it thinks for god, speaks for god, acts as god. Their god changes form depending on what god is supposed to do in their name.

I have failed again, to avoid torturing the language in this last paragraph, but when behaviour and thinking twist and turn themselves inside out and upside down - and I wish the language had more than these two variants to be able to capture the full complexity of reality - the language has no hope of catching all the constantly changing nuances, and again, the blame for serpenticity is not all mine. When meaning becomes the primary driving force, language as is, may not be able to cope which is why some scientists may be prone to the dreaded *faux pas* if their linguistic ability falls short of their scientific competence or if they are using a second language when their knowledge of this languages is not sufficiently nuanced.. We are all infinitely creative, *homo creativus* is a tag I have favoured for a long time to try and catch our extraordinary talent *to make things up,* if I can use the wonderful expression used all the time by our parents when I was very young, as an accusation, but never unfortunately, as praise for creativity. We, all of us, including those with no formal education and also very young children, twist and turn and change meaning into every which shape, and language may lag behind, often notoriously, and not just in the case of children. It is often futile running around playing *catch-up*, as we sometimes must in the worlds of blasphemy, when absoluteness and the infinite capacity to spin and swivel in a vortex of change may be the default. This is why religious blasphemy was originally chosen to illustrate semiotics. Religion is often more manifest and overt, and honest, than the secular worlds in both institutional and personal contexts, if only because they are often securely encrypted to guarantee lack of transparency, but also because they are also sometimes camouflaged by blatant hypocrisy and dishonesty; but especially in the case of the personal, as we all know, and not only when we inadvertently break the multiple rules of what is not to be said in any explicit way.

It is also unfair to give examples here from Islam, because reams of background knowledge are needed, about the origins of Islam and differences in doctrine and practice in history and also between different factions, if there is to be any understanding on the part of those who come from outside this world; but also, this type of ideational explanation cannot guarantee even minimal emotional sensibility which may often be of absolute importance. The often fractious and sometimes violent relationship between the two major *denominations* within Islam - one a sometime aggressive minority, the other a sometime aggressive majority which claims dominance as of right - would be totally outside any kind of emotional understanding, if I were not Irish and brought up in the rigid and fractious religionism of Ireland in the 1940s and '50s; and if I had not experienced in all kinds of ways, the random hatred from various religious groups in Northern Ireland and the Republic of Ireland shouting at each other across the borders and airwaves. Which included especially, a group on the fundamentalist wing of Protestantism which had none of the restraint which might be found in the official, more genteel, Protestant *Church of Ireland* whose members were then the establishment north of the border, and in certain contexts south of the border as well, in the Republic.* But also if I had not become more and more aware from my teenage years onwards, that Irish and Catholic was not a happy chain of words in Britain, or in America in the '70s, even when I worked in the university in an American city where *Irish* was the dominant political force. When I began to accept, emotionally and intellectually, quite early in the research, that *my people* - and there was no equivocation in this, I was not given a choice, they were my people, whether I liked it or not - came to be defined centuries ago as not human, and therefore, not entitled to the most basic of human rights, that I was able to develop an initial framework for understanding symbolic violence.

*Our superiority was of the very easy natural kind. We had always been in authority, they had come on the scene much, much later, and as a consequence of not very moral behaviour in the case of our nearest neighbour which always negated anything they might say on their own behalf.

It is not just that human rights were denied to the Irish, whoever they were deemed to be, there was no question of accrediting human rights to *such people*, as the English of a certain class can say like no other. My particular young Irishness was one of easy and sometimes endless joy - and which has not changed one iota in half a century - and had no traces of nationalism or *betterism*, of any kind, which made the journey to accepting that my tribe was not regarded as human a painful one, and sometimes a desperately sad one. But the pain and sadness was vicarious, for them, for the people who were regarded like this, and treated accordingly; the real religious culture of my upbringing had a very simple, simple in the best sense, principle of equality, and this despite the parallel message of our peculiar hierarchical, religious aristocracy that we were also subjects, their subjects, which we also happily accepted. There was always also the utmost admiration that countless Irish people did not live in the semiotic cage the colonial masters had constructed for them and that they had campaigned endlessly and peacefully in the first decades of the nineteenth century in Ireland - my own part of the south of Ireland was particularly involved for some reason - and in the second half of that century in America, for representation and fundamental human rights. This could also include those who had not been allowed access to a literacy which some of their ancestors might have enjoyed centuries before this - in the context of writing and not just reading - as part of their normal life; but the people I am talking about often worked far and away beyond what is human to better themselves, in every sense, and not just materially, at home and abroad.

Going to America even in the mid-nineteenth century, for instance, was often no different from throwing the dice in a thick fog on the top of the mountain to decide which way to go down, and women and men risked everything to have a life, including their own lives and the lives of their young children, which is as good an example as any of contradiction in the real world. Everyone and everything had to be risked if you wanted to have any chance of a life human beings should have (and, of course, they knew this might be a life that was barely a life). And yes, I am honoured to be from these people, and this is honoured, not proud, and, as a good Catholic born in the faith, I would know very well the difference between pride and honour. And if you know a little of early American history and immigration, Irish and Catholic did not necessarily help your prospects in a context where the descendants of Irish immigrants from the northern counties and who were of Scottish Presbyterian lineage, shared political dominance with Scots and English colonists; the latter were always in the majority but predictably, as often happens in the case of minorities, the Irish not of Catholic background also had to couple religious ascription with national origin, to avoid any possibility of confessional miscegenation. As might be predicted, these Irish Presbyterians around the time of American independence were often particularly conscious that they were not just a different Irish, or a class apart, but, in practice, a different species, which hovered between literal and figurative, as often happens when this type of symbolic violence is in play. Even now, some two hundred and fifty years later, those who were of that peculiar Irish background make great play of their contribution to independent America in the latter half of the eighteenth century and to the subsequent framing of the first American constitution, while also referencing those who have occupied the White House from their caste. It would be a long, long time before the first Catholic would become President, he was number thirty nine - an American friend said the Irish were not even allowed to wait on the street outside the famous White House - and had served less than three years when he was assassinated in 1963.

But the journey to that world where being human was denied to my people was also a kind of pilgrimage to a secular semiotic universe which regards all such symbolic violence as belonging in worlds beyond where reason and logic could ever reside; and which are ridiculous and ludicrous etc., when viewed outside the context where they are designed and created, and where they often subsequently thrive. In my way of thinking, this was a script which might be written for theatre, it screamed *symbol land* and would have been far beyond what I knew as reality except for one peculiar factor. It was no different in practice from when we were eight, ten, twelve, and calling other ten to twelves names from an endless list which welcomed endless innovation and creativity which we had in abundance when it came to insulting each other in our chosen *you are stupid* games. We used every channel of communication long before I had any idea what channel means in this context, but maybe this was my first silent lesson in how important it is to be able to transfer the world from thr implicit into the explicit, if we are to see all its parts and understand it some kind of adequate way. The games were fun and helped us pass the time happily, but they also served as a peculiar form of temporary recidivism from the boredom which seemed to be imposed on us from everywhere. Without some such rite of passage in terms of religious, ethnic, racial experience, I do not see how there can be any appreciation of what is happening within Islam today but also in the wider world because of the sometime mayhem in Islam, including for me who lived through a similar story of an inter-group, inter-religious violence, but one which pales in comparison in all kinds of ways in terms of what absolute can mean with regard to how different forms of ultimate meaning are assigned and where *ultimate* can include end of life in ways which breach every way of thinking in their endless, often casual cruelty against any group which is defined as *not them*.* There is also the possibility that cultural understanding will be difficult as well, because the Islamic and Muslim story is intellectually complex and historically difficult, and sometimes conceptually *strange* and different to what is the life of the vast majority now in the West. *Strange* of every kind, can cause so much distress for children, and can also catch all of us unawares dramatically when we are far beyond our childhood and adolescence. But *strange* also because of a subconscious, cognitive type of block, including one which decides expressly or implicitly, that this, whatever the *this* may be, makes *no sense*, or worse, that this is not religion or even that it is a blasphemy against God and religion itself. There is also the recurring, often fallacious assumption that knowledge, whatever it is, brings understanding, and when it only creates prejudice or exacerbates the partiality and predisposition already in place, we may feel we now have nowhere to go.

*This is no longer the Irish, Jews, Catholics, this is whoever is not them. This is not a new concept, far from it, but it is now explicit, and is being communicated very clearly, and sometimes very dramatically, in verbal and non-verbal mode.

(Note: To add to the betterism comment just above. There was also no trace of inferiority, because my own Cork culture that I was born into, does not do statutory inferiority. We did not work with the assumption that others - no matter who they were - were in principle, better than us. If anyone at the back of the class is sniggering at this, you might resign yourself to never understanding identity, because identity lives primarily on the ground, as it were, and not in any assumed superior higher ground. My heart is not proud, Lord, my eyes are not haughty; I do not concern myself with great matters, or things too wonderful for me might be taken as the text of the day, every day, if you want to work in the goldmine that is identity; and to make sure that feet stay firmly fixed on the ground and eyes do not look too much in the clouds, because that is where those who assume superiority always fix their eyes. Secondly, even in Ireland which has recently and sometimes almost frantically moved on culturally to a somewhat post-religious phase, no emotional understanding is often a guarantee of a closed mind, which makes having a barely adequate understanding of some of what has been happening in Islam recently in many places extremely difficult, if not impossible, which is a very ominous thing to say.

There is also an additional problem for me because highly educated Muslims may say I do not really understand Islam or fractious Islam, and my answer is always the boring same, if I were to breach the rules of good manners. In Ireland we had more than seven centuries of fractious religion - as the youngest in the family, I would never say we are also the older brother religion - which was sometimes extremely violent as well and in all kinds of ways, and this provides a rather long period to study such a contrary and intractable religious phenomenon. And while it is predictable to say an outsider cannot really understand, this is often a protective gambit to not deal with what is said and something we all use in all kinds of circumstances, including with the self. It is a terrible thing when what is integral to your very identity becomes an embarrassment; the only thing I can say is that when the most abominable violence was being committed in my name in Ireland, I said very quietly that after the centuries of oppression my people suffered, I not only repudiate the gun now in Ireland, but much more importantly, I choose who speaks in my name which is the basis for the democracy my people articulated from the early 1800s. In many Islamic environments now, however, saying I repudiate the gun and I choose who speaks in my name would be a very dangerous way to live your life, and your family's life, and maybe the life of yout entire community as well).

[2] It seems, similarly, that those of us who worked for some time in Communist countries in Eastern Europe inside the system as visiting academics, for instance, but who were not *fifth columnists* or *fellow travelers* or some such, often suffer from the same syndrome. At staff meetings in the university in America after I had just left Communist Eastern Europe, I sometimes found myself still wondering who around the table would work voluntarily and enthusiastically for the security services if America was also Communist, who would be the *Party Secretary* cracking the whip in the faculty, and who would write the anonymous letters of denunciation, which was one of the most notorious means of control in such societies. The game is especially poignant if you have been able to be honest about what you would have done yourself, if you had been a citizen of such a country, if you accept, for example, and without any rancour, the fact that all kinds of people - including very dear friends, many of whom I still admire and respect absolutely - informed on you to the secret service, when there even seemed to be no immediate gain in volunteering such information. If they were asked they said what was needed because they did not want any negative comment about refusing to provide information in their ever bulging file (with all the potential consequences that could have for their parents, sisters, brothers etc. and not just for their own nuclear familiy, including their children's education).

I once said in a lecture on totalitarian systems such as that type of Communism, that bulging files on every citizen in the state, were an official form of *PCB*, *psychotic compulsive behaviour* on the level of the state, and also a symptom of a desperate, bordering on the neurotic, need to pretend everything was under control. I never fooled myself - my Irish

Catholic religion schooled me well about the stupidity of empty pride, a pride which lurks, at best, just below the surface in all of us, waiting to emerge - that I would behave any differently, if I were in their shoes, including reciting solemn odes to the *The Titan among Titans* and his consort, *The Genius of Science*, as my close friends had to do. I work with a general assumption in semiotics that in any area other than a number of aspects of pure theory, you can only do semiotics if you regard yourself, in principle, as no different from others, which is said out of absolute humility and sounds totally pompous at the same time, which sometimes may be the only proper mix in this kind of context. Advocating equality as the intellectual, semiotic default, can sometimes carry its own ultimate existential price, but I am absolutely easy with being, at the very best, no better than anyone else. It is as if I constantly reprise that fiercely democratic aspect - we are all equal - of my religious upbringing.

[3] THIS LAST part would be consonant with the very violent strand of Protestantism which preached doctrines based on a principle of arbitrary exclusion, a kind of lottery by birth, but in the context of traditional Catholic doctrine, this is crass blasphemy. I heard it first when I was a teenager and I still find it, in a strange kind of way, physically shocking. But the people who make such theological and doctrinal decisions and arbitrations, have given themselves, in principle, the right to assign any meaning they like, and to assign meaning any way they like, not just to whichever category they like, but also to whichever category they create, or nominate for this purpose. This is also the sometime crazy world - *everyone over 1 30 centimetres, with one blue eye and one brown eye, and who wears a chain on the left ankle* - comedians create for their audience, for a laugh and their

reward. This right to assign any meaning they like, to whoever they like, and however they like, is what gives those who preach doctrines of the arbitrary exclusion type, almighty power on earth. And why they are a kind of *tableaux vivants* and a living textbook for semiotics. The doctrine, for instance, mentioned in the first sentence, above, in this note, which says that some people are destined for eternal damnation just by being born, makes many of the worst forms of racism benign.

P.S I have a sometime habit of using very English phrases such as *not having a very healthy attitude to* violence, not because I do not know about the reality of the various forms of violence, including in history, but I use them sometimes unconsciously to avoid having to talk explicitly about violence with no limits).

[4] WE HAVE ALWAYS KNOWN about the Popes, but the murderous and sexual antics of certain Popes in the past never seemed to bother us in the least, which itself is hilarious in an absurd, disturbed kind of way. And all the more strange if you remember I was brought up under the regime of Pope Pius XII, the noted Canonist who we heard about all the time for some reason when I was growing up, as if he was managed by a publicist from Fifth Avenue. Homes had his picture in a gallery, a kind of reliquary of sacred icons, which would also feature the Virgin Mary in blue, and also Jesus Christ, our Saviour, with His Sacred Heart in red, on the outside of His clothes. The shrine might also have a small, permanent, electric red light. But in contrast, while Pius XII might have the premature status of a saint for us ordinary people in Ireland while he was still alive - I

was just finished the state school system when he died in 1958 -
I also remember the principal of my secondary school, himself a
Canon of the Catholic Church, telling us in class when I was
fifteen or sixteen about one of the Borgias, my memory says it
was Alexander the Sixth, going in solemn procession up the
aisle of St Peter's in Rome for his Papal inauguration, holding
the hands of his two *bastards*, a boy and a girl. We were
expected to laugh - I am not sure I did - but if I had said the *b*......
word, anywhere, in or out of class, I would have got a monu-
mental mauling from him, open palm, the full menu. My
mother might have thought our house was having a visit from
the devil himself. The word has never ever been in my portmanteau of colourful words, and even now, I think I would use the
Italian pronunciation which somehow takes away *the bad word*
aspect. He also told us this story apropos of nothing in a Greek
language class. Even Joyce at his most outrageous, would not
make up such a story, so it must be true.

Semiotics has indeed an impossible task in trying to figure
out how we construct and reconstruct our worlds of meaning,
and how we manipulate the concept of time, for example, in the
example just given about the Borgia Pope. That is badly put.
Semiotics does not have an impossible task, it is we will have the
difficulty if we do not start out with the assumption that there
are no boundaries and no limits to the complexities, in the
worlds of meaning we create, and not only when we want to
deceive ourselves and others. We design and construct them
and any system that aspires to capture our creation in the coils
of language is going to have an insoluble problem because many
of the meanings we create are not in the verbal world, which is
as it says, non-verbal. And, secondly, because the meanings in
large parts of the verbal world may sometimes, often, be
implicit, depending on circumstance. In addition, we are not

always explicitly conscious of the fact that expressing the meaning of the non-verbal world in verbal form may be impossible, or inadequate, at best, which is why we often choose the non-verbal - including physical violence - in contexts when the meaning is of great importance. Language is almost always inadequate, especially written language, which is why poetry exists, and spoken language as well, except, sometimes, in drama, including, more rarely, great oratory.

If I had voiced the slightest criticism of the contemporary Church, which I could not and would not have done, the thrashing I would have got from this particular priest would have not been the worst part. I would have been a pariah in the eyes of everyone. My family, including all of the vast extended family - I had twenty two aunts and uncles - my closest friends, all of my extended families' closest friends, all the neighbours, everyone in my home town, would have been aghast at the *scandal* I had committed. Religions of every kind have always regarded reality as blasphemy, when necessary, which is hardly surprising when it also says what reality is, at any given time. If those of you who are *outsiders* do not understand that blasphemy may also decide what reality is and that this is where its power lies then there can be no understanding of what it is, what it does and it can do. Blasphemy is a perfect case-study for semiotics because it decides what reality is, and in case anyone in the back of the class is harbouring a smirk, I am not saying this essay is perfect. Trying to write it has sometimes not been good for my poor bashed around ego and it sometimes seems like a dreadful mistake. If this essay had appeared in the early to mid-60s when I finished in university, there would have been deep worry about my psychological state among friends and family, which is the more interesting reaction semiotically, because it is this reaction which could enable the statement I had originally made, as *nothing less than the ravings of someone who is not properly balanced*: which, incidentally, has often proved to be a perfect protection against deviant ideas, and why it was always popular in Soviet Russia and similar types of governmental arrangements. The range of people who knew, would be confined to local circles which would be defined mostly by *perceived* social class, because - in a special Irish blend of could not and would not which was popular in the media at the time - blasphemous stories carried the highest level of taboo.

[5] I AM TALKING GENERALLY ABOUT monotheistic religions and denominations which have strict hierarchical power structures, including the cardinal power of truth; of deciding what is true, of assigning the additional meaning of true, as a value added to whatever they chose, a power which sometimes was, is, in practice and in theory, more important than the power of life and death. Other religions and cults can also, of course, betray similar characteristics, especially when they are in a fundamentalist phase, as can the *hard talk* secular ideologies, including many of the various types of Communism in Europe until the late 1980s and early 1990s, and which are still found elsewhere.

[6] I COULD HAVE SAID with more than a fair degree of accuracy what would constitute political, ideological, and cultural blasphemy in the university when I worked in Romania, but I would have no idea what would even take on the trappings of blasphemy for my students now in Ireland, other than forms of

gross unfairness, for instance, and paedophilia and extreme forms of physical cruelty in general. There are no religious or political *paper tigers* or *sacred cows*, or any other variety of animal, whatever the accompanying qualifier, with the result that virtually anything can be said now about religion and religious, and politics and politicians, but custom and practice has now also made saying anything positive in the political worlds something of a taboo. The latter, secular group come out the worst because *aren't they all the same* carries every negative you can think of now, and all the ones you will think of in the eternal tomorrow.

It might be helpful to further our understanding of semiotics, and secular blasphemy, if we all compiled a list of what would constitute blasphemy in the different aspects of our personal and social lives, and in our work environment, past and present. I could immediately list a whole variety of secular blasphemies such as the related set of telling the naked, unvarnished truth in all different kinds of circumstances, saying exactly what you think always, telling someone in the early stages of a relationship that you have no intention of telling him or her everything, and which you know is always the case, telling *this same lucky someone* that anyone who thinks a relationship can afford the truth is a fool etc. Comedians harvest secular blasphemies, but they never have to exhaust their creativity. We give them all the stories, they tell them, we laugh, they get paid, and the whole thing begins again tomorrow, we give them the stories, they tell them etc.

----

[7] IN THE EARLY 1990s, much was written about the excesses of some of the leaders and their families in many of the former

Socialist countries, but when the over-riding principle in any forensic assessment of a society is semiotic, terms such as excess in such a context is highly prejudicial and has the same intellectual status as *finger wagging*. Applying such boundaries *post-hoc* after it disappears is often just a useless exercise, at best, if we are not prepared to be open about all such limits in our own lives, institutions and societies, including what can be said and not said, and if it can be said, how it said etc., and sometimes endless etceteras. The one predictable and depressing phenomenon was that many Communist leaders and their families and minions in Romania who often enjoyed power without let or hindrance, might also indulge in what are often now regarded as the most perverse and violent sexual practices, and every type of extravagant material indulgence as well, which is where I happily hand over to the psychologists and psychiatrists who deal with the extremes of this type of group behaviour, and who might also examine whether there were differences because of peculiar religious background between Catholic cultures and those with an Orthodox Christian background, for example, and also between the various Greek and Russian Orthodox dispositions themselves.

ABOUT THE AUTHOR

Martin Croghan was born in Bantry in West Cork, Ireland a couple of weeks before WWII. He was educated in universities in Ireland, England and America. He has lectured in universities in Romania, America, Italy, Egypt, France and Ireland. He is the author of numerous publications in article and book form, and co-edited two collections of studies in Irish literature.